IMAGES
of America

EVESHAM TOWNSHIP

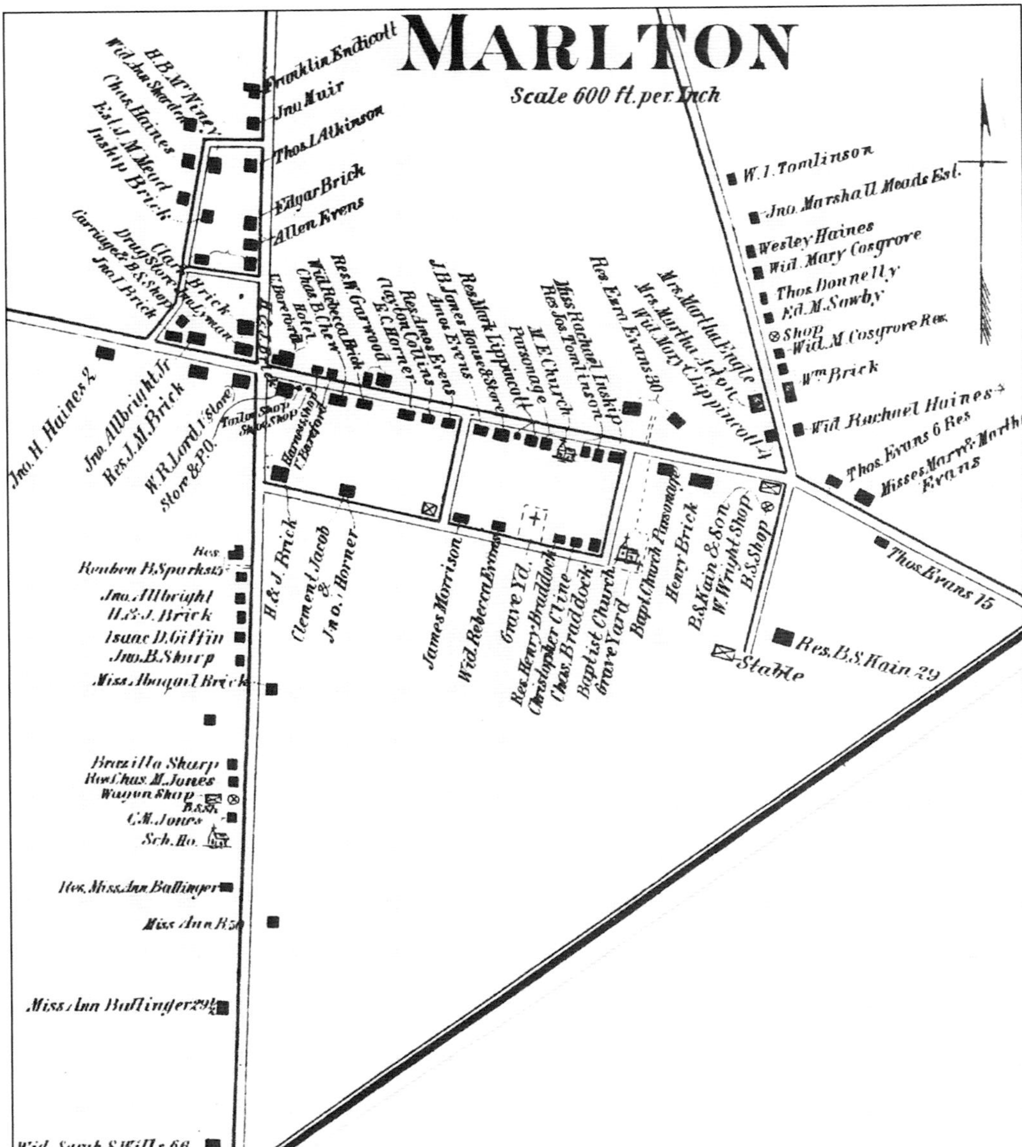

This map of the village of Marlton is from the late 1880s. (Author's collection.)

On the Cover: Workers are shown here picking peaches in 1951 in an orchard on the Byron Roberts farm. The farm's main crops were apples and peaches. Early on, it also grew some vegetable crops. This was Evesham's largest farm during the township's later agriculture years. (Courtesy New Jersey State Archives, Department of State.)

IMAGES
of America

EVESHAM TOWNSHIP

John S. Flack Jr.

ARCADIA
PUBLISHING

ISBN 978-0-7385-9753-9

Published by Arcadia Publishing
Charleston, South Carolina

Printed in the United States of America

Library of Congress Control Number: 2012937059

For all general information, please contact Arcadia Publishing:
Telephone 843-853-2070
Fax 843-853-0044
E-mail sales@arcadiapublishing.com
For customer service and orders:
Toll-Free 1-888-313-2665

Visit us on the Internet at www.arcadiapublishing.com

This book is dedicated to those who helped make Evesham Township, New Jersey, the fine community it is today.

Contents

ACKNOWLEDGMENTS

I would like to express my gratitude to the following for providing advice, images, information, and support: Dolores Wirth for allowing me use of her mother Edna's research material, Connie Evans, Guy Thompson, historian Paul Schopp, my mother Joan Flack, Pat Dougherty, and the Evesham Historical Society. This book would not have been possible without their assistance. I would also like to thank those who provided material for my Internet history site, which was helpful in compiling this book. Unless otherwise noted, images are from the author's collection.

INTRODUCTION

Evesham Township, New Jersey, is a community about 10 miles from Philadelphia in the southern New Jersey county of Burlington. Evesham was originally part of a tract of land between the Delaware and Hudson Rivers that belonged to Holland. In 1664, the English conquered the Dutch, and the Duke of York (later King James II) granted New Jersey to Lord Berkeley and George Carteret for their loyalty. Berkeley sold his share in 1674 to John Fenwick and Edward Byllynge, who bought the land to provide homes for the Quakers who endured continuous persecution in England.

The first dwelling in Evesham was supposedly a cave where William Evans and his wife, Elizabeth, first lived in 1688. In the same year, the Burlington Court established Evesham Constabulary as one of 12 municipalities. Incorporated on February 21, 1798, the large township once included all of Mount Laurel and Medford Townships and parts of Hainesport, Lumberton, and Shamong Townships. The New Jersey State Legislature gradually reduced the size of Evesham by creating the other townships in 1802, 1847, and 1872.

Many members of the Society of Friends, also known as Quakers, first settled Evesham. They found it to be a place where they could worship freely. When the Quakers arrived, they found the Lenape Indians, also known as Delaware Indians. The Quakers paid the Native Americans for their land, thereby establishing a good relationship with them. This was the only part of the country where Indians were paid for their land.

Many of the colonial homes belonging to the descendants of the original settlers still stand today, as well as Quaker meetinghouses. Evesham is considered one of the crossroads of the Revolutionary War. The British army passed through Evesham during the retreat from Philadelphia in 1778; troops camped along Greentree Road in an area that is now the Woodstream development.

The first post office in the township opened in 1808 as Evesham Post Office. The post office name was changed to Marlton on August 6, 1845. Marlton became a village, which became the commercial center of town. The names Marlton and Evesham have since become interchangeable.

The mining of marl began in the 19th century. A green sandy clay containing a high level of calcium and magnesium carbonates, marl is used as a fertilizer by farmers. It was mined in seven locations and was very profitable until the 20th century, when chemical fertilizers came into use. The industry was revived during World War I, when many chemicals imported from Germany became unavailable. From its beginning, Evesham's main business was agriculture. This began to change during the 1950s, when developers bought farms and built Evesham's first residential developments.

In 1988, Evesham Township created a twinning relationship with Evesham, England. This started when a tax bill sent to a resident of Evesham, New Jersey, turned up in Evesham, England. Thus began a friendship between the two towns.

One

Early Years

Evesham was part of a tract of land between the Hudson and Delaware Rivers that belonged to Holland until England defeated the Dutch in 1664. The same year, the Duke of York (later King James II) granted New Jersey to Lord Berkeley and George Carteret to repay their loyalty. Berkeley sold his share in 1674 to John Fenwick and Edward Byllynge, who purchased the 4,695 acres to provide new homes for the Quakers, then under persecution in England. The Quakers dealt fairly with the Lenape Indians then inhabiting the land. The first settlers were William and Elizabeth Evans, who arrived in 1688. That same year, present-day Burlington County was divided into eight townships. Evesham was incorporated in 1798. At that time, the township included Medford and Mount Laurel and portions of Hainesport, Shamong, and Lumberton.

For most of its history, Evesham Township has had a local economy based on farming. Its other industries included glass, charcoal, soap, marl fertilizer, and gristmills and sawmills. In 1881, the railroad arrived, crossing Old Marlton Pike at the Cherry Hill border. This was a tremendous help in moving the township's farm and industrial products to markets, as well as providing transportation to residents. Named for the marl that was discovered there, Marlton became the principal village in Evesham.

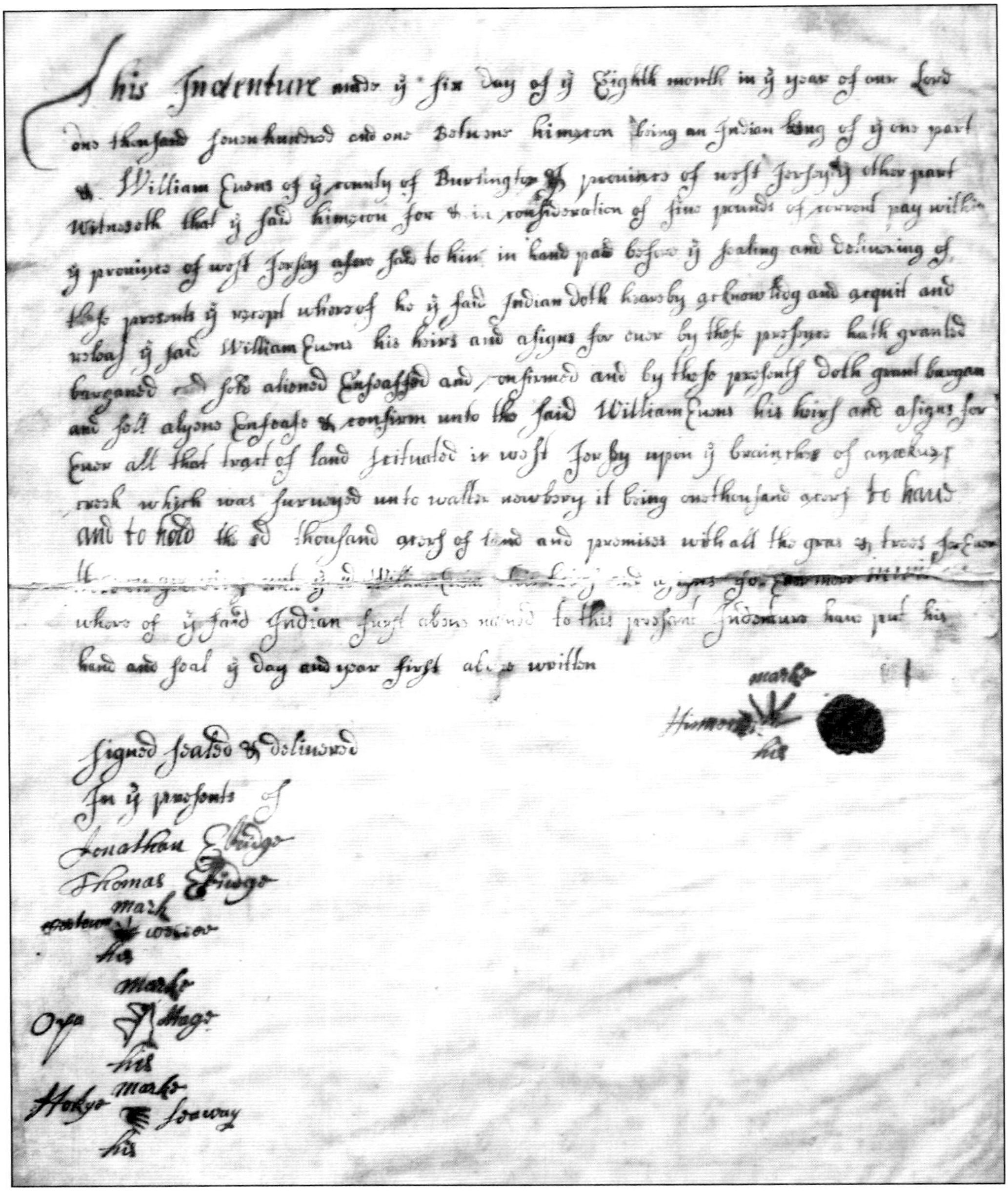
This Indenture made ye six day of ye Eighth month in ye year of our Lord one thousand seven hundred and one Between Himorou being an Indian king of ye one part & William Evans of ye county of Burlington & province of west Jersey ye other part Witnesseth that ye said Himorou for & in consideration of five pounds of current pay within ye province of west Jersey afore said to him in hand paid before ye sealing and delivering of these presents ye receipt whereof he ye said Indian doth hereby acknowledge and acquit and release ye said William Evans his heirs and assigns for ever by these presents hath granted bargained and sold aliened Enfeoffed and confirmed and by these presents doth grant bargain and sell alien Enfeoff & confirm unto the said William Evans his heirs and assigns for Ever all that tract of land situated in west Jersey upon ye branches of [illegible] creek which was surveyed unto walter newbery it being one thousand acres to have and to hold the sd thousand acres of land and premises with all the [illegible] trees [illegible] [illegible] whereof ye said Indian first above named to this present Indenture have put his hand and seal ye day and year first above written

Himorou his mark

Signed sealed & delivered
In ye presents of
Jonathan Eldridge
Thomas Eldridge
[illegible] his mark
[illegible] his mark
[illegible] his mark

Thomas Evans received a patent for a tract of 1,000 acres in Evesham Township soon after its establishment. His survey was recorded in the proprietor's office in Burlington. Shown is the deed he had drawn up in 1702 for the Native Americans to sign, releasing the land for £5, or $25. These Indians were not versed in English when they signed the deed and used pictograms as their signatures. The original document is still held by the Evans family. (Courtesy Connie Evans.)

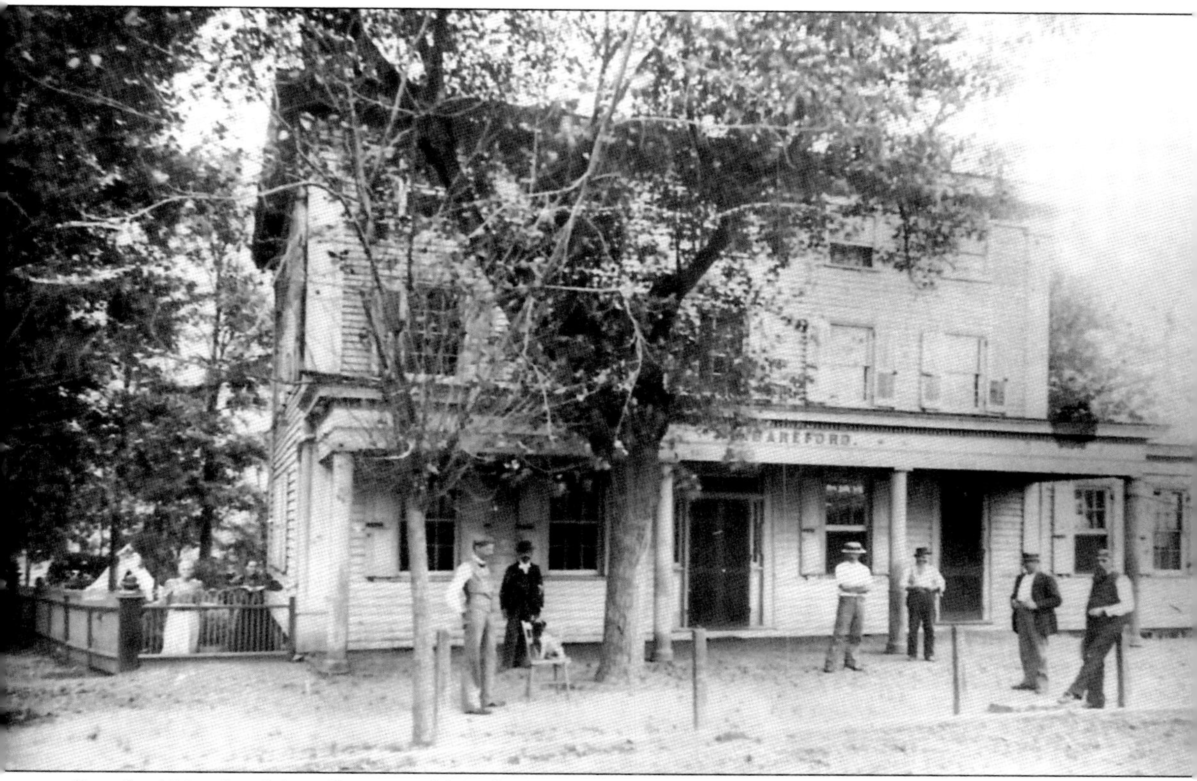

Bareford Hotel at Main Street and Maple Avenue was a favorite carriage and stage stop en route to and from the shore resorts. In 1850, Joseph Shivers built the 26-room hotel as an addition to the front of the Rising Sun Tavern. Samuel Swain built the tavern in 1820. Swain was instrumental in changing the name of the post office to Marlton in 1845. The Bareford family purchased the building in 1865. The town's first post office was located here, and a racetrack was added to the property. Jack Jones, shown on the far right, was proprietor at the time this late-1800s or early-1900s photograph was taken. He was a son-in-law of Uriah Bareford. (Courtesy Edna Wirth.)

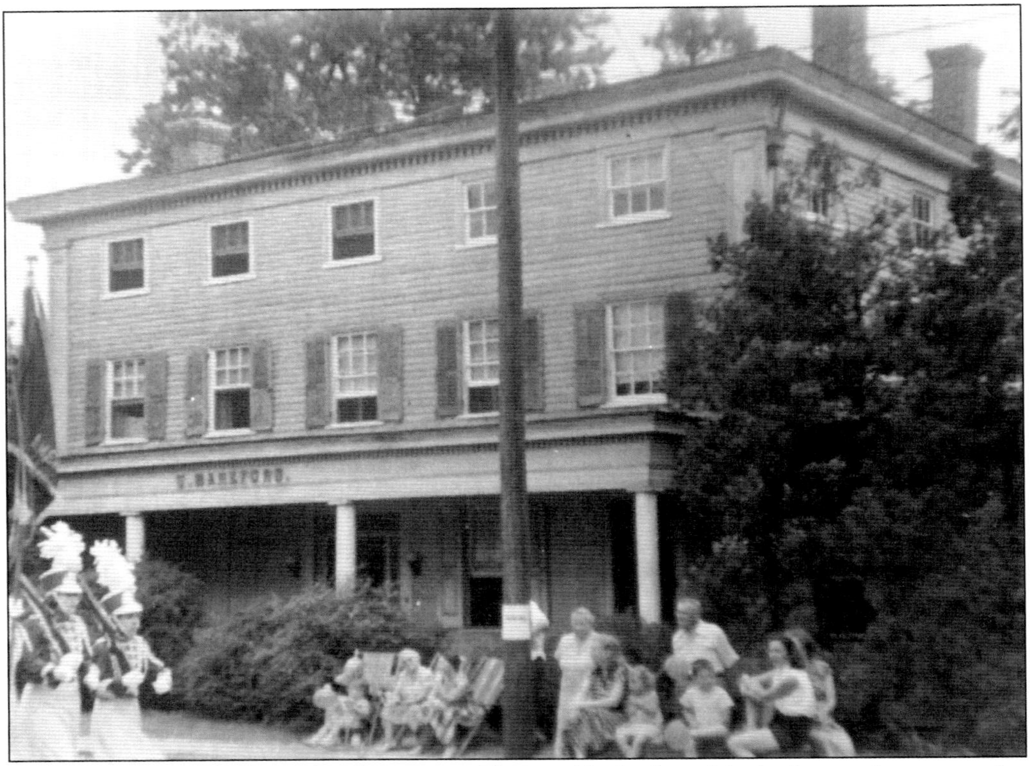

Shown is the Bareford Hotel in later years. The marl hole along Maple Avenue by present-day Route 70 was part of the Bareford property. The hotel passed down through several generations of Bareford descendants. Its use as a hotel gradually waned, and later the building served as a residence for several members of the Bareford family. The family sold the building in 1965. After it was razed, a 7-Eleven convenience store was built on the site. (Courtesy Edna Wirth.)

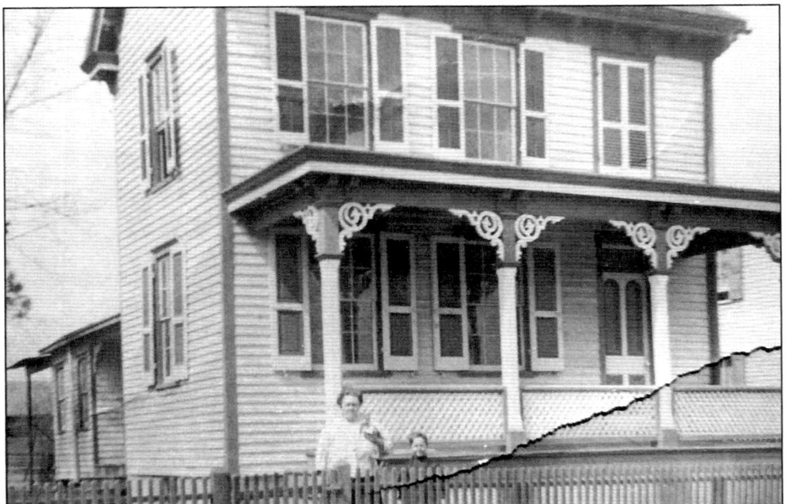

This house was built in 1847 at the Kresson Glass Factory and was used as a worker's residence. Franklin Endicott purchased the house and moved it around 1875 to 24 North Maple Avenue for his residence. Endicott later had the house enlarged. (Courtesy Edna Wirth.)

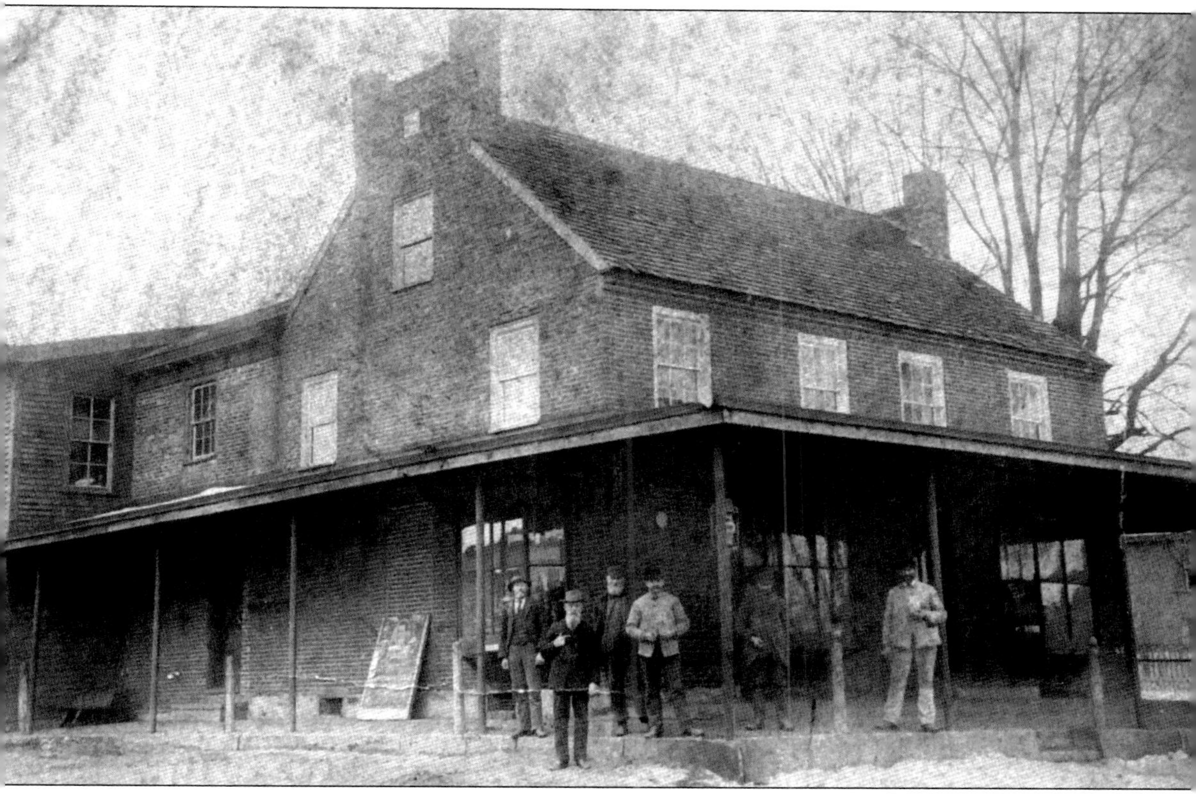

Isaac Stokes built this store at Main Street and Maple Avenue in 1823. He operated a general store and post office here. The store changed ownership several times. The last grocer to own it was William McNaul, who purchased it in 1946. McNaul operated the store until the early 1970s, when it then housed Paula's Place craft shop. During renovations in 1982, a log house was discovered within this building. (Courtesy William McNaul.)

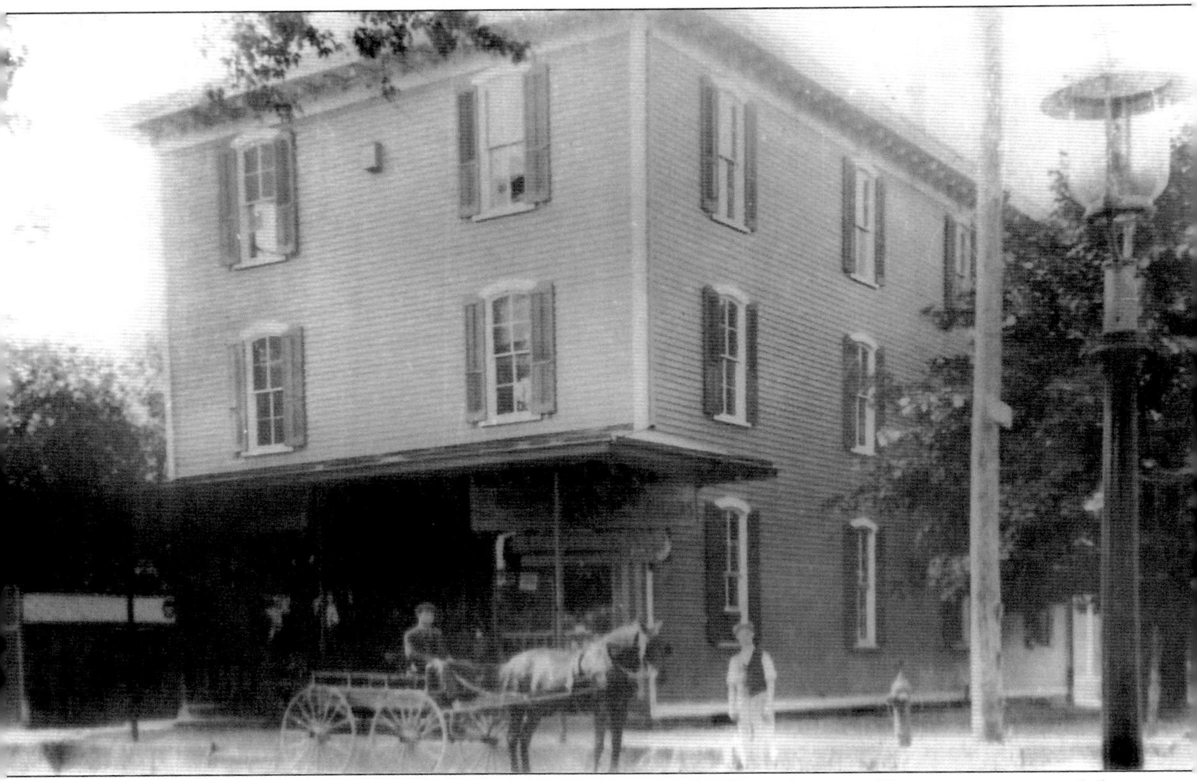

Shown here is Brick's General Store at Main Street and Maple Avenue. Four generations of the William Brick family operated a successful business here for a total of 115 years. A gas streetlight can be observed in this scene. The Marlton Light, Heat, and Power Company installed these lights after its founding in 1903. Young boys lit and extinguished the lamps and were responsible for cleaning the glass globes once a month. (Courtesy Edna Wirth.)

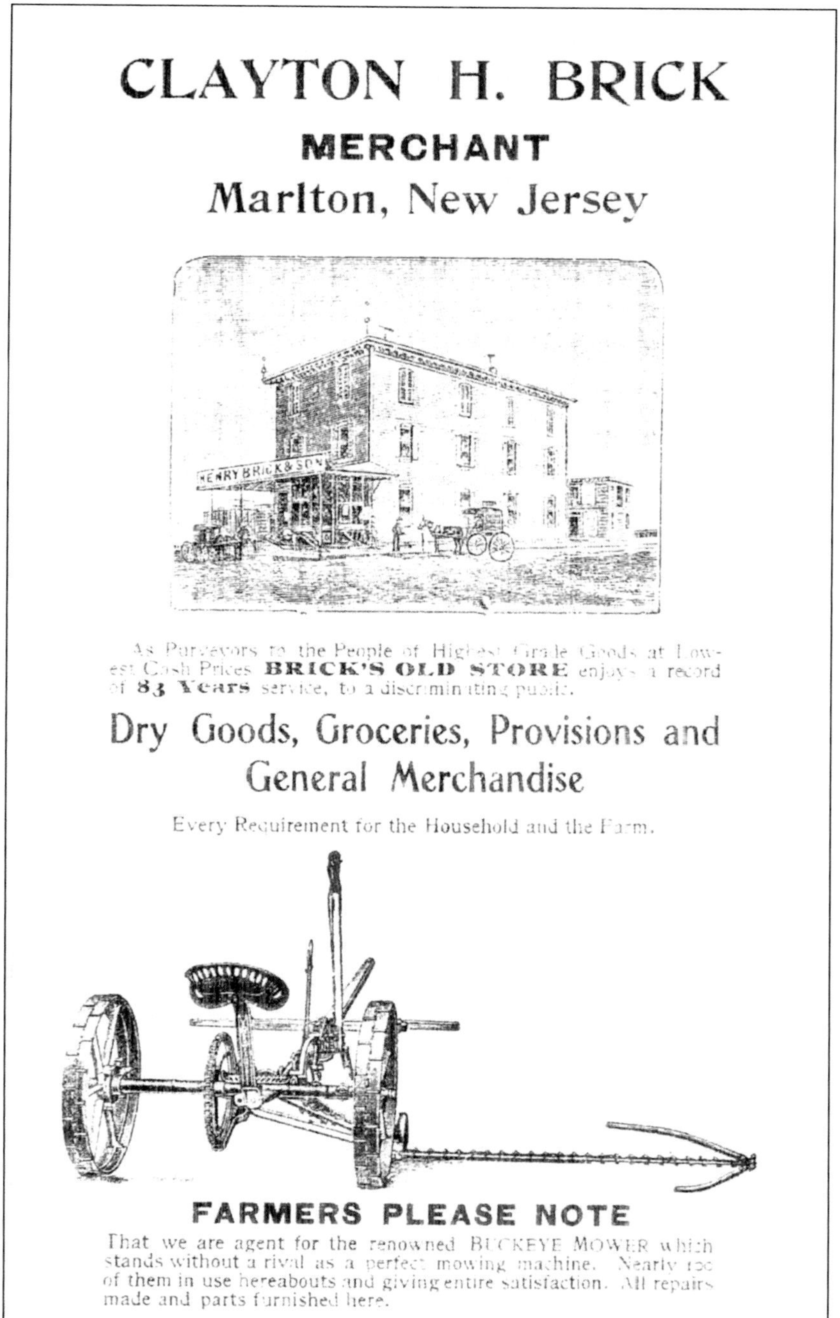

This is an ad for Brick's General Store from 1900. Brick's original store stood at Oak and Maple Avenues and was built in the 1830s. The family replaced that small store with the larger one shown in this ad at Main Street and Maple Avenue. The first two floors were used for general merchandise, while the upper floor served as a meeting and entertainment room. The Methodists held meetings here while their church was being built. The Bricks offered free concerts and stereopticon exhibitions with up to 400 people attending.

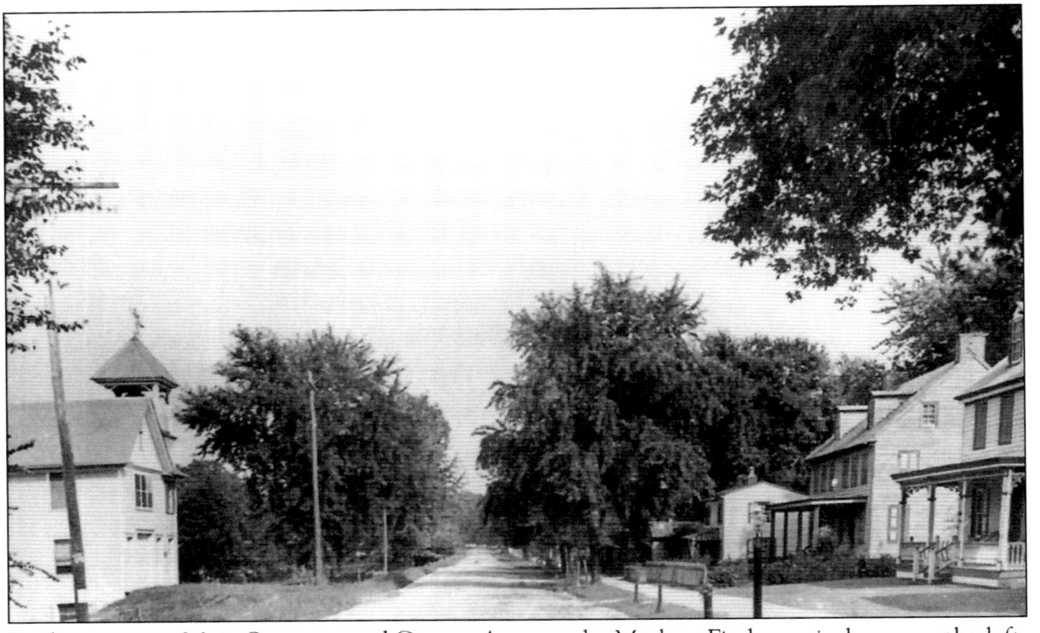

Looking east on Main Street toward Cooper Avenue, the Marlton Firehouse is shown on the left. Across from it are homes owned by John Evans and Isaac Stokes. (Courtesy Edna Wirth.)

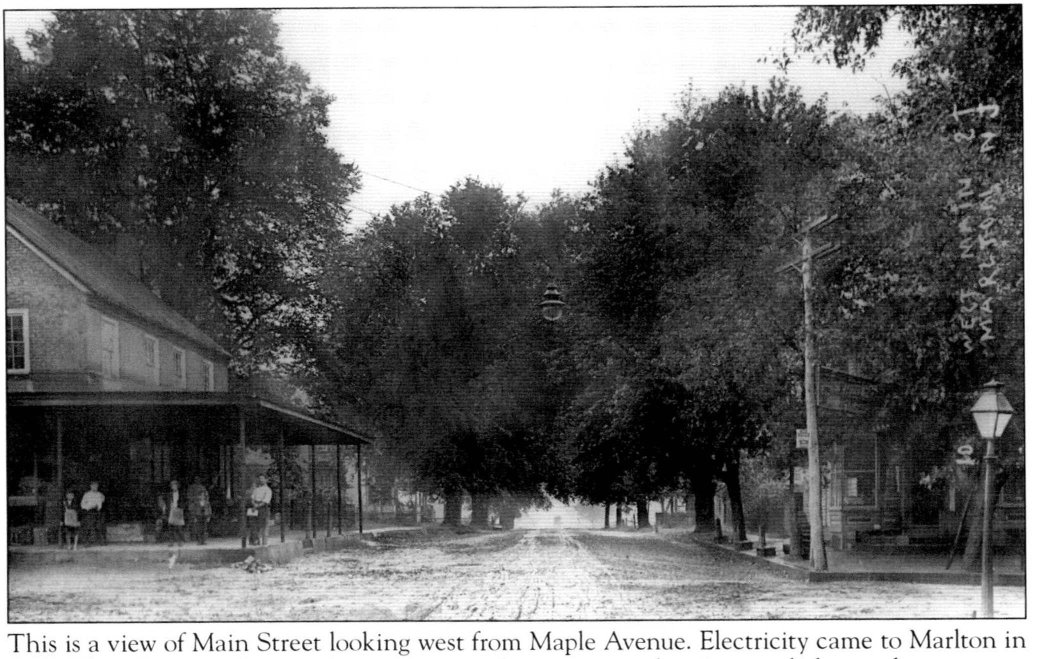

This is a view of Main Street looking west from Maple Avenue. Electricity came to Marlton in 1922. This photograph was taken sometime after, since an electric streetlight can be seen over the intersection. (Courtesy Edna Wirth.)

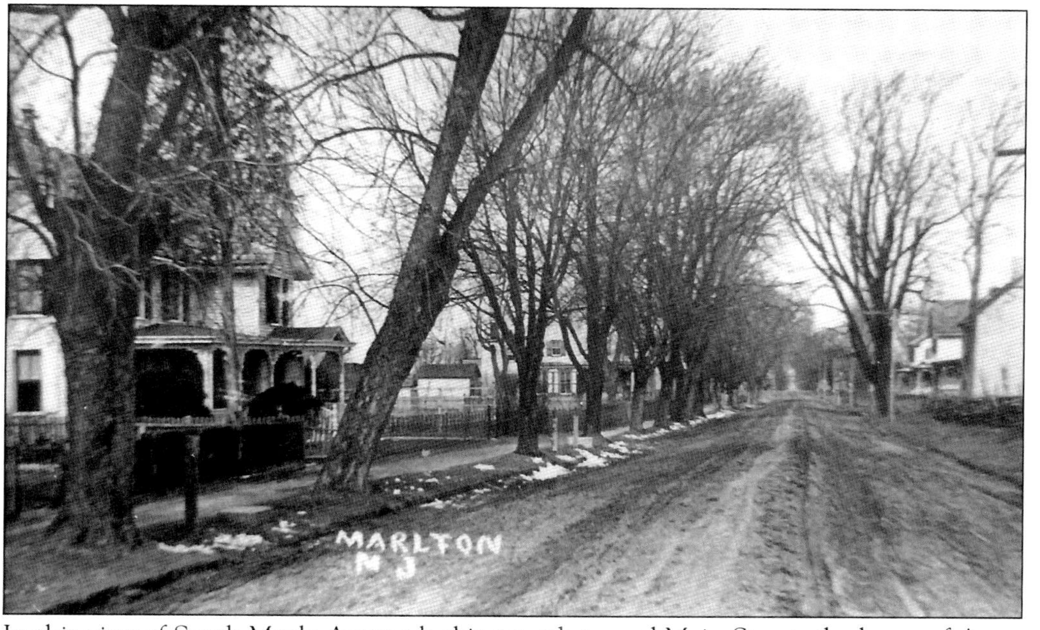

In this view of South Maple Avenue looking north toward Main Street, the home of Anna Morrison is shown on the left. (Courtesy Edna Wirth.)

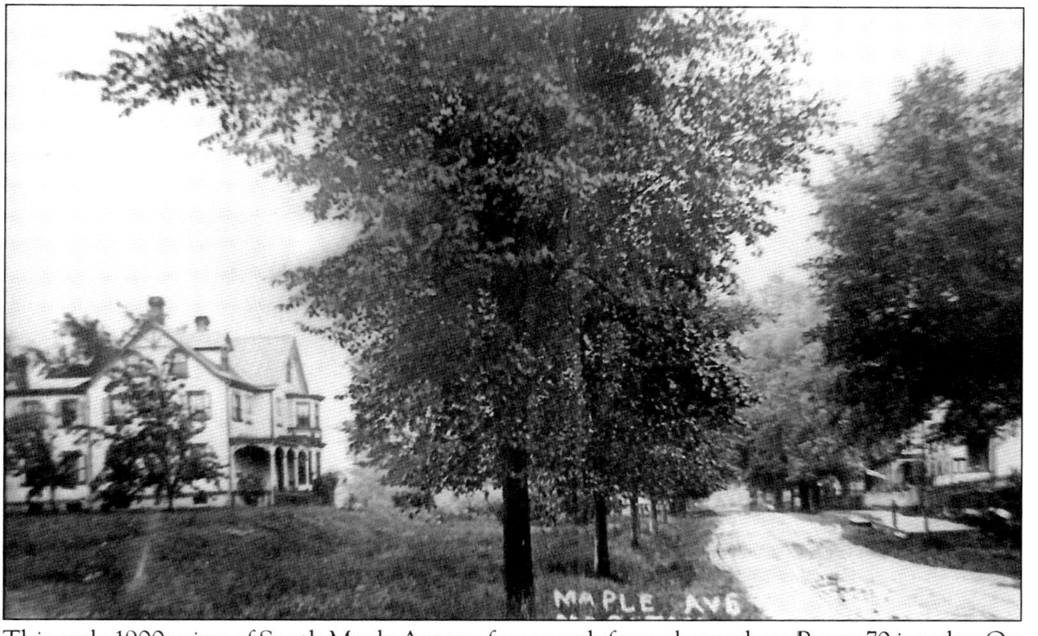

This early-1900s view of South Maple Avenue faces south from about where Route 70 is today. On the left is the home of George Middleton. The Franklin Endicott home is on the right, obscured by trees. (Courtesy Edna Wirth.)

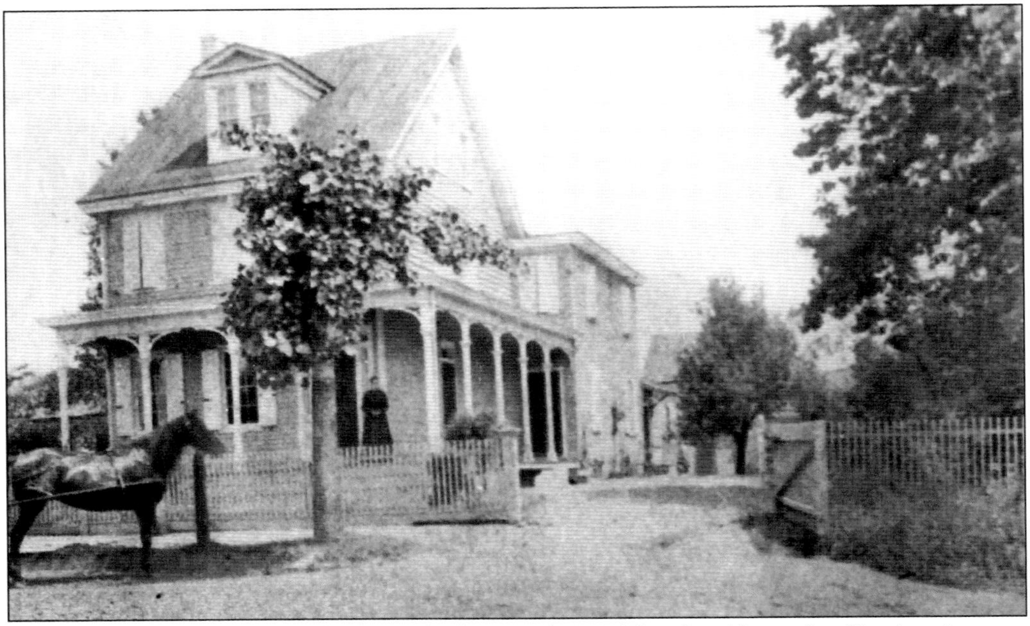

Charles and Sarah Kain had this home built around 1848. They lived here after Kain's retirement from operating a carriage shop on East Main Street. Later, it served as the home of Howard Evans, who held Marlton Grange meetings here. It then became the residence and office of the township clerk from 1949 to 1955. (Courtesy Edna Wirth.)

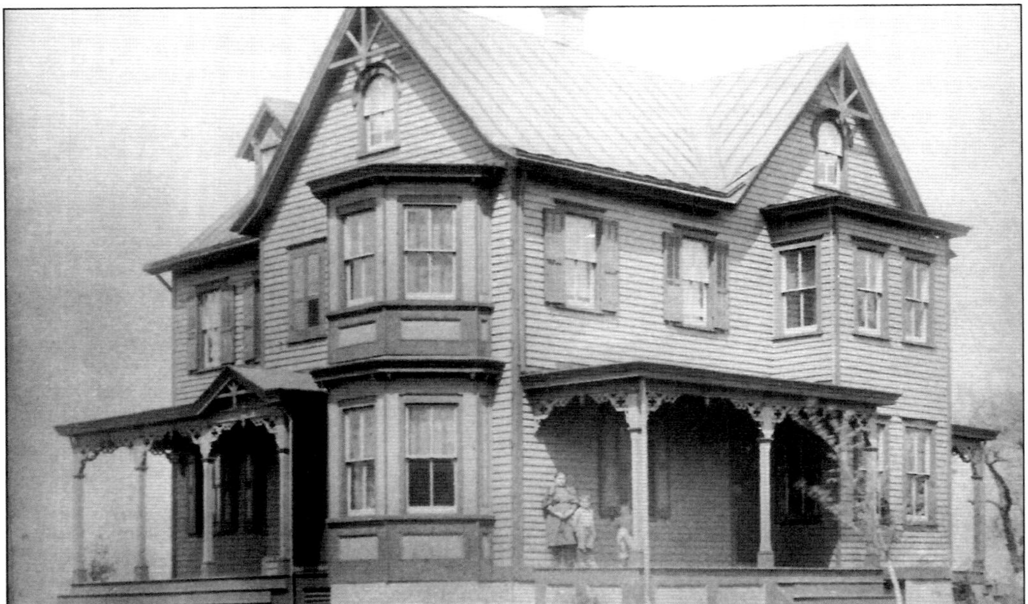

Shown here is the Middleton house at 25 North Maple Avenue, with Mrs. George Middleton and her two children. This property later became Watson's Lumber Yard before it was demolished. (Courtesy of Edna Wirth.)

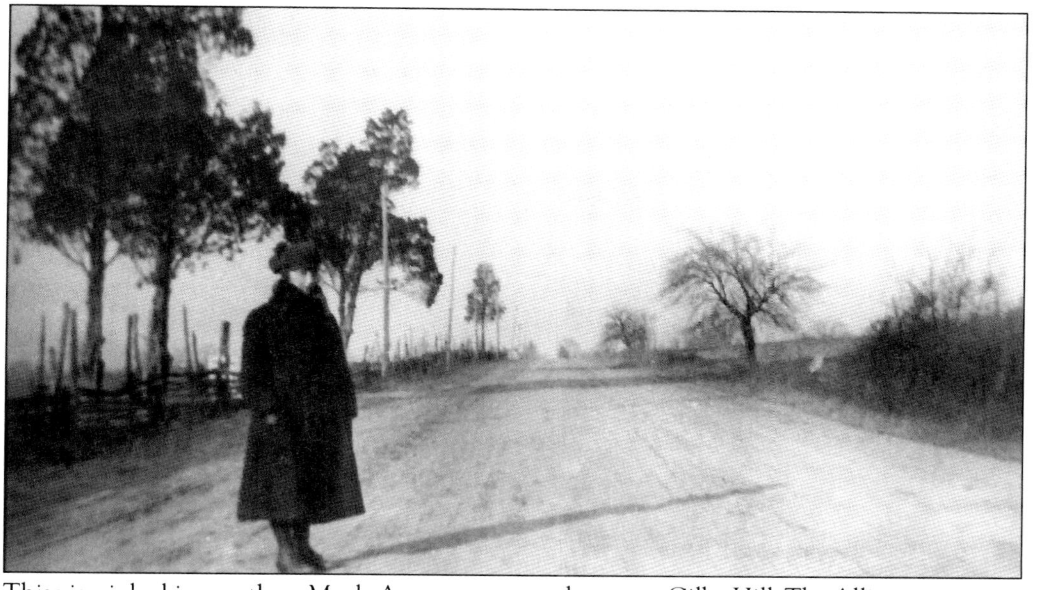

This view is looking north on Maple Avenue at an area known as Gilbo Hill The Allison apartment complex would later be built on the right side of this scene. (Courtesy Edna Wirth.)

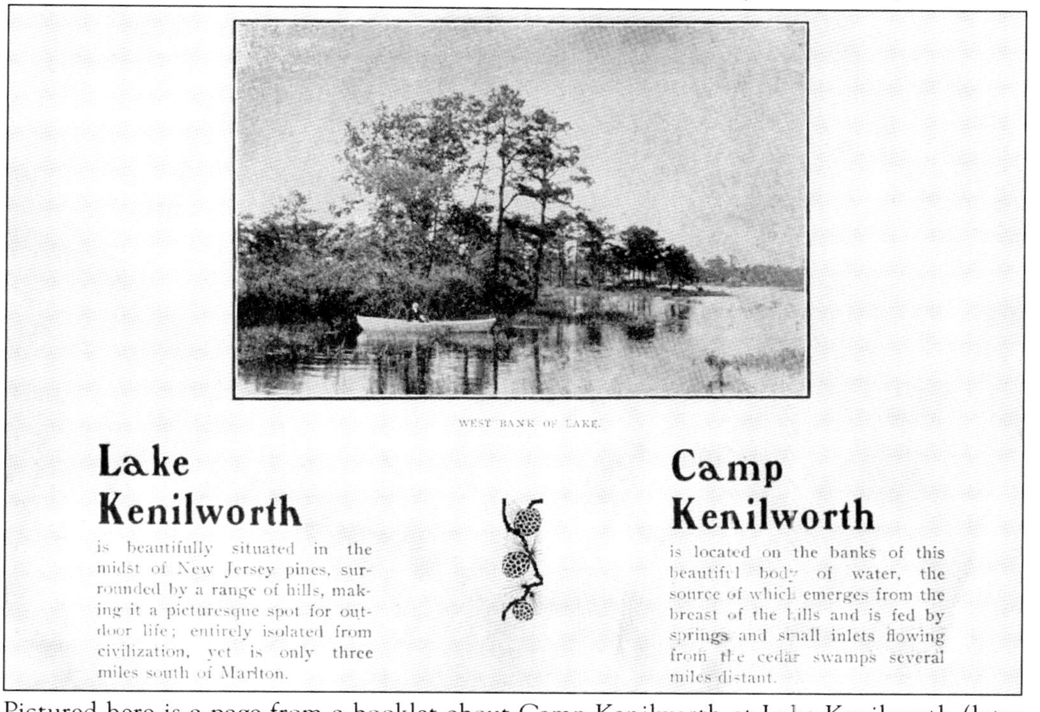

WEST BANK OF LAKE.

Lake Kenilworth

is beautifully situated in the midst of New Jersey pines, surrounded by a range of hills, making it a picturesque spot for outdoor life; entirely isolated from civilization, yet is only three miles south of Marlton.

Camp Kenilworth

is located on the banks of this beautiful body of water, the source of which emerges from the breast of the hills and is fed by springs and small inlets flowing from the cedar swamps several miles distant.

Pictured here is a page from a booklet about Camp Kenilworth at Lake Kenilworth (later Kenilworth Lake). Located below Braddock Mill Road, Camp Kenilworth was operated as a summer resort and promoted as a healthful spot to camp and vacation. Facilities on the grounds included a dining room, a cottage for inclement weather, horse stables, and an inn. Campers could sleep in either tents or bungalows and could enjoy fishing, boating, and swimming on the lake. (Courtesy Edna Wirth.)

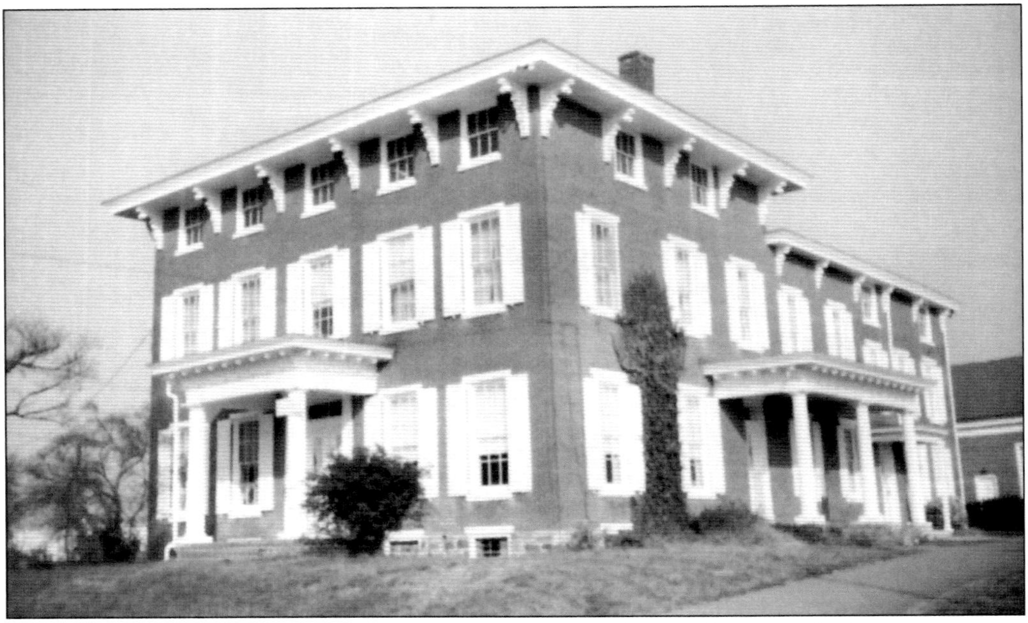

Built around 1860, William Tomlinson and his family owned this Italianate-style, 14-room mansion until it was purchased along with the surrounding land by the Marlton Methodist Episcopal Church in 1962. Local residents considered the mansion to be quite a showplace. A second-floor bedroom was used as a classroom for Quaker children between 1907 and 1911. (Photograph by Miriam Wurst, courtesy Edna Wirth.)

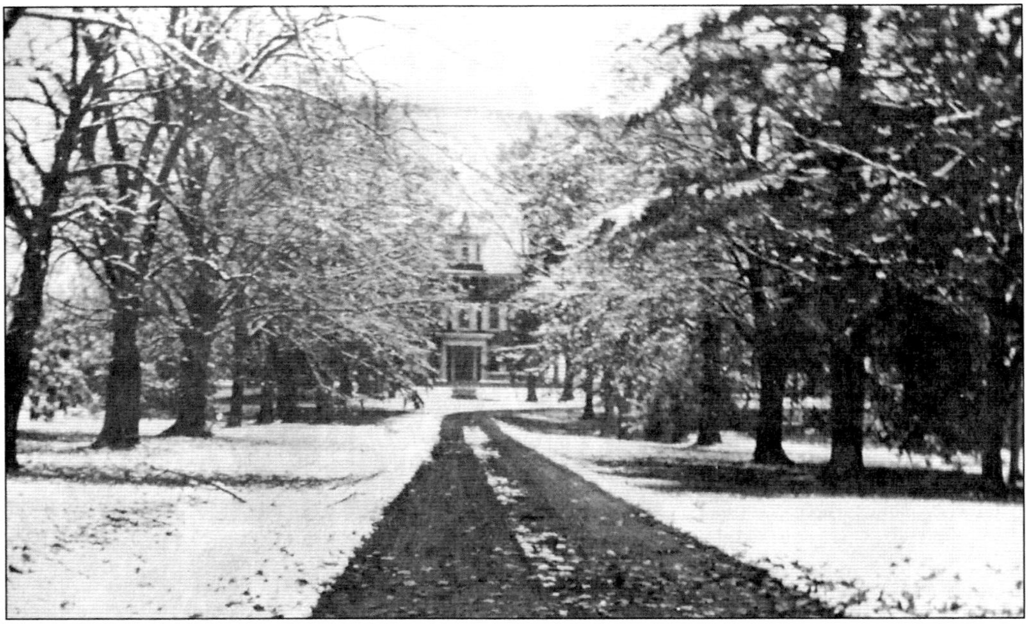

Shown here is the lane that connected the Tomlinson mansion to Main Street. With the construction of Georgetown and Heritage Village, part of this lane became Plymouth Drive. A small portion of the original lane connects the mansion to Plymouth Drive and is called Tomlinson Lane.

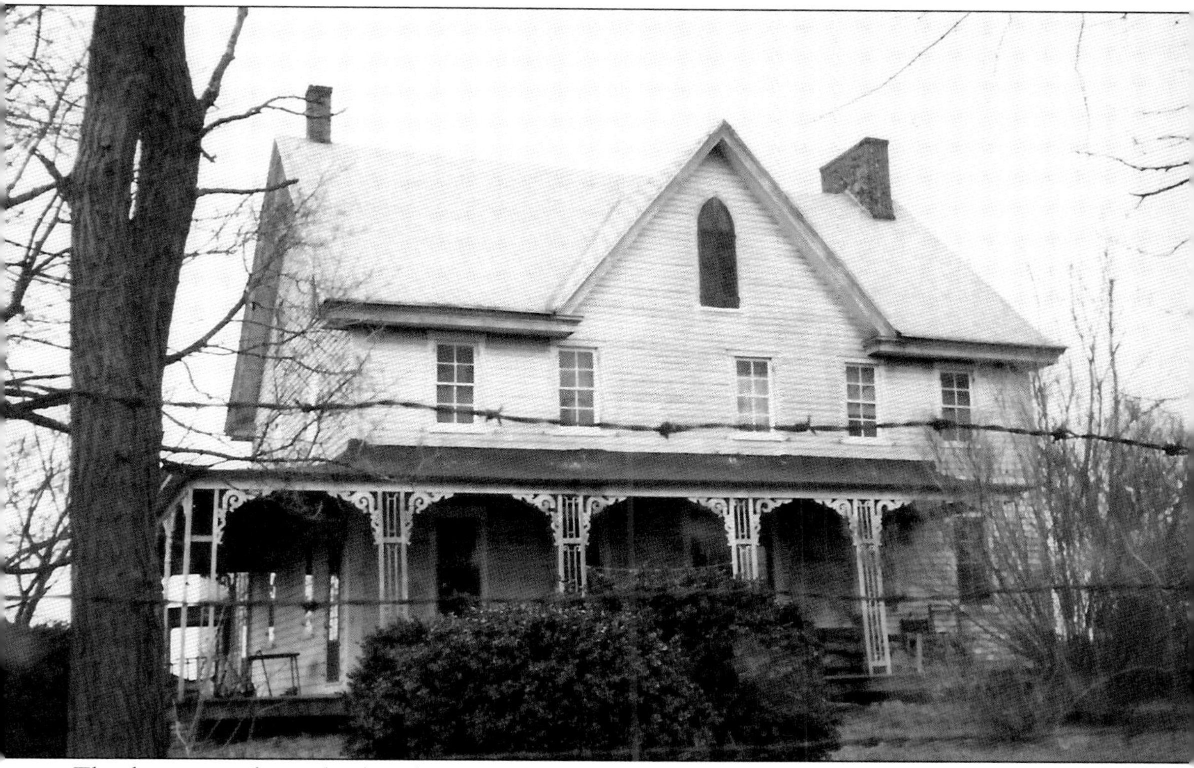

This house stands on the foundation of the original farmhouse, built in 1770. The house and surrounding land belonged to the Inskeep family until 1936, when Alfred and Helen Higginbotham purchased it. The house stood empty for 20 years after the Higginbothams' death, and the township scheduled it for demolition in 1988. Instead, the Evesham Historical Society obtained the house and restored it. (Courtesy of Edna Wirth.)

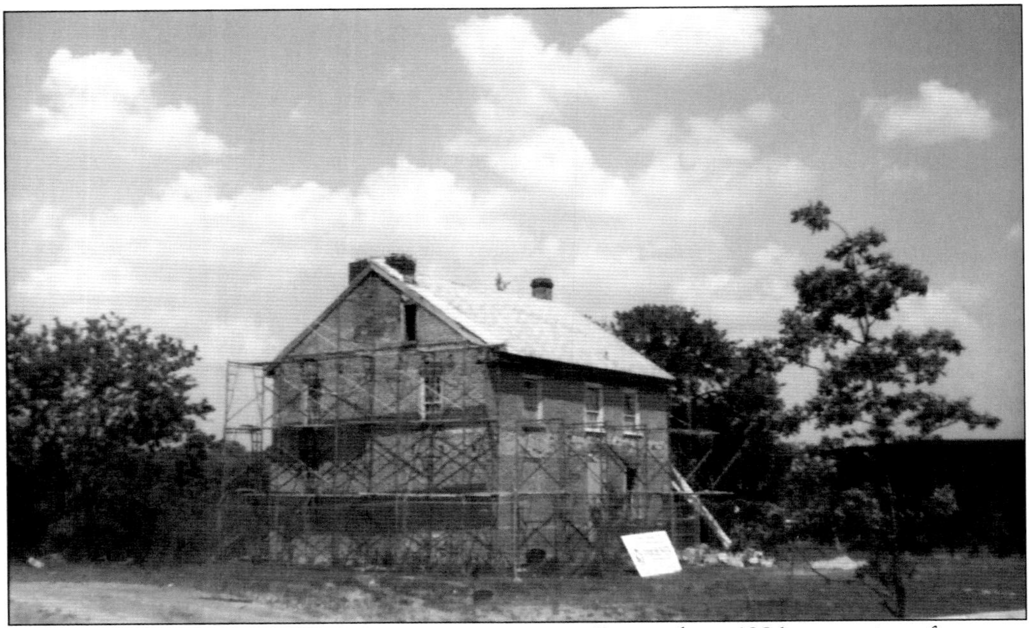

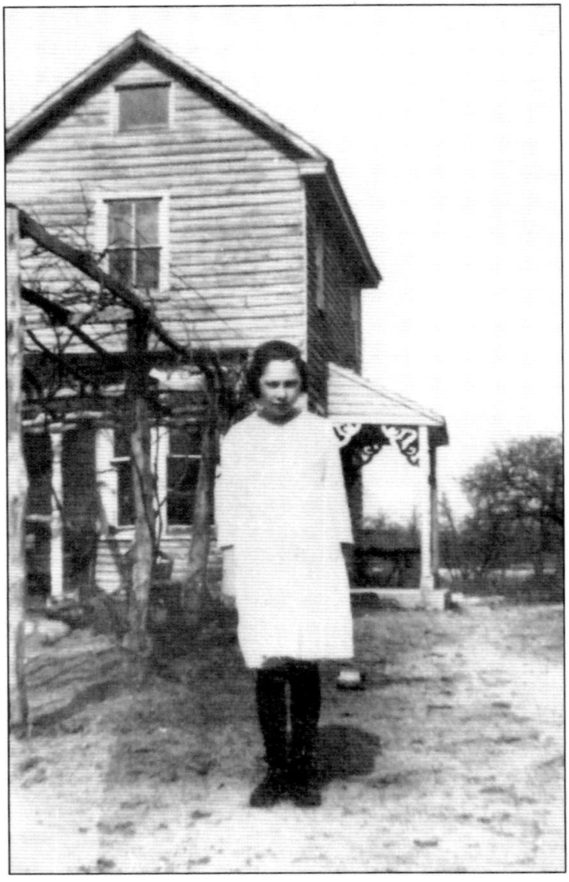

Pictured is a 1986 restoration of the Thomas Hollinshead house. Hollinshead built this house in 1776 on the 1,000-acre farm he inherited from his great-grandfather Thomas Eves. The last farmer to own this land was Edward Stow, who sold it to a developer in 1982 for the Evesham Corporate Center. The developer sold the house for $1 to Frank Messina, who did the restoration. It is now the centerpiece of the corporate center on Greentree Road. (Photograph by author.)

Here is the Wirth homestead on Kettle Run Road. John Wirth bought land here along a stagecoach route in 1859 and built a home, which burned down. He then constructed the replacement house pictured here, which was built in two sections. (Courtesy Dolores Wirth.)

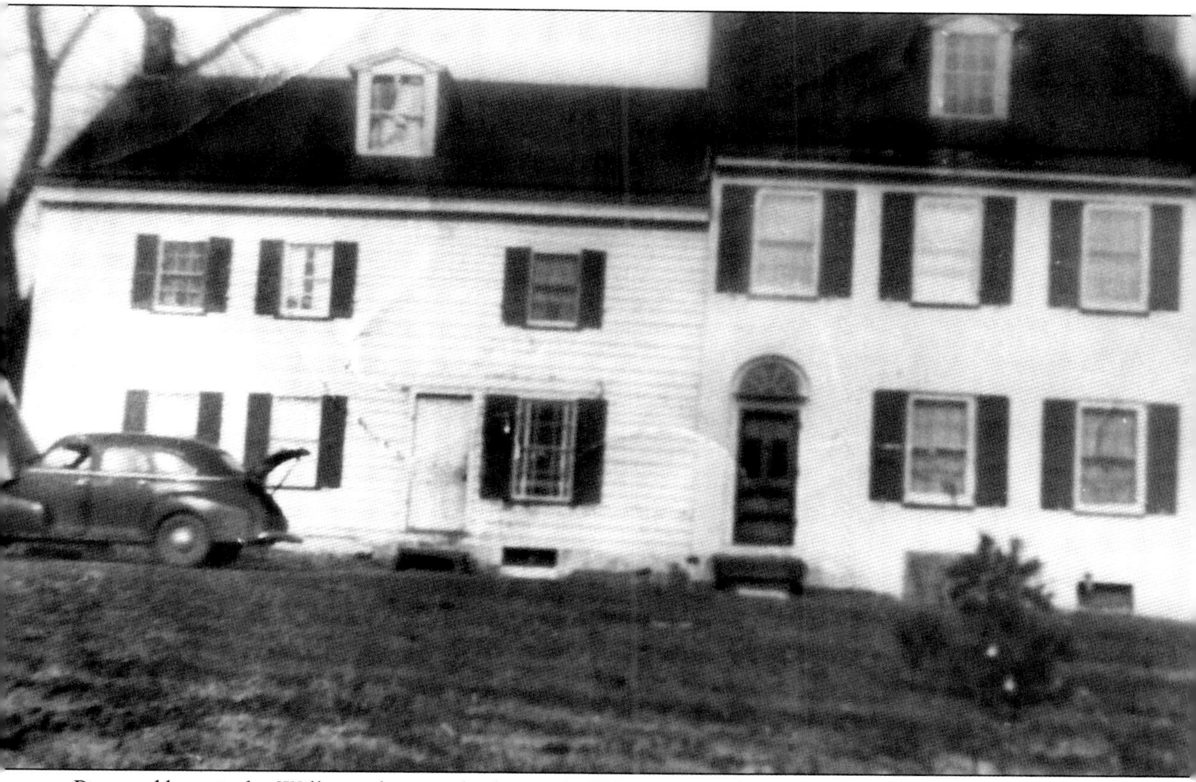

Pictured here is the Wills residence, which stood off Route 70 and across from the present Plymouth Drive. Zebedee Wills was justice of the peace and judge of the Court of Common Pleas in Evesham Township. He also served a term in the New Jersey State Legislature. (Courtesy Edna Wirth.)

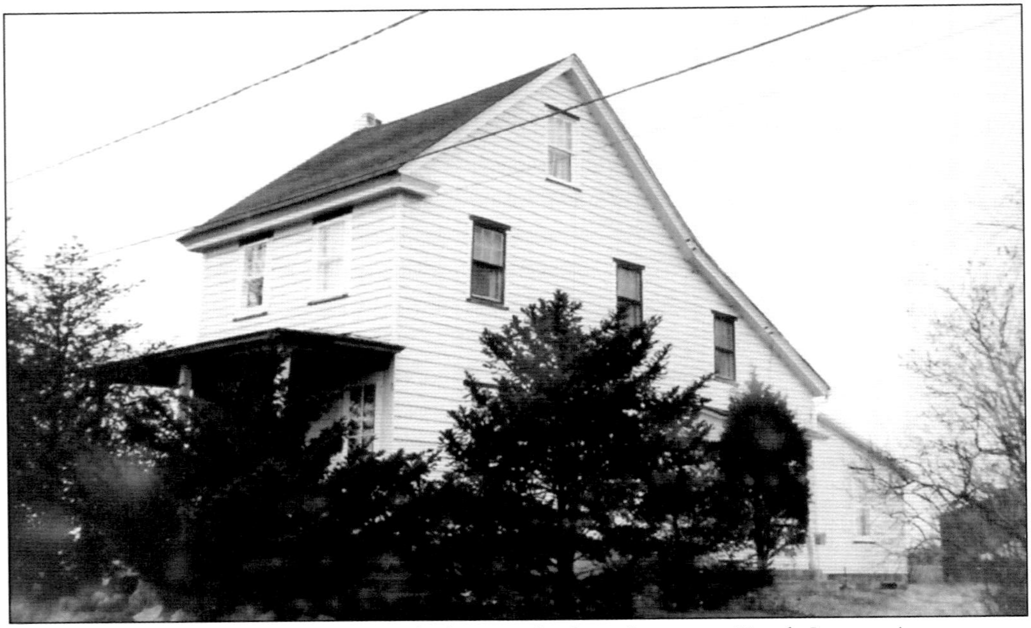

This is a 1975 photograph of the Linford Higginbotham house on North Locust Avenue near Greentree Road. (Photograph by Miriam Wurst, courtesy Edna Wirth.)

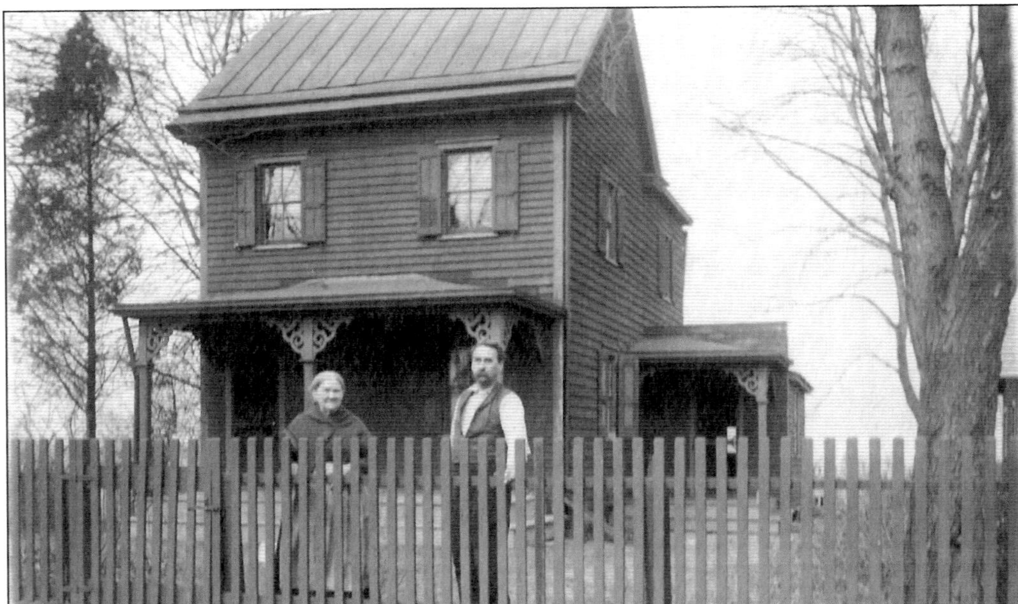

Seen here is the Heritage family homestead on Whisky Road, which is now known as Locust Avenue. Rebecca and Justin Heritage are standing in front of the home. A resident of the house found the date 1744 cut into a chimney in the attic. Justin's father, Jason Heritage, developed the Heritage strawberry, which the family grew on land that is presently known as Heritage Village. (Courtesy Edna Wirth.)

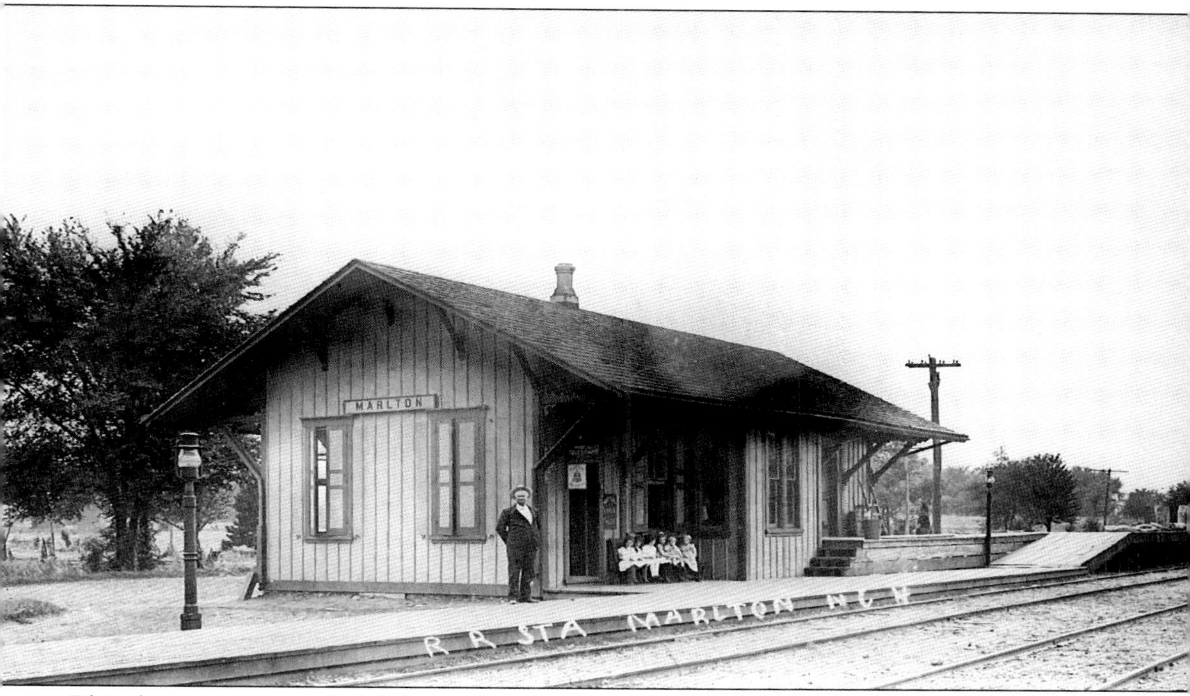

This photograph shows the Marlton railroad station at Cooper Avenue. In 1881, the Philadelphia, Marlton & Medford Railroad laid tracks through Evesham. The line was placed into service in October 1881, running between Haddonfield and Medford. The tracks entered Evesham from Cherry Hill at Old Marlton Pike and ran along present-day Route 70 to Medford. The route was originally planned to travel a course slightly to the north and would have run through the present Woodstream development to a site near the intersection of Locust Avenue and Route 70.

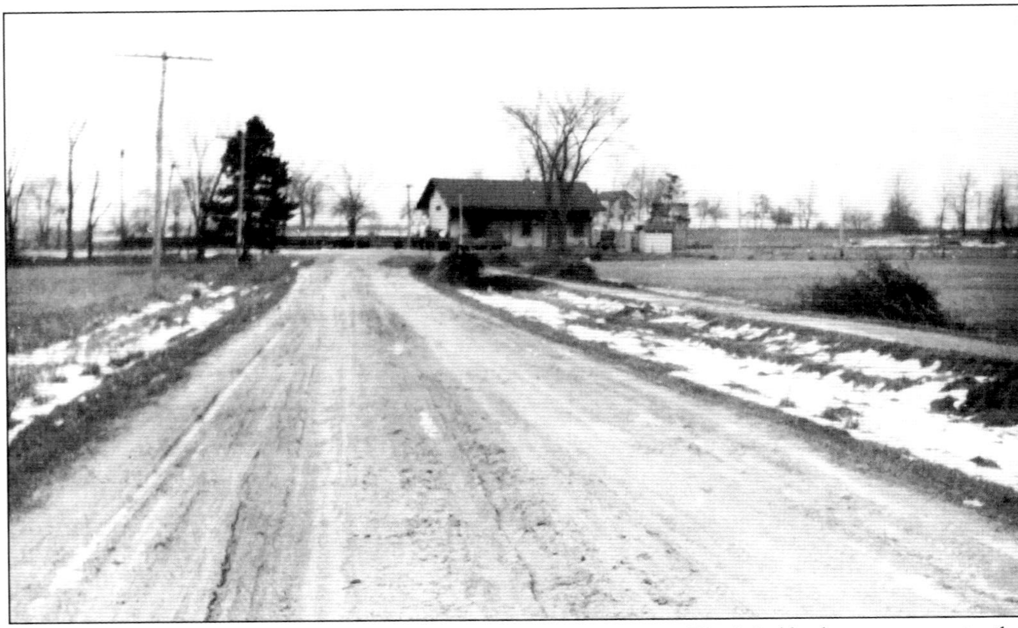

A 1920 photograph shows the back of the Marlton train station. The Medford station was similar to this building. The road running to it is Cooper Avenue. The need for rail service declined in the 1920s with the increased use of motor vehicles, and the Philadelphia, Marlton & Medford Railroad ended service on November 2, 1931. Passenger service had ended on the line in 1927.

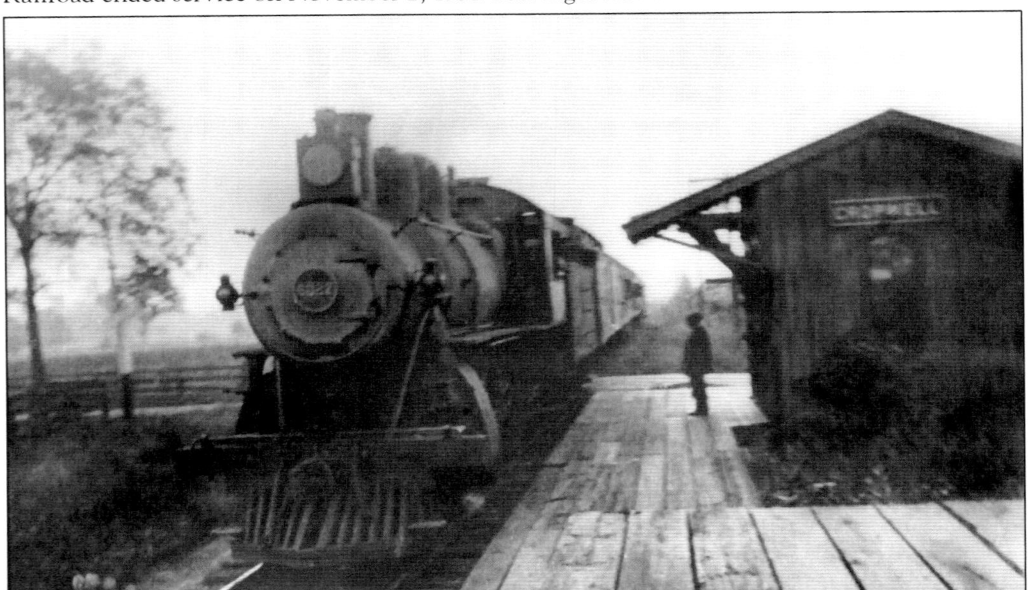

Here is the Cropwell station in 1910 that stood at the southwest corner of present-day Route 70 and Cropwell Road. The Burrough family moved the building to the southeast corner and used it as a farm stand. It was moved once again to a field across from the Kings Grant development on Taunton Lake Road. In 1988, the former station was accidentally demolished when the site upon which it sat was being cleared for a shopping center.

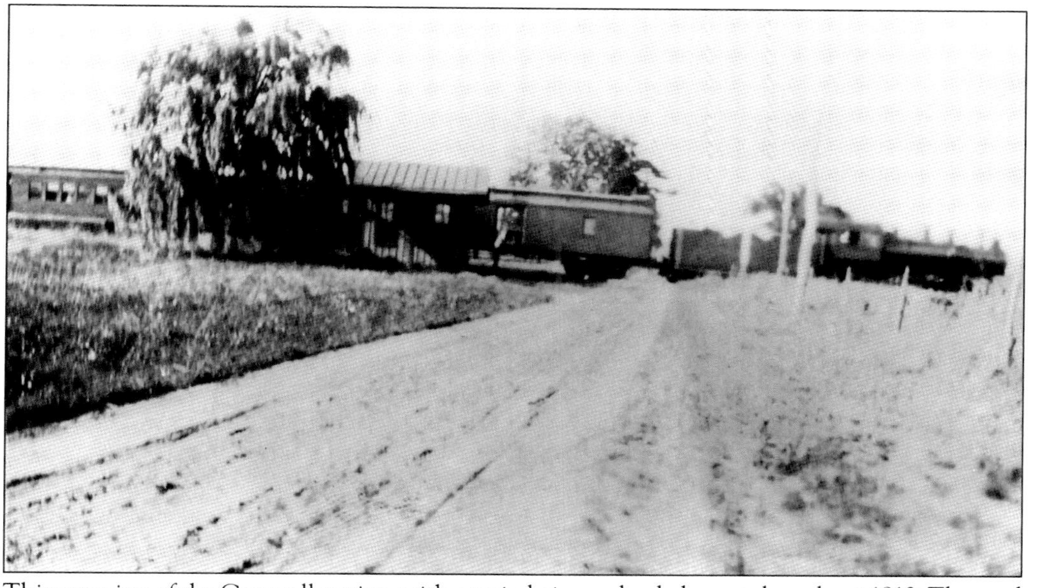

This rear view of the Cropwell station, with a train being unloaded, was taken about 1910. The road in the foreground is Cropwell Road. Freight on the line consisted mainly of agricultural products from farms along the route and shipments of marl from the Atlantic Potash Company.

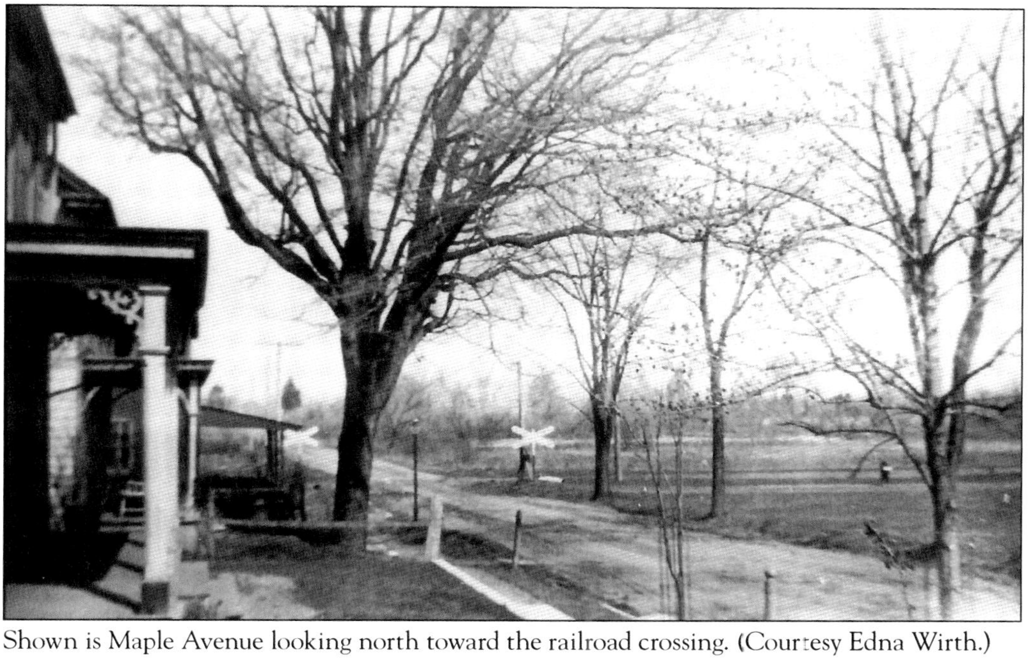

Shown is Maple Avenue looking north toward the railroad crossing. (Courtesy Edna Wirth.)

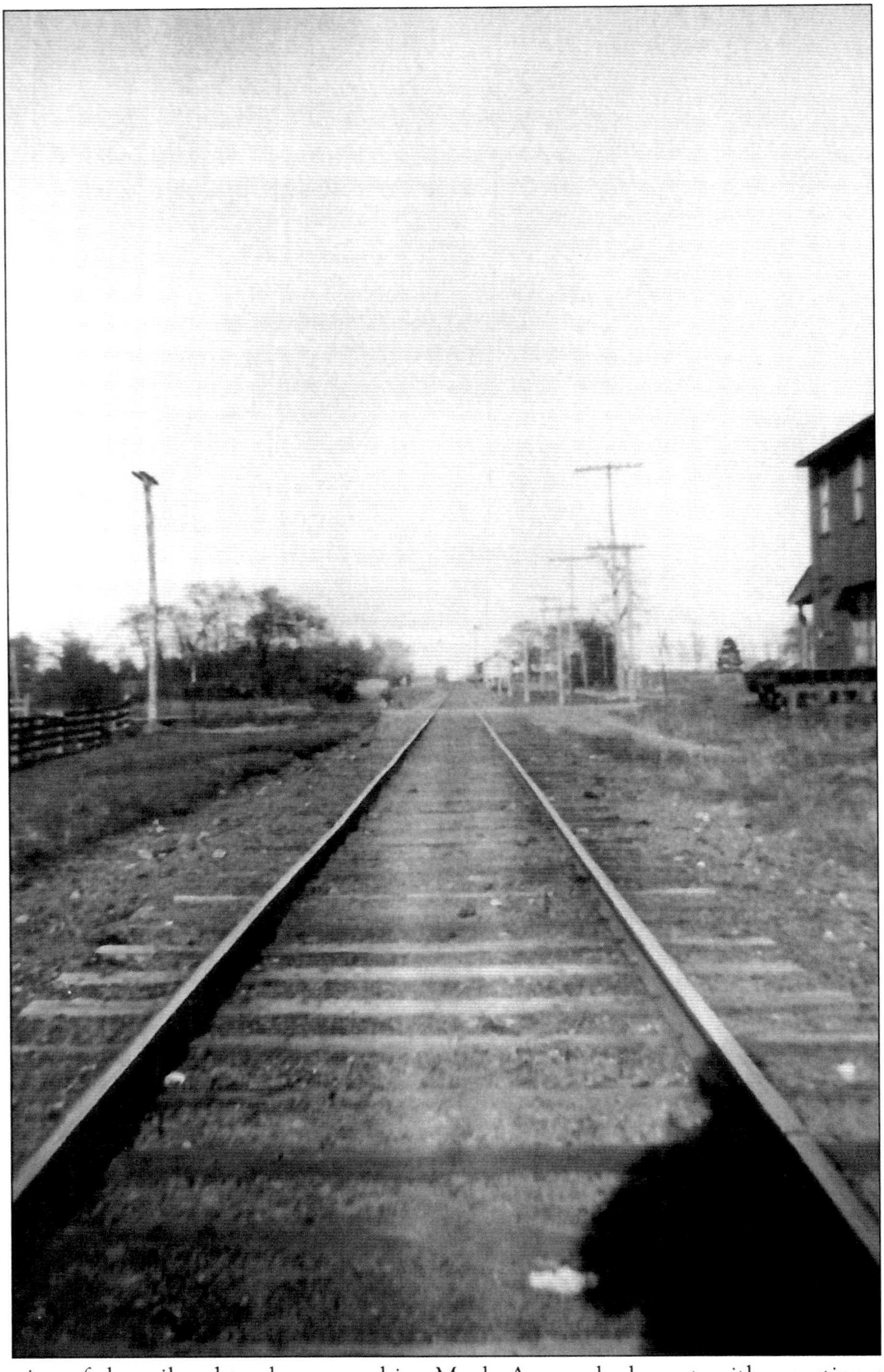

This view of the railroad tracks approaching Maple Avenue looks east, with a portion of the soap factory shown on the right. The Marlton station can be seen in the distance. (Courtesy Edna Wirth.)

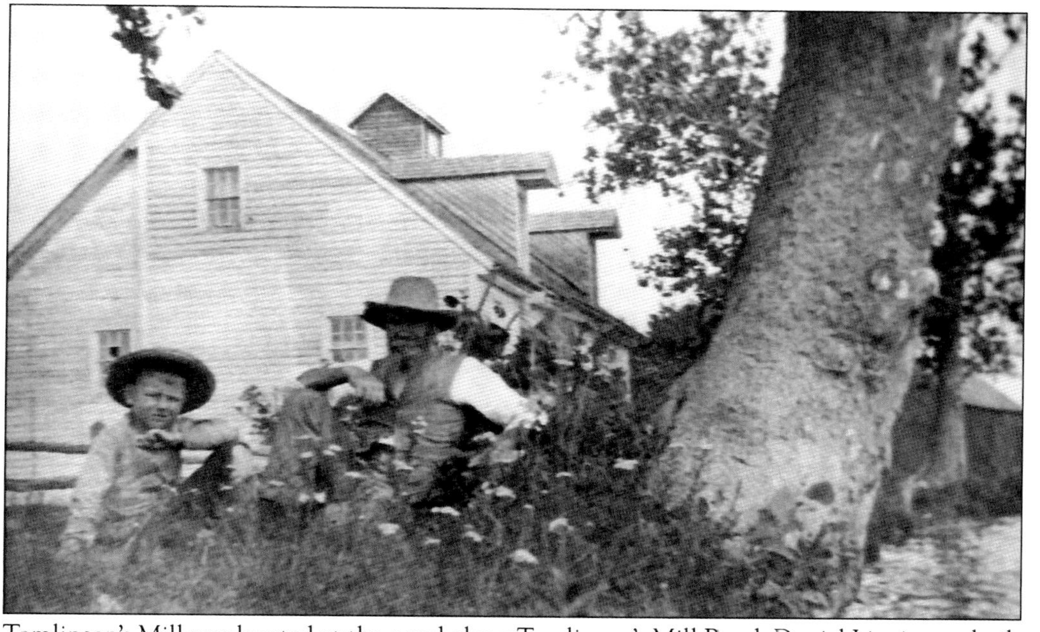

Tomlinson's Mill was located at the pond along Tomlinson's Mill Road. Daniel Lippincott built the mill after purchasing the land in 1737. The Lippincott family owned the mill for 84 years. The Evans family later owned the mill. (Courtesy Edna Wirth.)

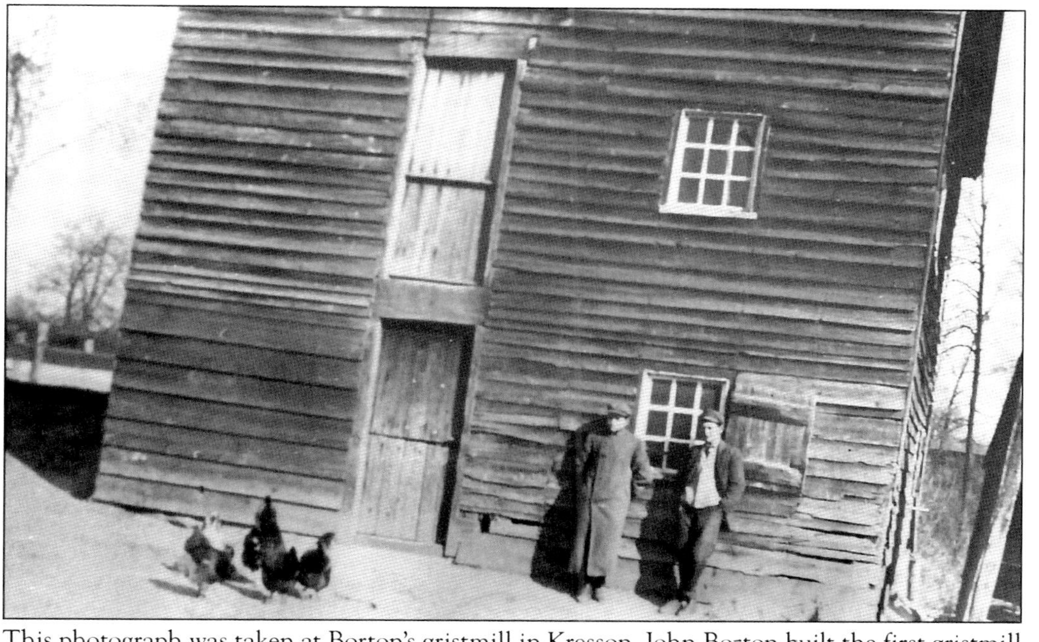

This photograph was taken at Borton's gristmill in Kresson. John Borton built the first gristmill here sometime before 1753. Borton's son Isaac constructed the mill shown here. The mill remained in the Borton family until 1808, when Reuben Matlack purchased it from the estate of Isaac Borton. Ownership of the mill changed several times before operations shut down in the 1930s. (Courtesy Edna Wirth.)

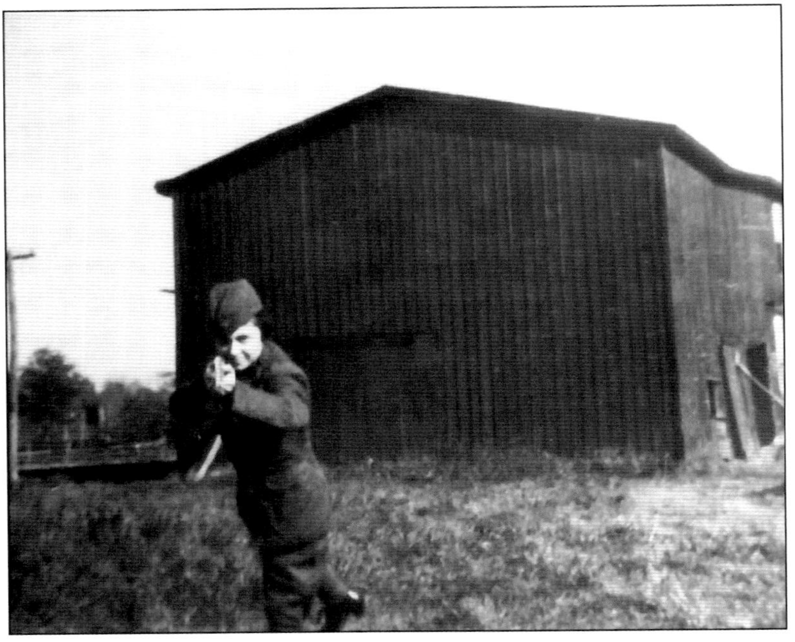

Joseph Dumphey constructed this large building, known as the soap factory, about 1890 along the railroad tracks at Maple Avenue. Along with the manufacturing of soap, a machine shop operated here as well as a manufactory of toys and plant pills. School classes were held here while the first addition was being made to the Marlton School. (Courtesy Edna Wirth.)

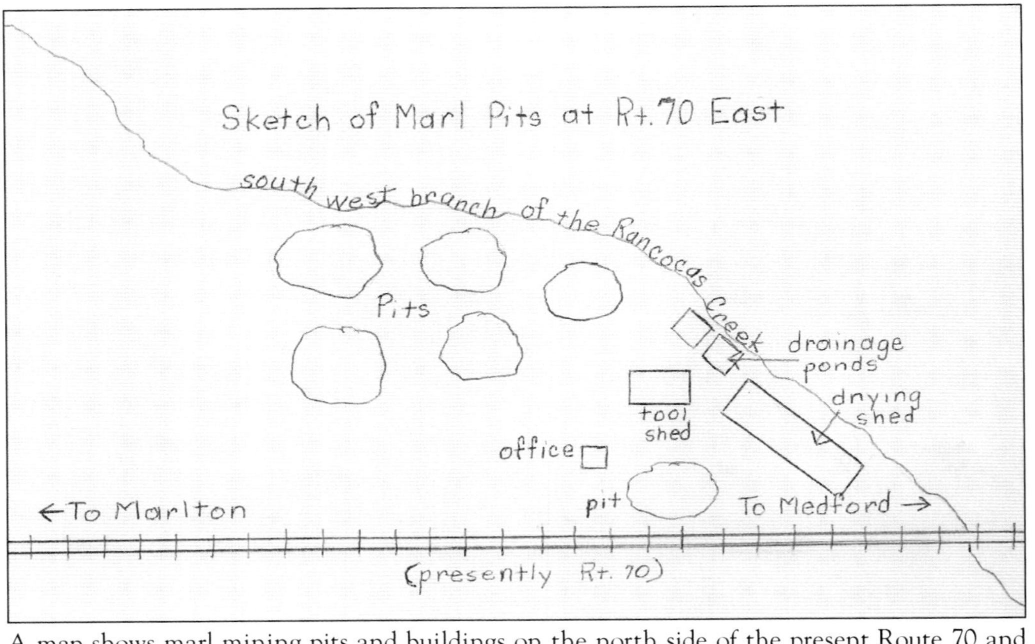

A map shows marl mining pits and buildings on the north side of the present Route 70 and Radnor Boulevard intersection. Some of these pits reached 90 feet in depth. Workmen lowered a six- or eight-inch pipe with flexible joints into the pits and then pumped out marl in a liquid state, which spewed on the ground. Workers shoveled the marl onto a wire screen for straining. The strained marl was then dried in a shed until it became a fine powder. The pits closed around 1930. (Courtesy Edna Wirth.)

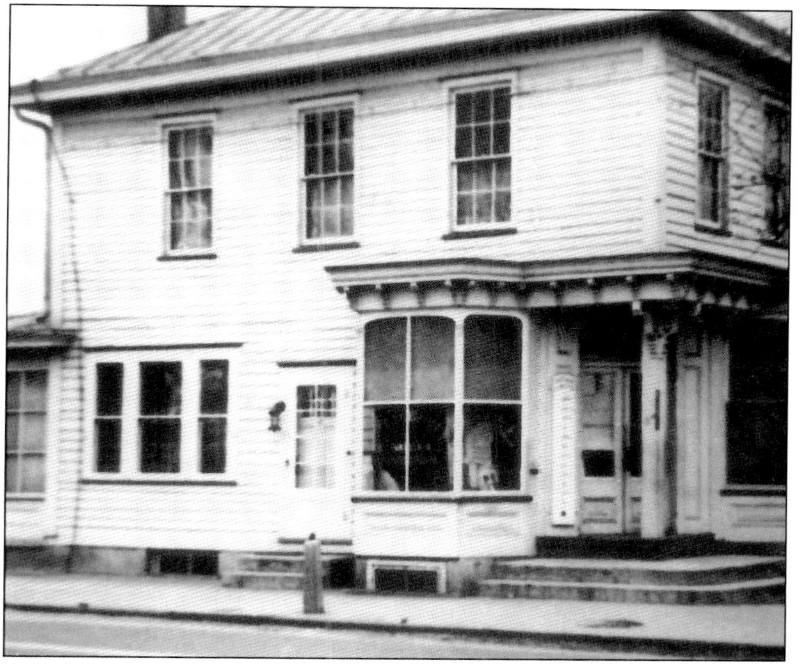

Shown here is 2 West Main Street before it became the Cranberry Scoop ice cream parlor. William Hammet constructed this building. William Zelley purchased it in 1877, and it became Zelley's Drug Store. Zelley also served as postmaster in Marlton. (Courtesy Edna Wirth.)

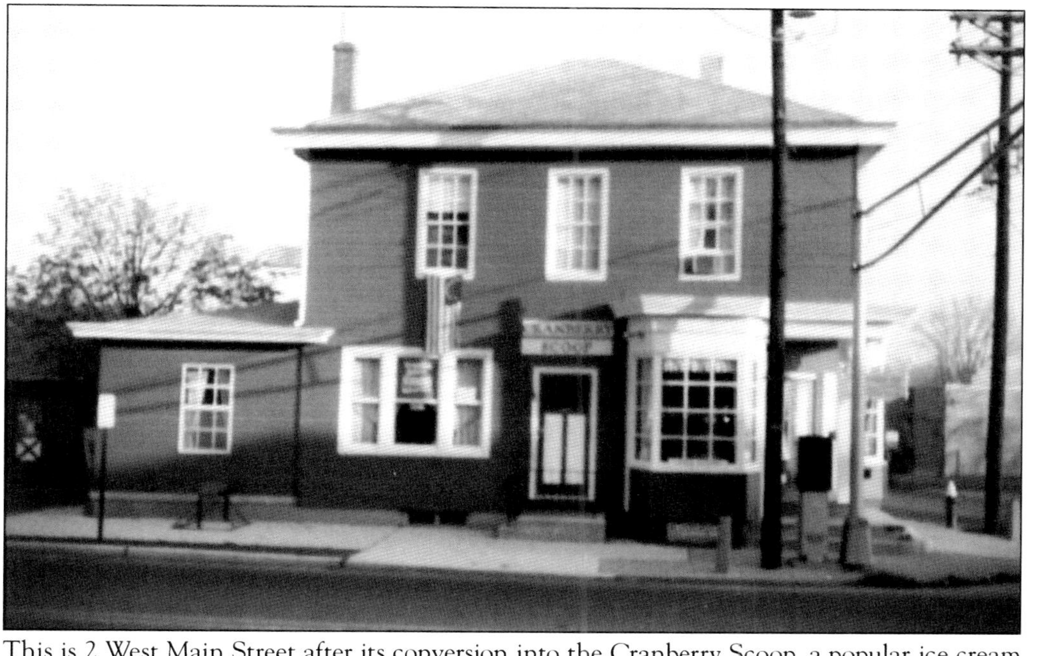

This is 2 West Main Street after its conversion into the Cranberry Scoop. a popular ice cream parlor in the 1970s and early 1980s. (Courtesy Edna Wirth.)

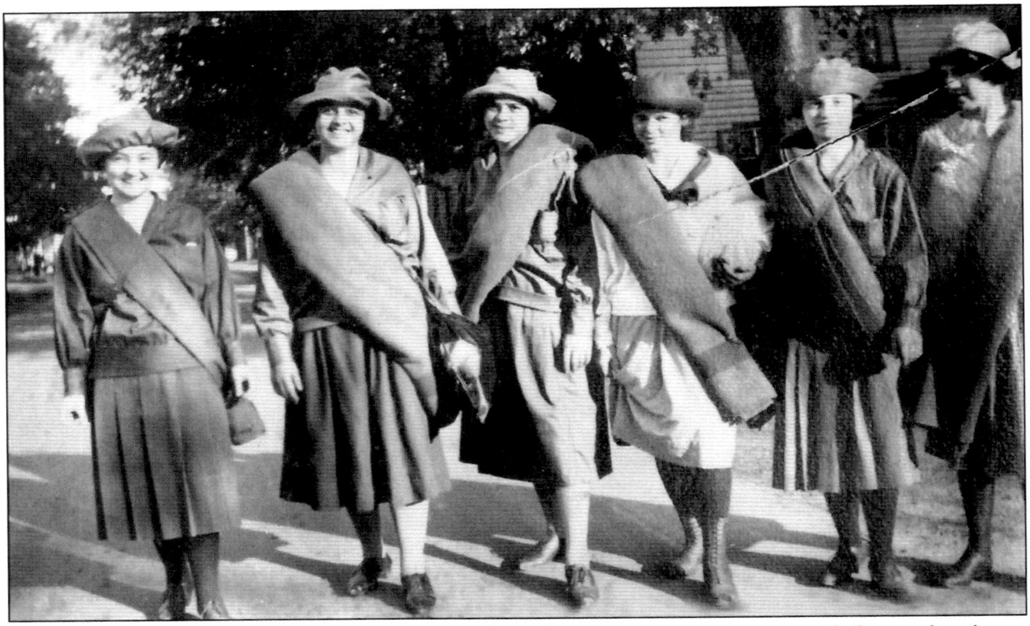

This June 1922 photograph shows a group of Marlton women starting on a hike to the shore. Pictured are, from left to right, Emily Donahue, Alice Endicott, Ethel Wells, Hannah Wells, Ritchie Wells, and Francis Endicott. (Courtesy Evesham Historical Society.)

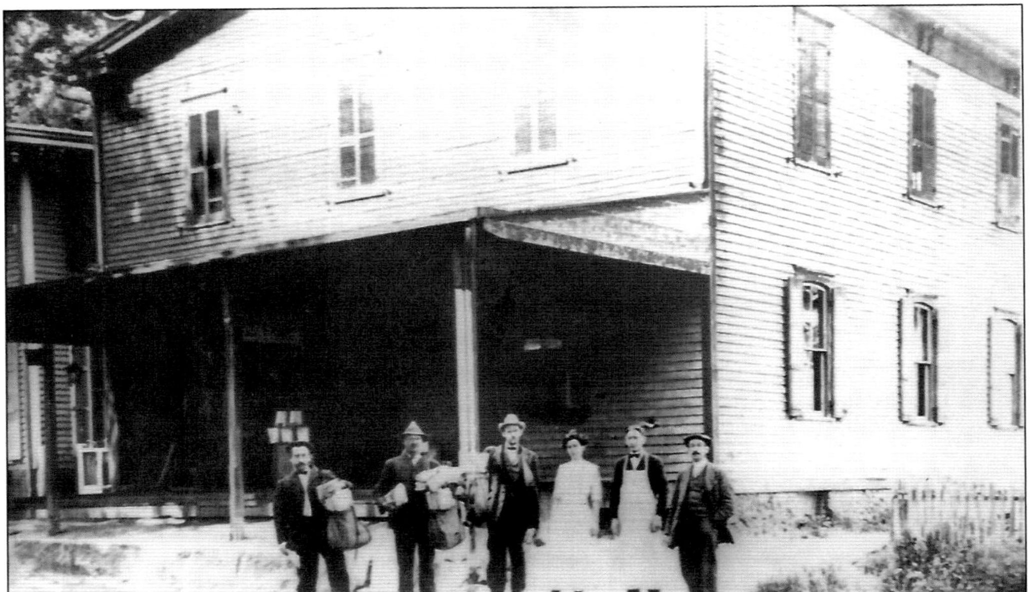

Seen here are, from left to right, Ed Vennel, Howard Wells, Walter Winner, Annie Wells, R.W. Ripple, and Charles Middleton. They are standing in front of a building at 6 North Maple Avenue that housed at different times the Grange Hall, Endicott's store and post office, and Marlton General Hardware. In the late 1970s, the building was moved to Route 70 and was converted into the Old Marlton Inn. Later, in the 1980s, it became the Marlton office of Weichert Realtors. (Courtesy Edna Wirth.)

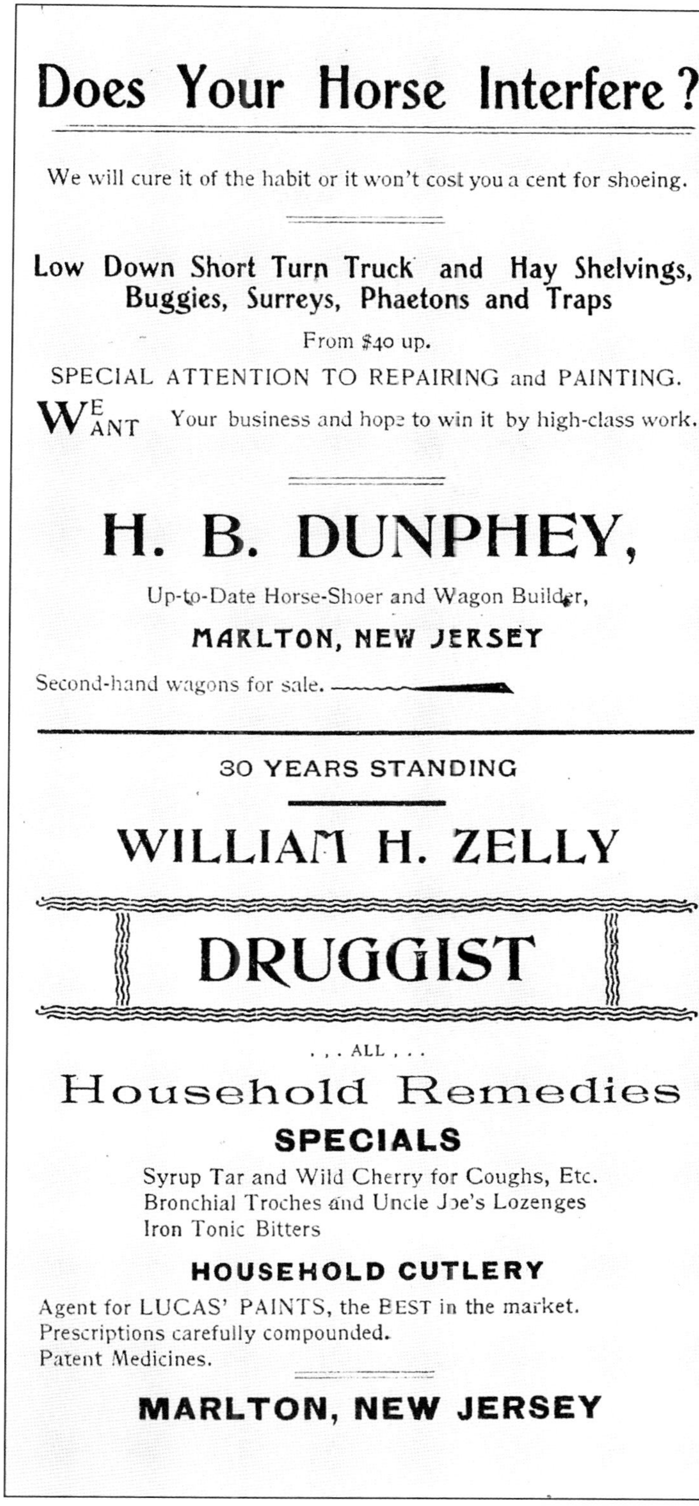

Does Your Horse Interfere?

We will cure it of the habit or it won't cost you a cent for shoeing.

Low Down Short Turn Truck and Hay Shelvings,
Buggies, Surreys, Phaetons and Traps

From $40 up.

SPECIAL ATTENTION TO REPAIRING and PAINTING.

WE WANT Your business and hope to win it by high-class work.

H. B. DUNPHEY,

Up-to-Date Horse-Shoer and Wagon Builder,

MARLTON, NEW JERSEY

Second-hand wagons for sale.

30 YEARS STANDING

WILLIAM H. ZELLY

DRUGGIST

. . . ALL . . .

Household Remedies

SPECIALS

Syrup Tar and Wild Cherry for Coughs, Etc.
Bronchial Troches and Uncle Joe's Lozenges
Iron Tonic Bitters

HOUSEHOLD CUTLERY

Agent for LUCAS' PAINTS, the BEST in the market.
Prescriptions carefully compounded.
Patent Medicines.

MARLTON, NEW JERSEY

These are advertisements for H.B. Dunphey and William Zelley from 1900. Dunphey was known for his fine workmanship building wagons, buggies, and carriages. He opened a blacksmith shop in 1893 on West Main Street.

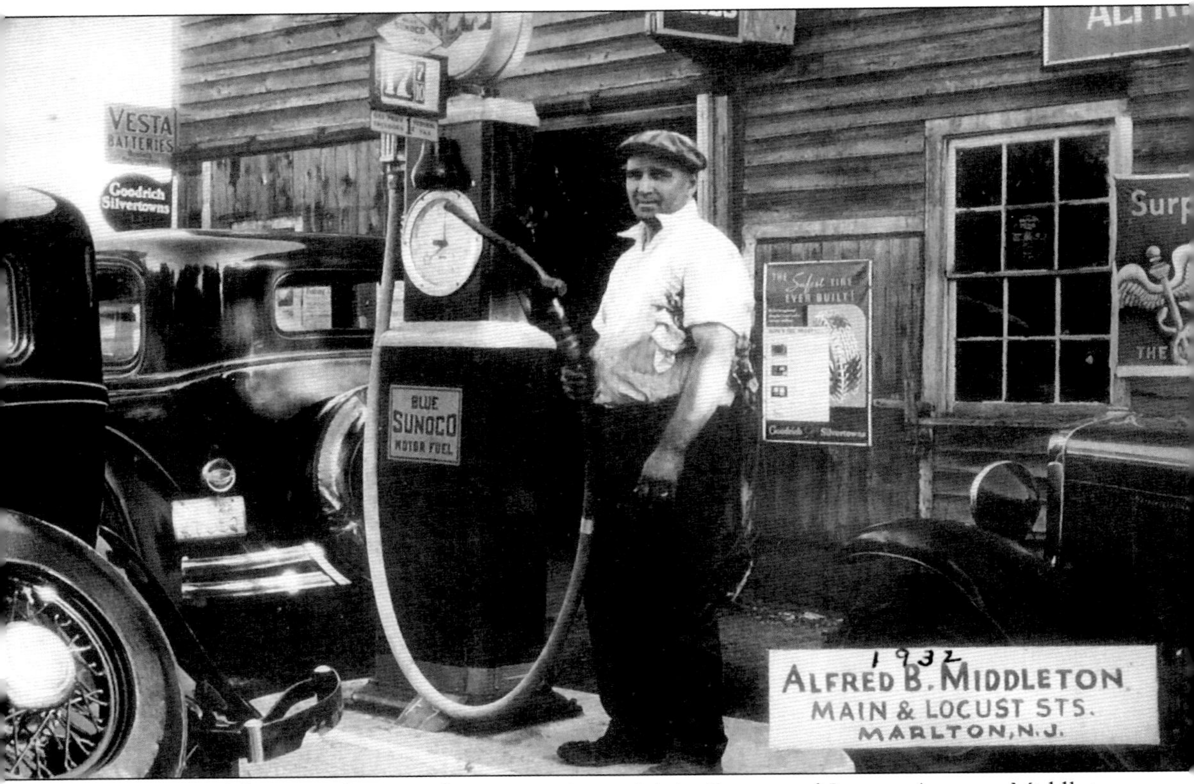

Alfred Middleton is shown at his gas station at Main Street and Locust Avenue. Middleton converted the old carriage shop originally owned by Benjamin Kain and later George Haines into a garage and added gas pumps. Blacksmith Harry Ross continued to work in a shop in the back of the station until he retired in 1953. (Courtesy Evesham Historical Society.)

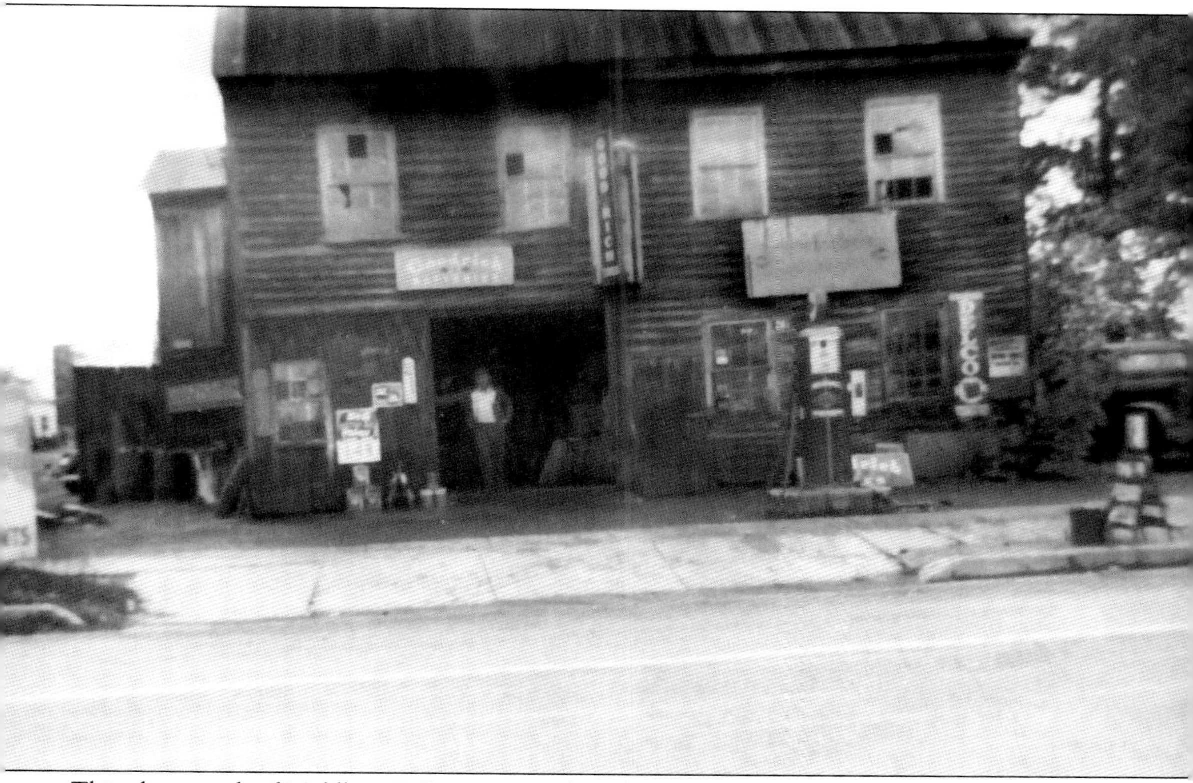

This photograph of Middleton's Garage was taken about 1949 with "Nabe" Middleton standing in the doorway. In 1953, this building was demolished, and a new service station was built. An automobile service shop still operates here. (Courtesy Evesham Historical Society.)

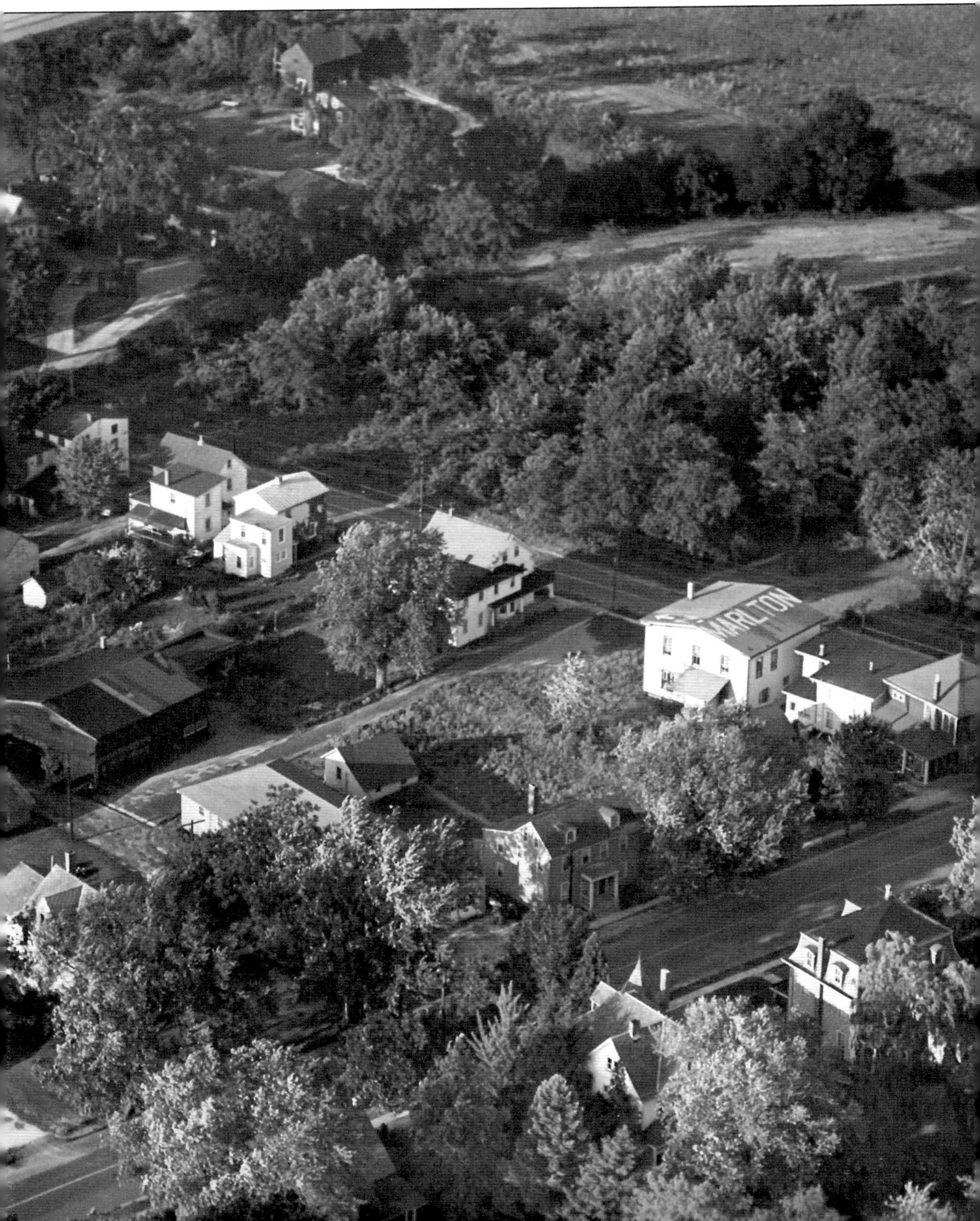
MARLTON

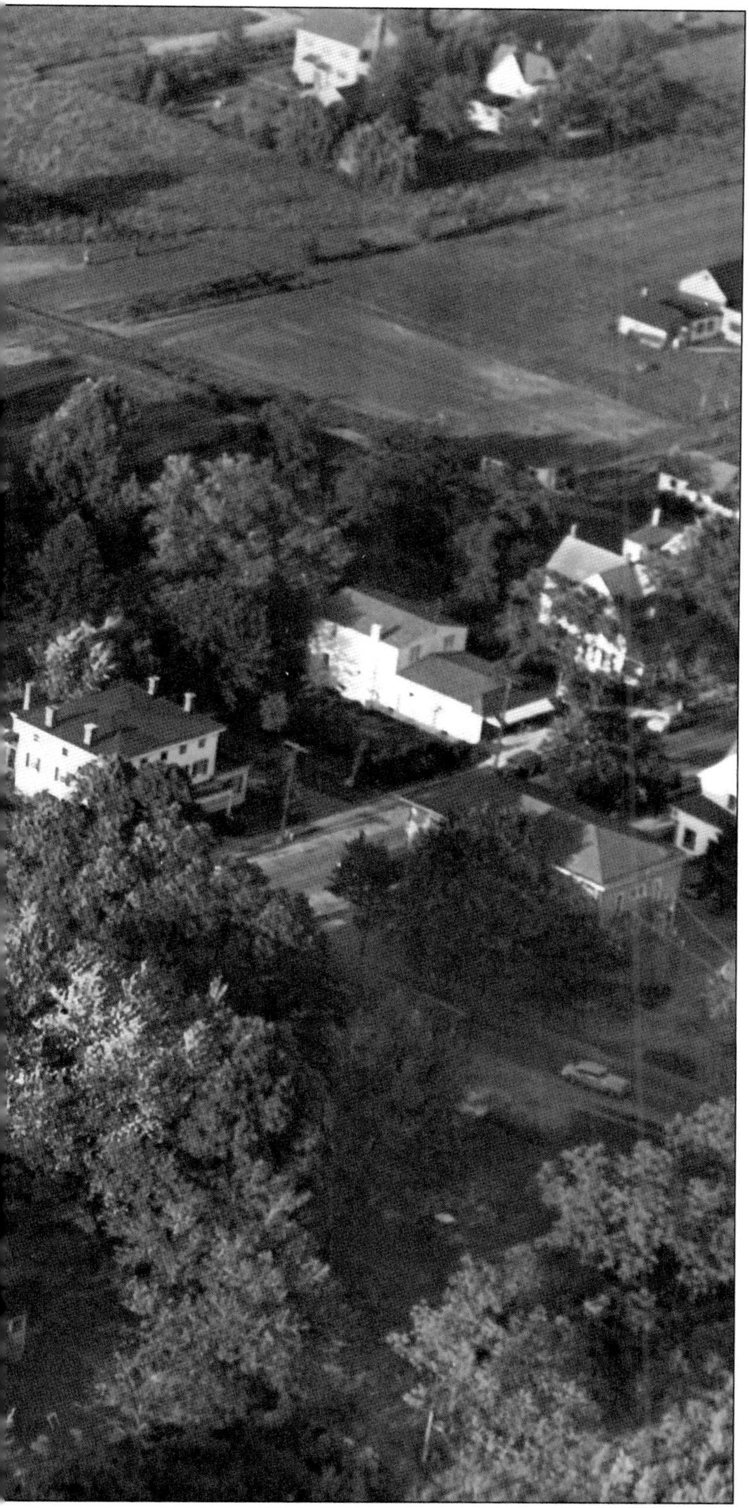

This aerial view shows the center of Marlton. John Inskeep III opened a store in 1758 that may have given birth to the village of Marlton. The south boundary of his plantation would become Main Street in Marlton. Inskeep recognized a need for a store, since the area was completely rural at that time. The third generations of the Lippincott, Eves, Evans, Hewlings, Troth, and Wills families were arriving and would need a place to buy supplies. Customers could buy meat, cheese, butter, hardware items, tobacco, dry goods, and clothing. Marlton was originally known as Rising Sun, named after a tavern in the village. The discovery of marl near the village in 1806, and the industry it created, started a building boom. Marlton soon boasted about 30 homes, two churches, a schoolhouse, and more businesses. Marlton then became the commerce and social center of Evesham. A post office opened here in 1808. It was Evesham Post Office until 1845, when it was named for the village of Marlton. The road that became Maple Avenue opened in 1813, and its intersection with Main Street became the hub of Marlton. After 1900, a water company, fire company, gasworks, and a newspaper served Marlton. (Courtesy Evesham Historical Society.)

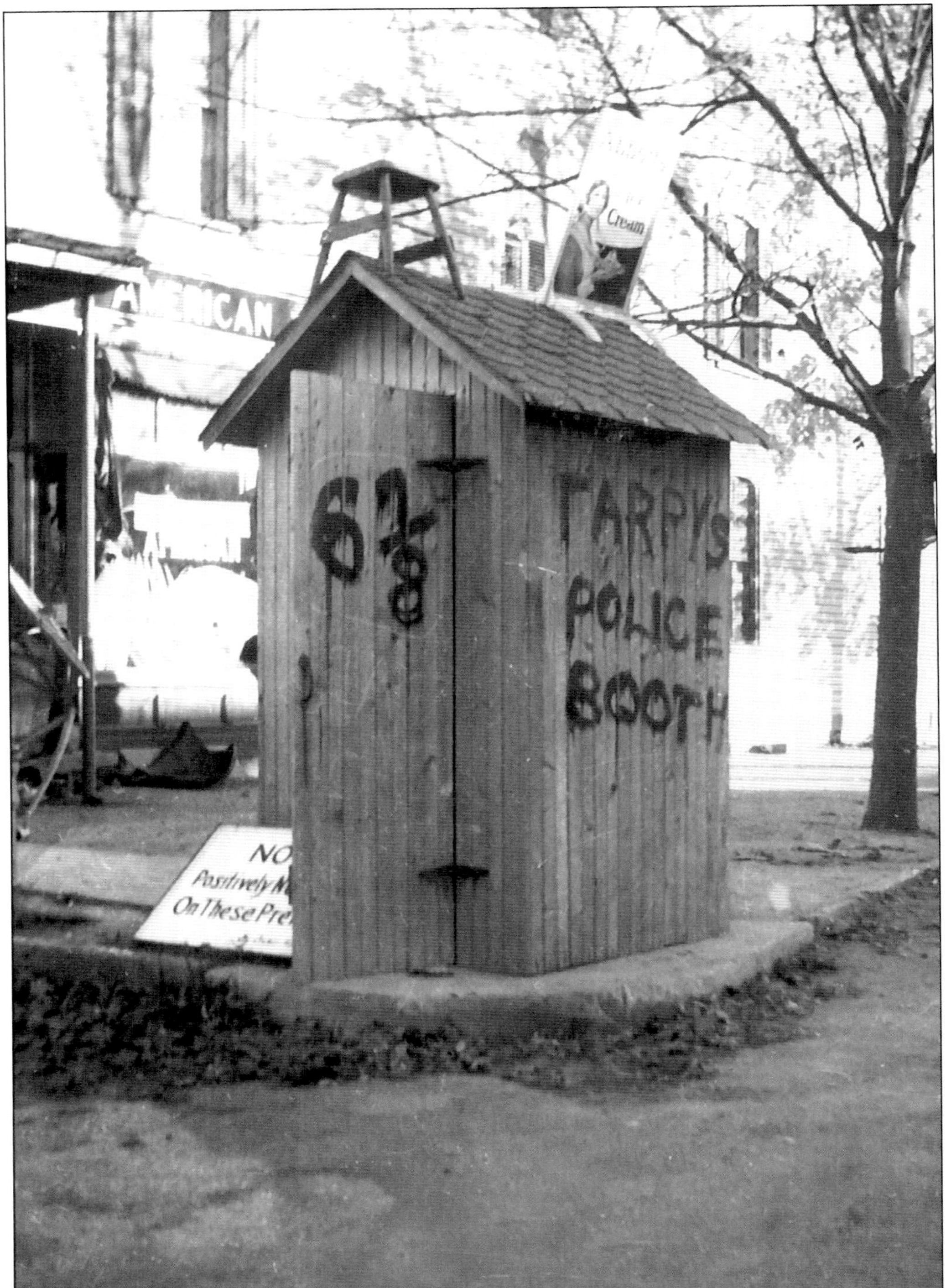

For a late-1930s Halloween prank, the outhouse at Cline's Barber Shop was moved to Main Street and Maple Avenue and marked as the police chief's booth. (Courtesy Evesham Historical Society.)

Two

CHURCHES

The Society of Friends, or Quakers, established the first organized worship in Evesham Township. In England, the Quakers had suffered religious persecution and departed for the New World in hopes of finding friendlier shores. In 1760, the Quakers built a meetinghouse in present-day Mount Laurel, which at that time was part of Evesham Township. The Cropwell Friends Meeting House dates to 1809. Friends also met at Quaker schools and homes in the area.

Other denominations began to build their houses of worship. The Baptists constructed their church in 1805, followed by the Methodists in 1824. Religious growth continued through the 20th century with the addition of the non-denominational Wiley Mission and St. Joan of Arc Roman Catholic Church. This Catholic parish served all of Evesham Township until increasing numbers of parishioners required St. Isaac Jogues to be built in 1996. The Prince of Peace Lutheran Church was established in the 1960s as well as Marlton Presbyterian Church. In recent years, a synagogue, Congregation Beth Tikveh, and several non-denominational places of worship have been added. This religious growth through the years supports the Quakers' original theory that they and others could enjoy religious freedom in this area.

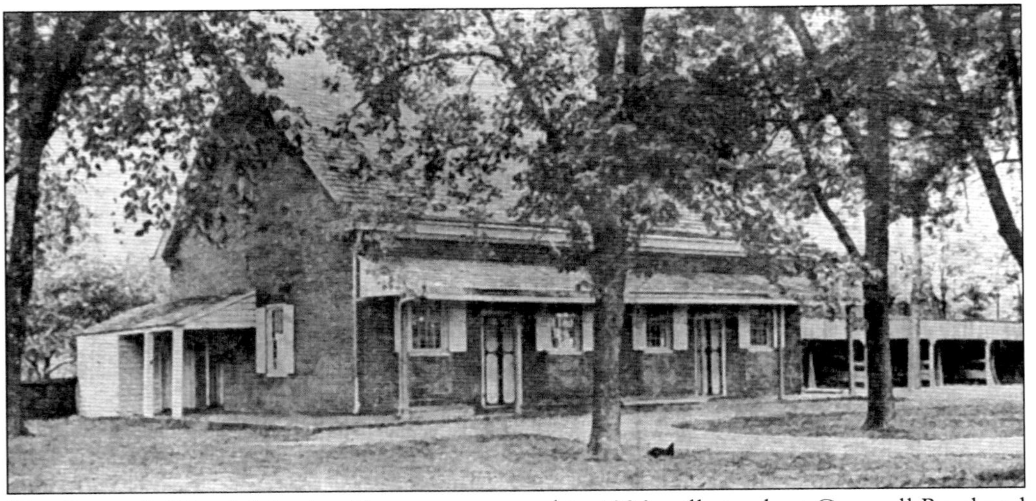

The Cropwell Friends Meeting House, constructed in 1806, still stands at Cropwell Road and Marlton Pike. It provided an overnight stopover for Quakers traveling from Philadelphia to Tuckerton. Prior to constructing the meetinghouse, the friends held their services in a one-room schoolhouse built on the grounds in 1785.

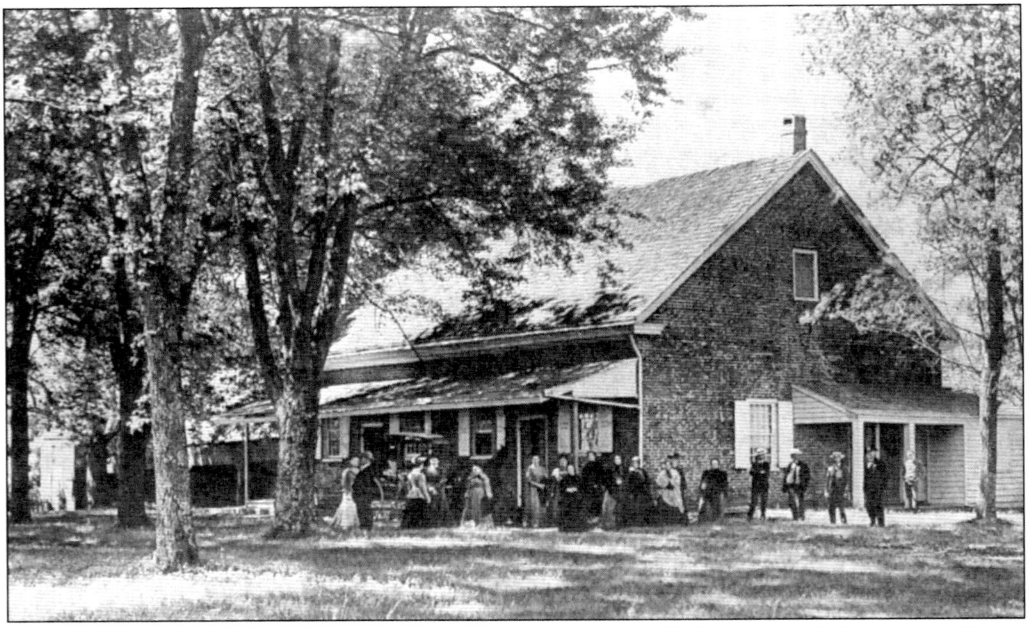

Shown is the Cropwell Friends Meeting House on August 17, 1905. Quakers built this meetinghouse to avoid traveling to Haddonfield or Mount Laurel to attend meetings. The building remains unchanged today, with the exception of electricity being installed. (Courtesy Jeffrey Auchter.)

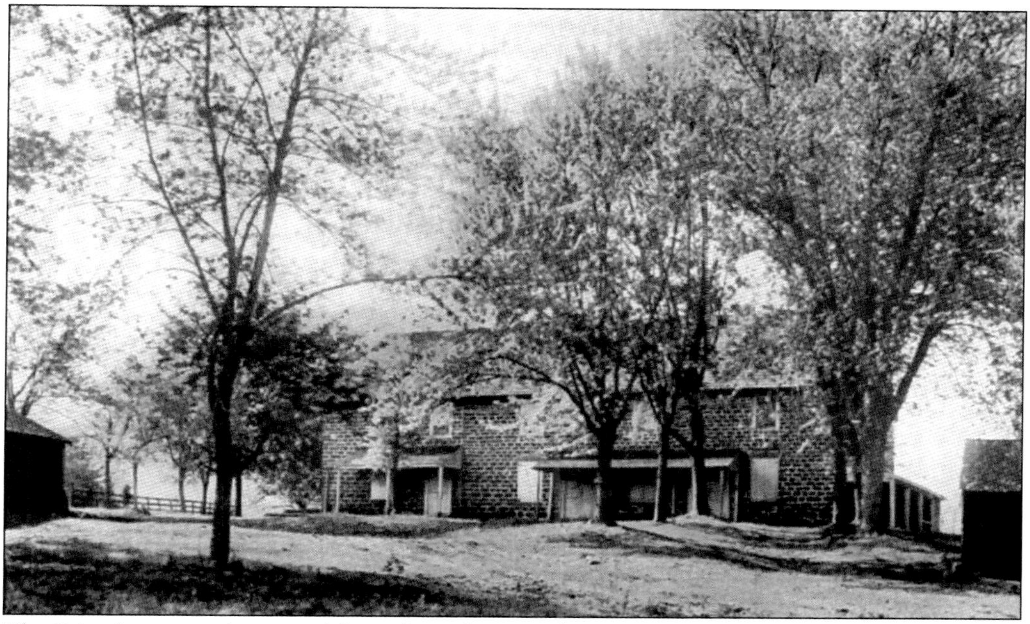

The Friends meetinghouse at Mount Laurel is seen here. Built in 1760, the Quakers called this building the Evesham Meeting House, since Mount Laurel did not become a separate township until 1872. The sandstone used for the building was quarried on Mount Laurel. Early settlers of Evesham would travel here or to Haddonfield to attend meetings. Mount Laurel is the oldest meetinghouse still standing in Burlington County and is still in use.

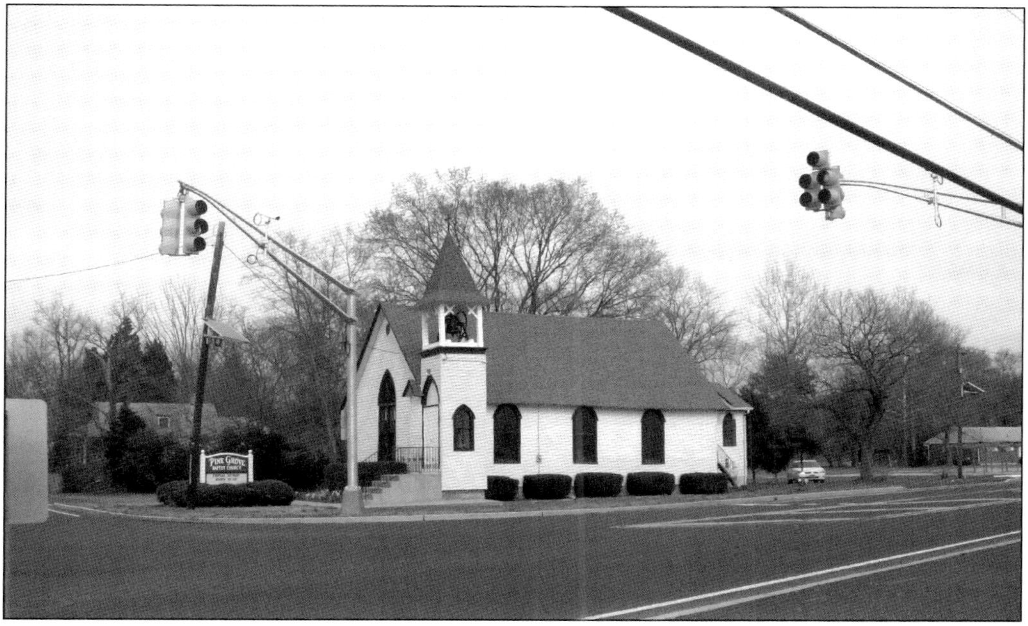

The Pine Grove Baptist Church is shown in 2012. This church, built in 1906, still stands on part of what was the Whittaker farm. Before being built, the congregation met in what was a former Friends schoolhouse on Paul Avenue, which later became the parsonage. (Photograph by author.)

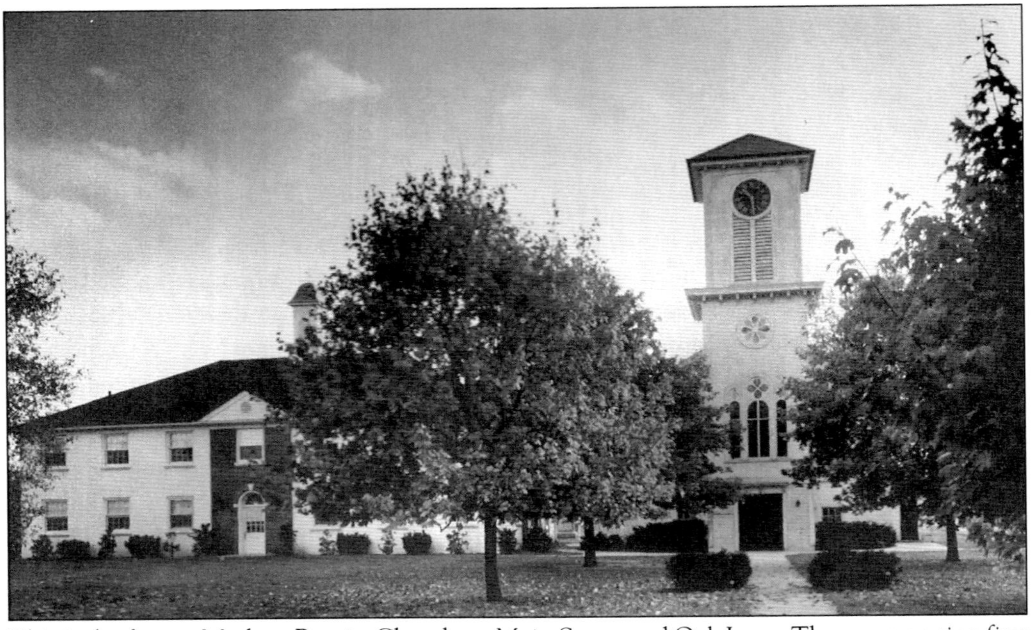

This is the former Marlton Baptist Church on Main Street and Oak Lane. The congregation first met about a mile east of Marlton as Evesham Baptist Church. They constructed this building in 1839 and changed the name to Marlton Baptist Church. The structure on the left dates to 1959 and served as an educational building and a fellowship hall. This congregation disbanded in the early 1990s, and the building then became the Calvary Chapel.

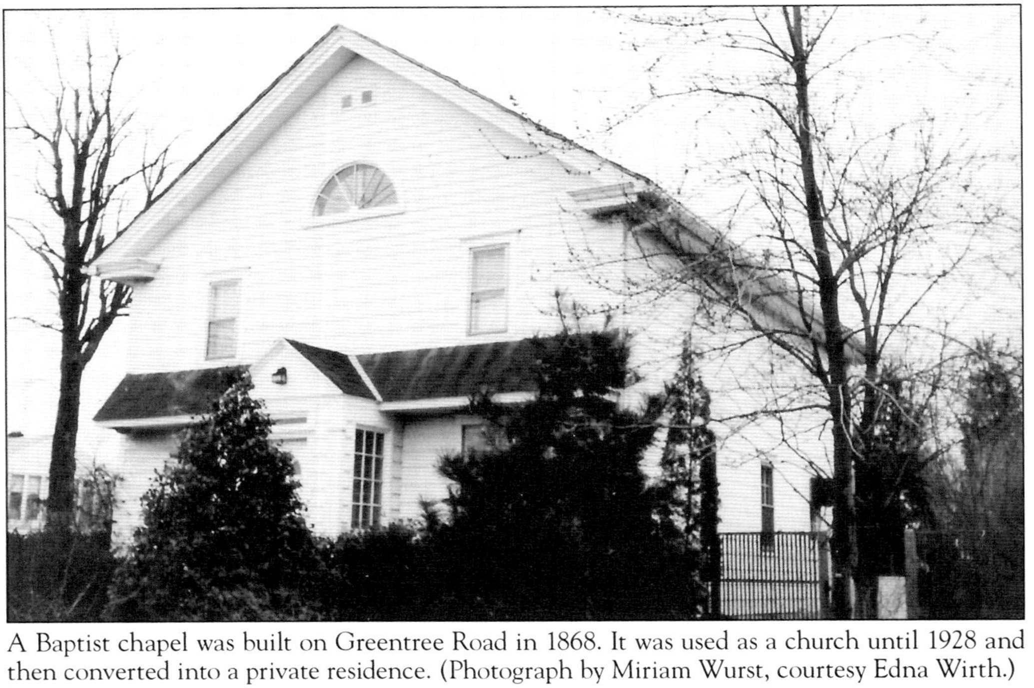

A Baptist chapel was built on Greentree Road in 1868. It was used as a church until 1928 and then converted into a private residence. (Photograph by Miriam Wurst, courtesy Edna Wirth.)

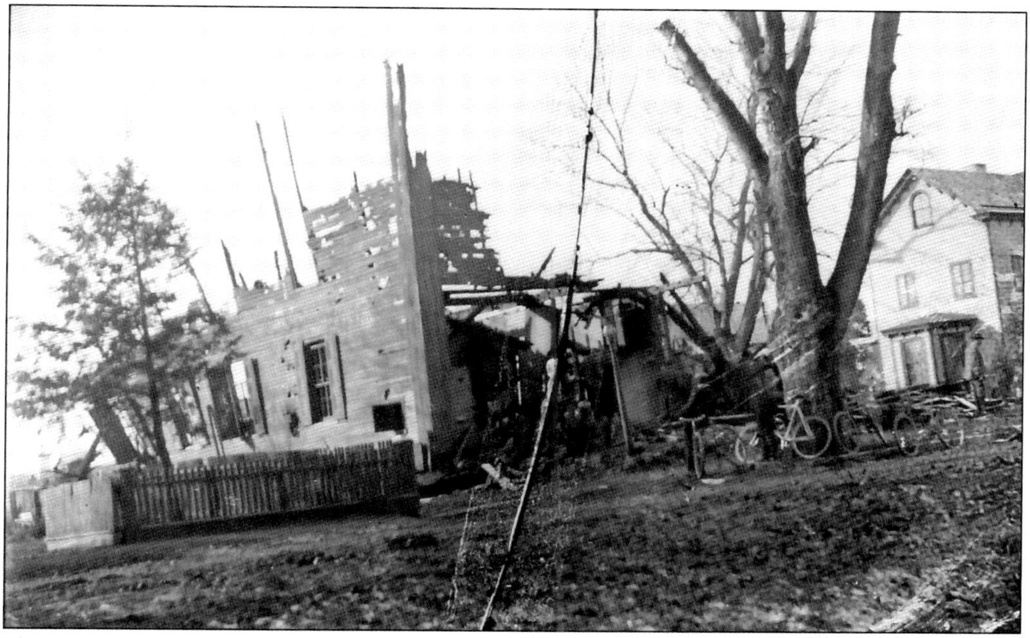

Shown are the remains of the Marlton Episcopal Methodist Church after a fire struck in December 1898. This was the first blaze fought by the Marlton Fire Company, which was formed earlier that year. After removing the ruins at 43 East Main Street, the congregation built and dedicated a replacement church in 1899. (Courtesy Edna Wirth.)

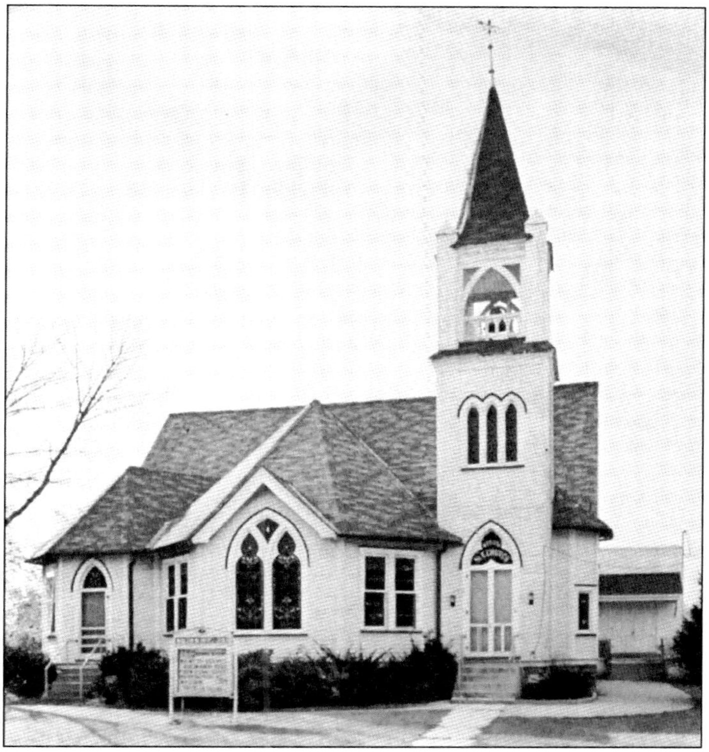

The Methodist Church in Marlton began in 1824 when members met in homes. The Marlton Methodist Episcopal Church was incorporated in 1838 and constructed a temporary building at 43 East Main Street. The congregants completed a larger church in 1858. The Methodists sold the temporary church and moved it farther west on Main Street. A fire swept through the 1858 building in 1898. The building shown here replaced the one that burned and was completed in less than a year.

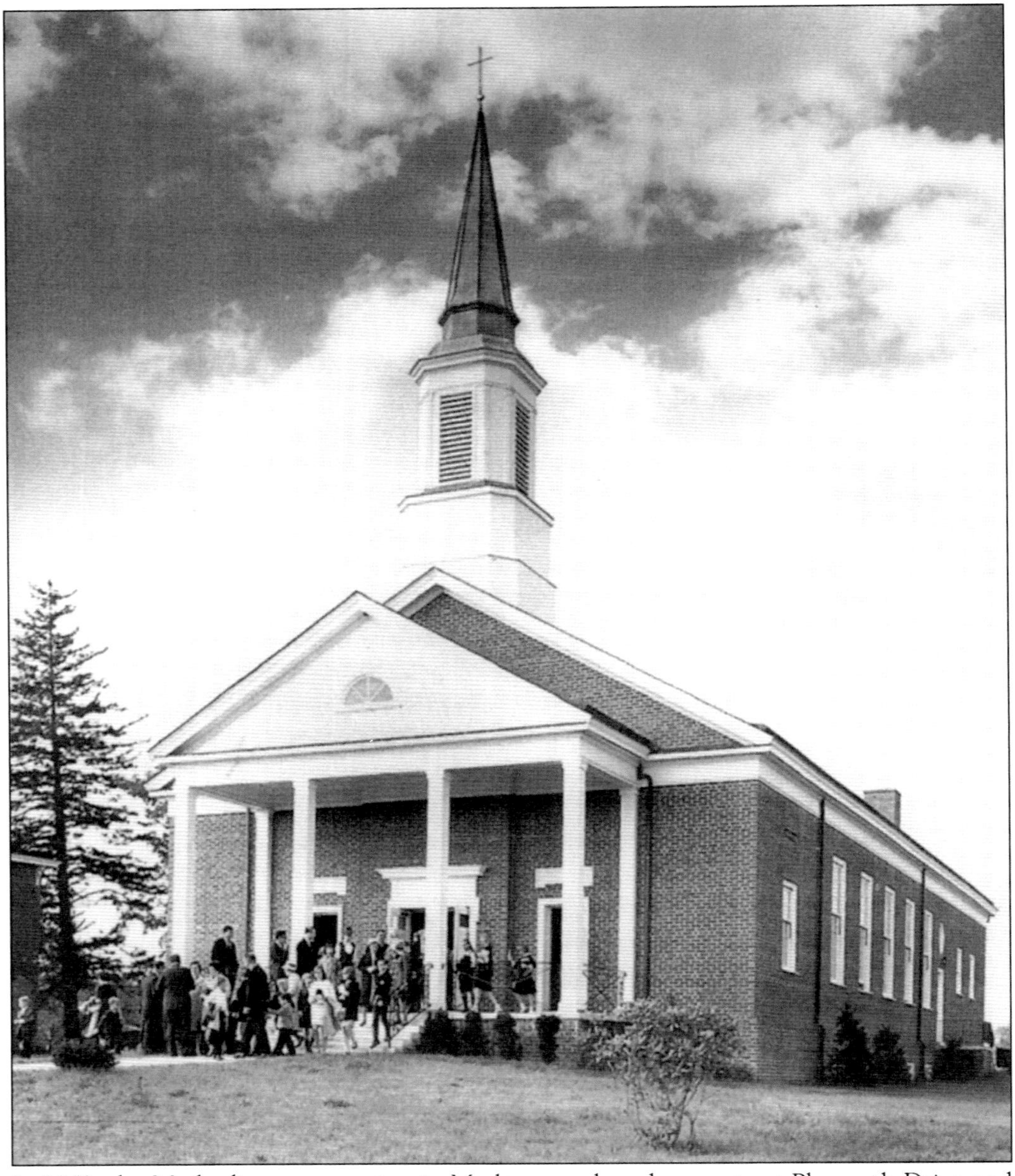

In 1962, the Methodist congregation in Marlton purchased property at Plymouth Drive and Marlborough Avenue and completed a new church building there in 1964 to replace the Main Street church. The congregation held its first service on Good Friday in 1964. The church became Marlton United Methodist Church in 1968 following the merger of the Methodist Episcopal Church and the Evangelical United Brethren Church. (Courtesy Marlton United Methodist Church.)

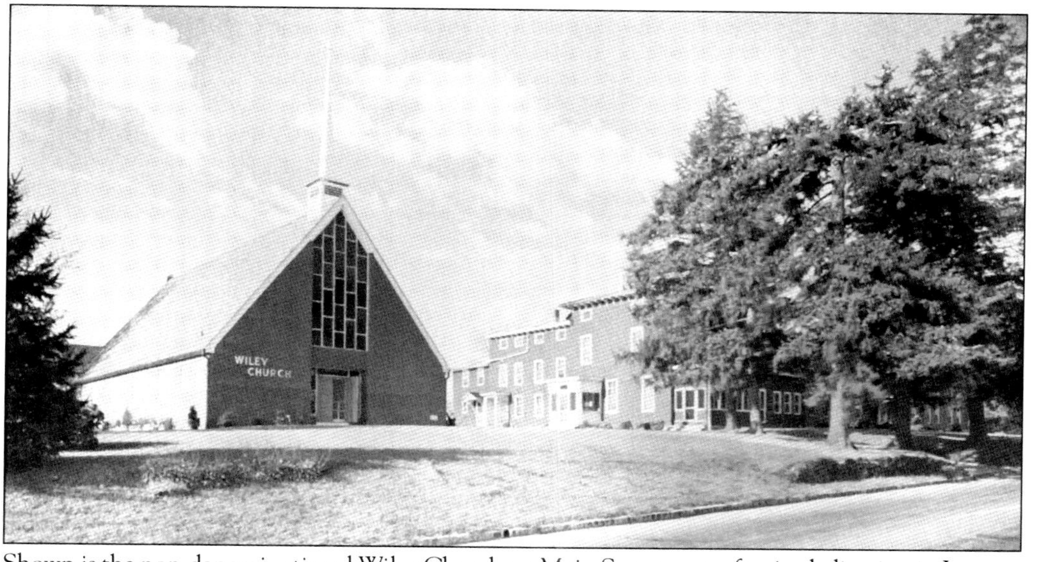

Shown is the non-denominational Wiley Church on Main Street soon after its dedication in January 1962. The church stands adjacent to what is today the Wiley Retirement Community. The Wiley residents, as well as people from the surrounding community, attend this place of worship.

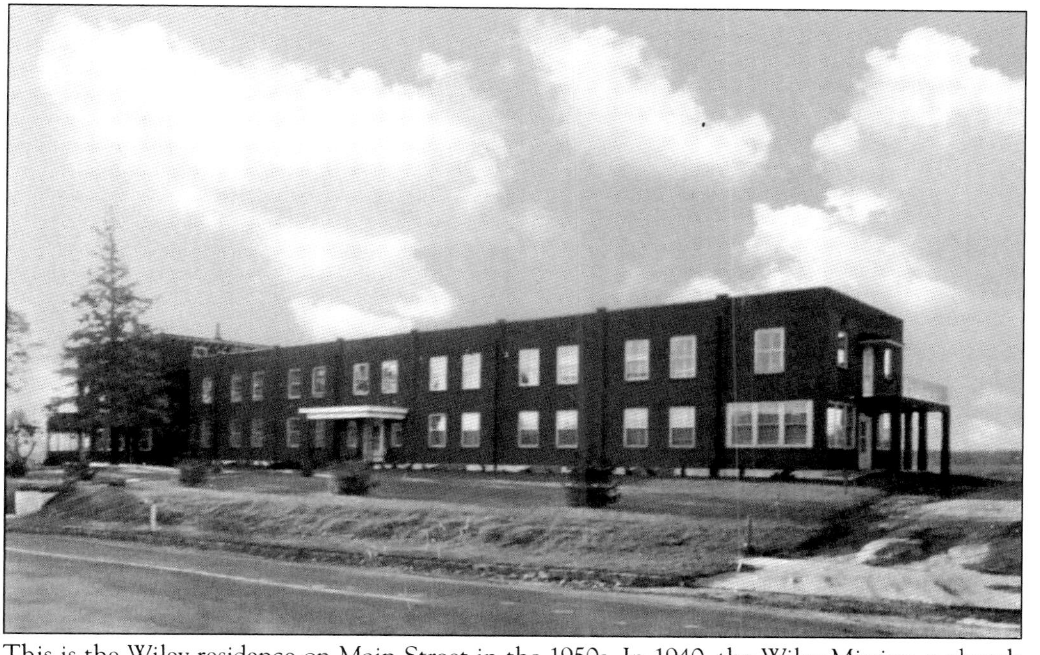

This is the Wiley residence on Main Street in the 1950s. In 1940, the Wiley Mission, a church first founded in Camden in 1929, purchased 70 acres on Main Street in Marlton. The church renovated a 19-room home there to become the Wiley Home for the Aged. The home then expanded to 27 rooms in 1942. Plans were drafted and work begun in 1949 for a 37-room addition. (Courtesy Wiley Mission.)

WILEY HOME

of the

WILEY MISSION, Incorporated

99 EAST MAIN STREET

MARLTON, NEW JERSEY

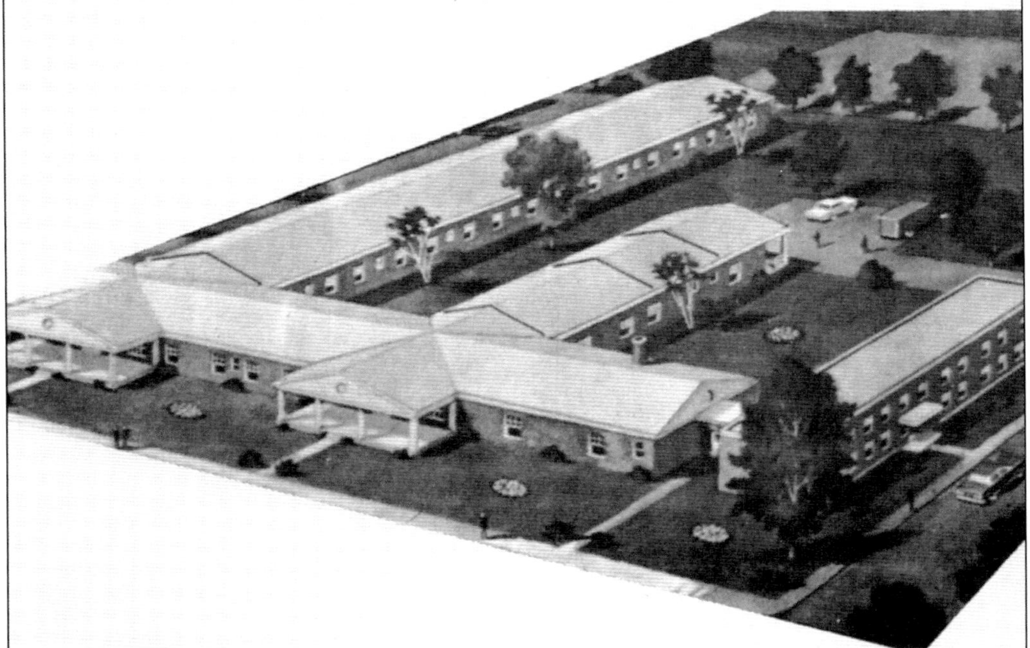

DEDICATED TO THE GLORY OF GOD

APRIL 3, 1966

3:00 P.M.

In April 1965, Wiley Mission broke ground for a 58-room building. Dedication of this building occurred in April 1966. (Courtesy Evesham Historical Society.)

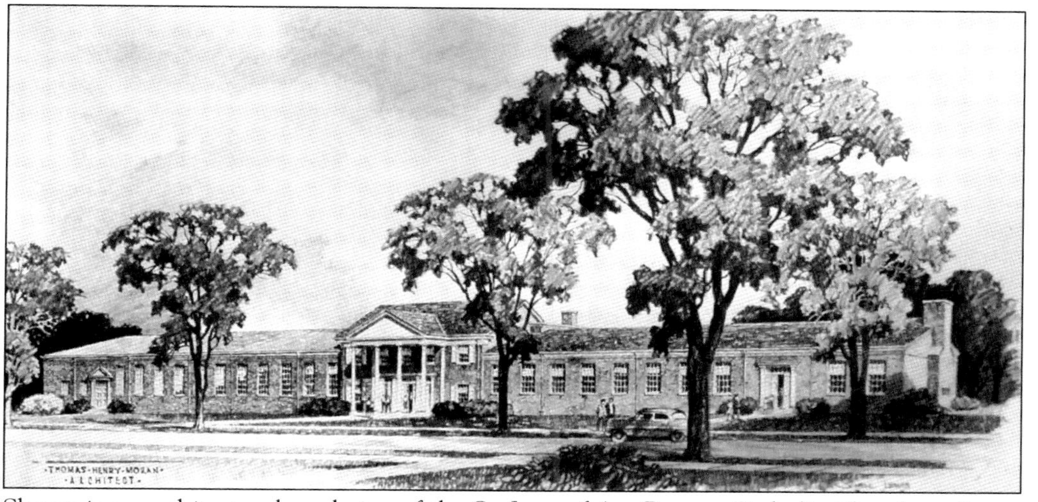

Shown is an architectural rendering of the St. Joan of Arc Roman Catholic Church on Evans Road. The Trenton Diocese established the parish in June 1961, and the congregation first held Mass at the Evans School. Ground was broken for the Church on October 17, 1962, and completed in 1963. The rectory was originally in the London Square development and later moved to a building on the church grounds along Willow Bend Road. St. Joan of Arc School opened in 1965 for grades one through five and expanded to eighth grade in 1968.

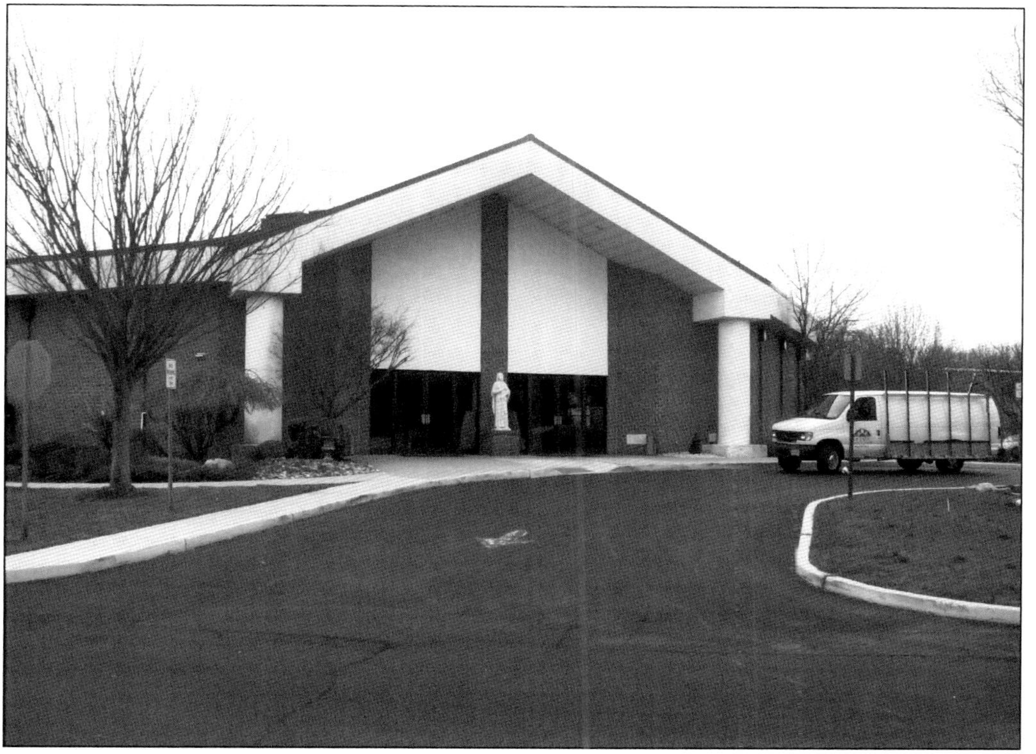

St. Joan of Arc built a new church in 1988 behind the original building. (Photograph by author.)

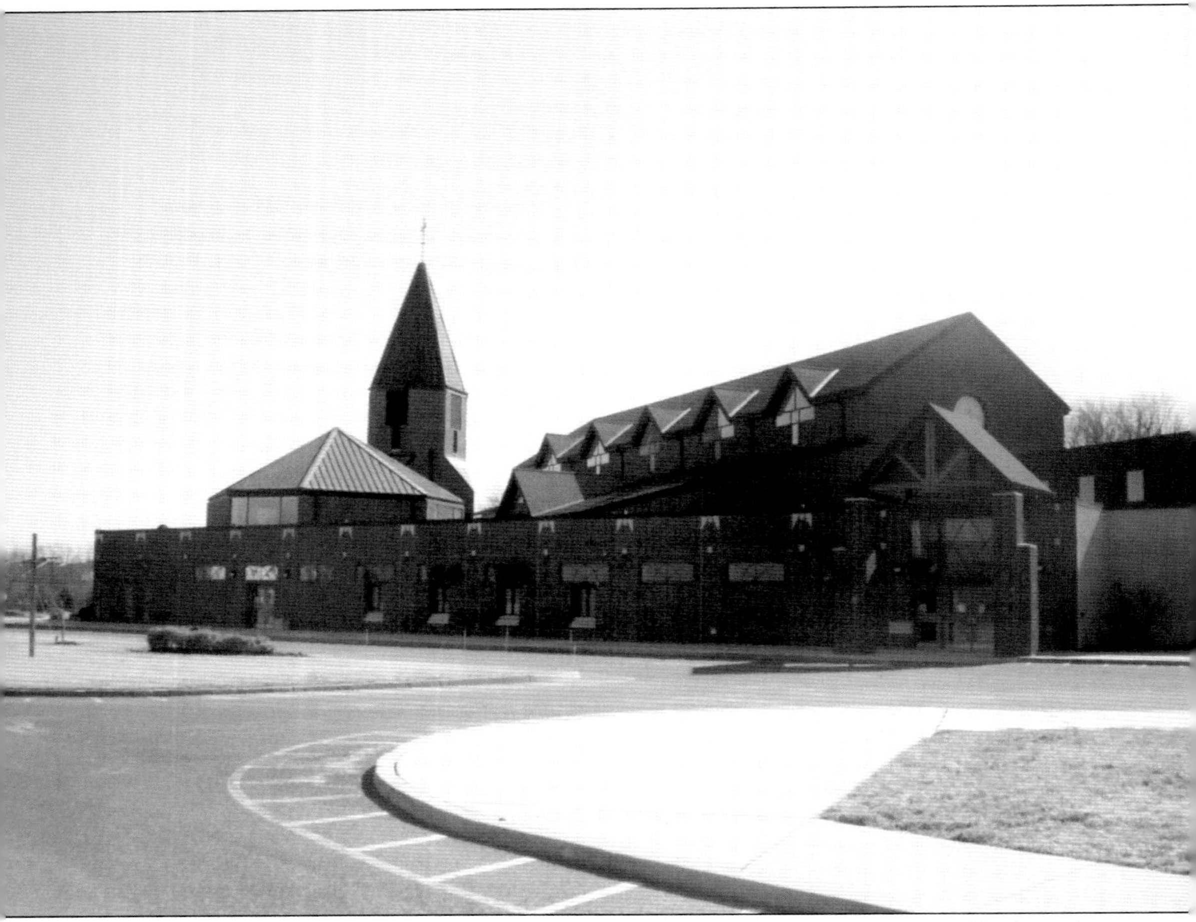

This photograph shows the St. Isaac Jogues Roman Catholic Church on Medford-Evesboro Road. The diocese founded this church in 1996 after the splitting of the St. Joan of Arc parish. (Photograph by author.)

Three

Farms

Thomas Evans, the son of William Evans, the original settler in the area, received a patent for 1,000 acres in Evesham Township. It was located about two miles east of what is now the town of Marlton. He paid Native Americans $25 for this land. Over time, the Evans family divided the land into smaller farms. Most of it was wooded and needed to be cleared of trees and brush, which at that time was a huge task. They accomplished it with handsaws, logging wheels, and oxen. Some of the logs were transported to Philadelphia by way of the creeks and the Delaware River. After arriving in Philadelphia, sawyers cut the timber into lumber to be used for buildings and ships. Smaller streams running through the southern area became cranberry bogs, as the soil in that area was sandy and acidic and not suitable for other types of crops.

Other families, following the Evans' example, established their own farms. These included the Lippincott, Hewlings, Troth, Sharp, Inskeep, Burrough, Haines, Eves, Wills, and Venable family tracts, which were also divided into smaller farms through the years. Farming continued to be a major industry in Evesham until the 1950s, when the first farms were sold to housing developers. After a gradual decline, a few farms remained into the 1980s.

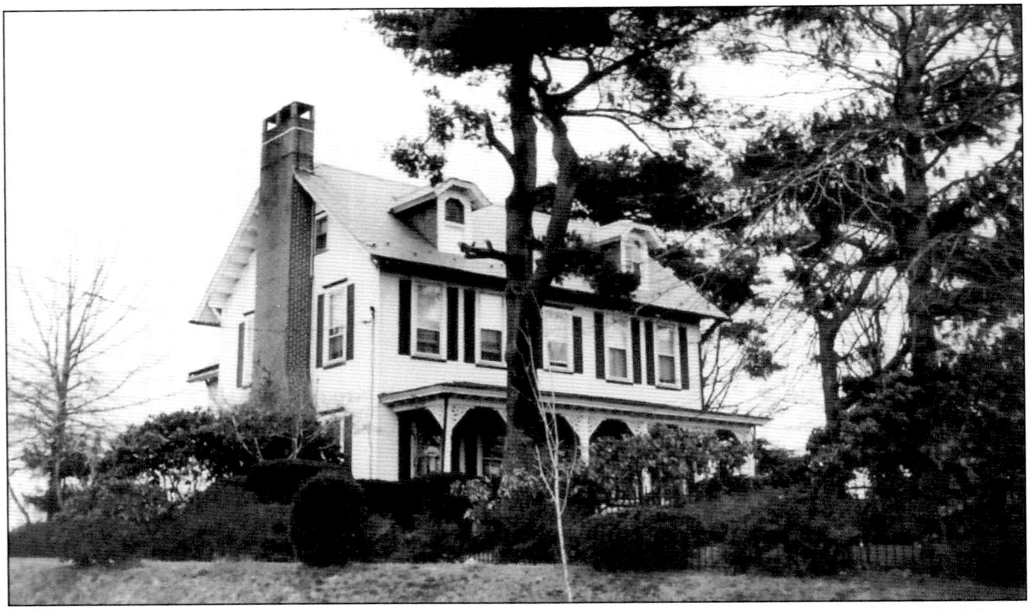

Samuel Lippincott was one of Evesham's first settlers, arriving about 1700. He had land holdings scattered throughout the town. This house belonged to a descendant around 1825 and had a driveway connecting it to Marlton Pike. It is now surrounded by a section of Woodstream. An addition was later made to the rear. This addition was separated in 1906 and rolled down a meadow on logs to create a separate dwelling, which later housed the G Boys Garden Center. (Photograph by Miriam Wurst, courtesy Edna Wirth.)

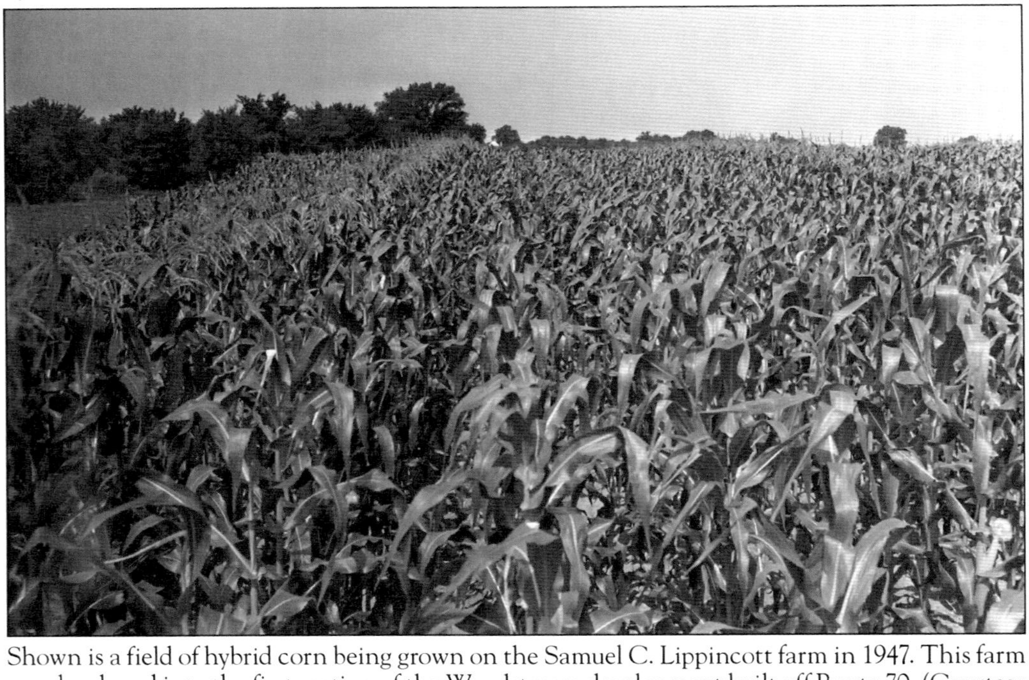

Shown is a field of hybrid corn being grown on the Samuel C. Lippincott farm in 1947. This farm was developed into the first section of the Woodstream development built off Route 70. (Courtesy New Jersey State Archives, Department of State.)

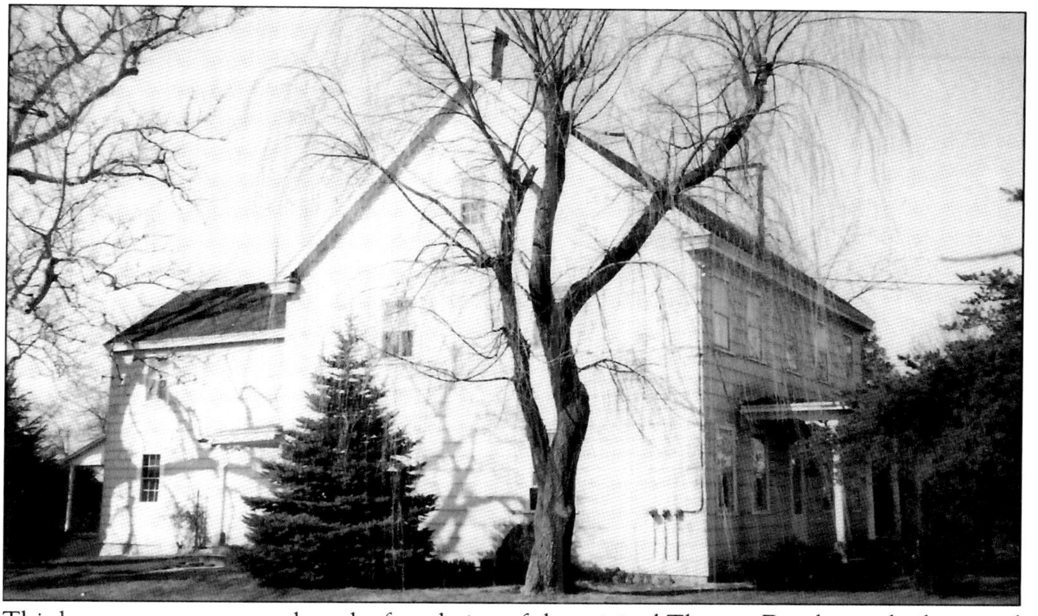

This house was constructed on the foundation of the original Thomas Eves home, built around 1720. A British commander slept here during the British encampment during the retreat from Philadelphia through Evesham Township in June 1778. John Lippincott owned the house and surrounding farm during the encampment. Percy Vennel was the last farmer to own this house. When he sold the farm, it became part of the Woodstream development between Greentree Road and Cropwell Creek. (Photograph by Miriam Wurst, courtesy Edna Wirth.)

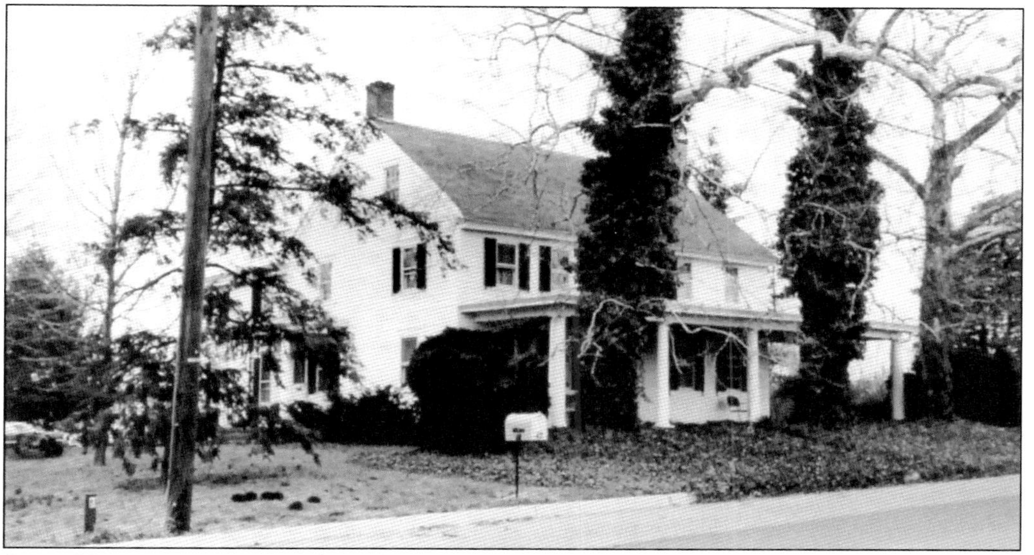

Samuel Lippincott was an early settler in Evesham Township. He took title of 1,000 acres in the northwest corner of the township, where he grew orchards. John Lippincott later received the farm by will and built this farmhouse around 1820 on Greentree Road near present-day Charter Oak Lane and Meeting House Lane. Barton Brothers, fruit farmers, purchased the 117-acre farm from the Lippincott family. The house was demolished in 1998 after a fire. Some custom homes have been built on the site. (Photograph by Miriam Wurst, courtesy Edna Wirth.)

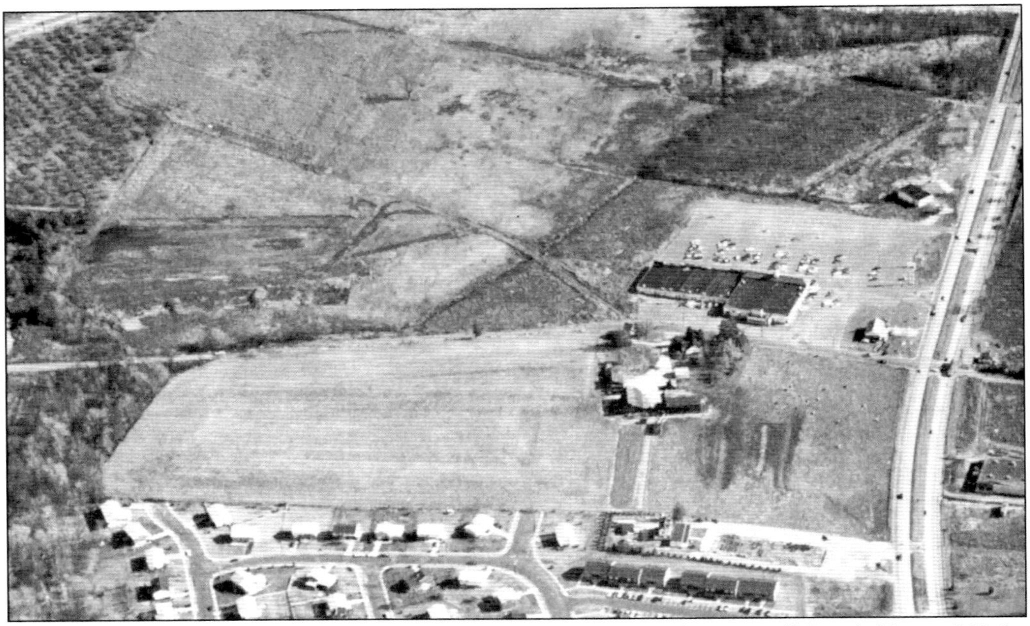

Here is an aerial view of the Holtz farm at Route 70 and North Cropwell Road. Howard Holtz purchased this farm from William Lippincott in 1928. It remained in operation by the Holtz family until the 1990s.

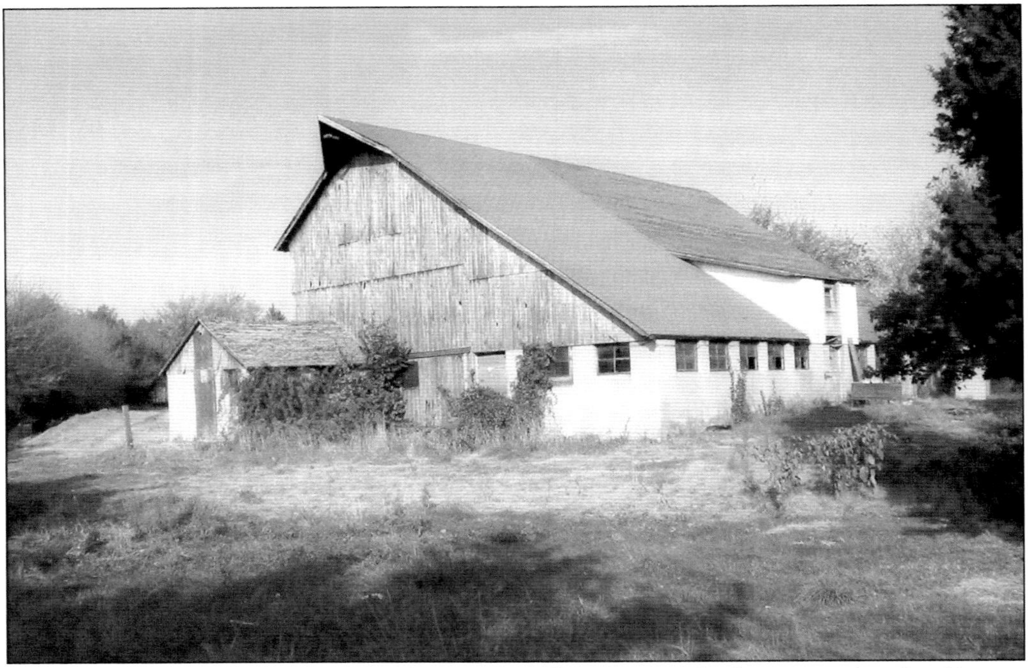

This is a view of the barn at the Holtz farm. Originally 100 acres, the farm was reduced to 21 acres after portions were sold off. This was the last remaining farm in this section of Evesham when it was sold in 2000 for the Brook View apartment complex. (Photograph by Guy Thompson.)

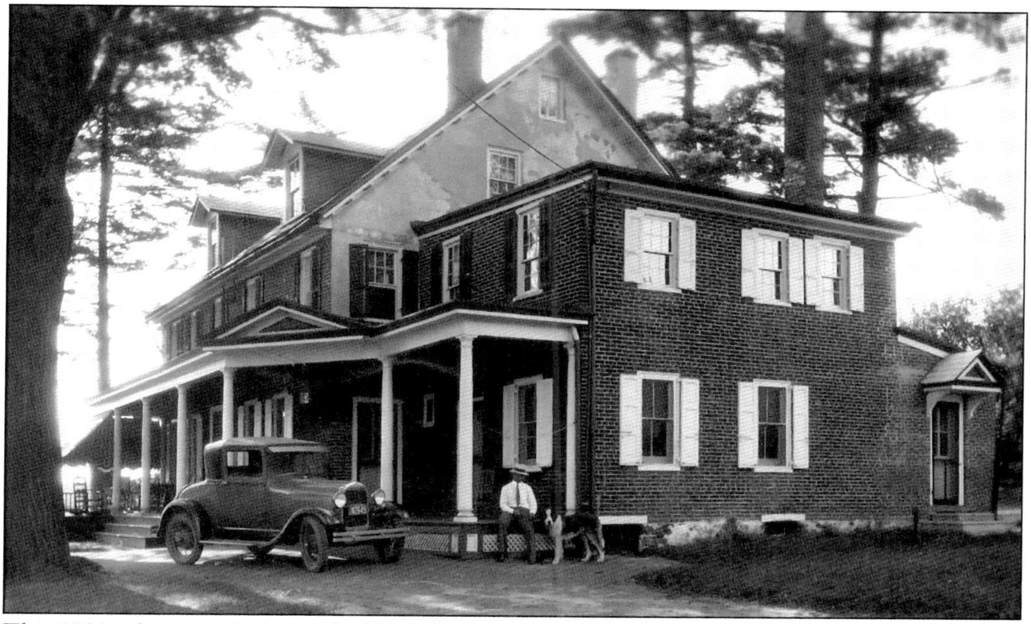

This 1930s photograph shows the Evans house at Hillside Farms, featuring Joseph Evans and his dog, Rex. This was the newest of the Evans farmhouses. The Evans family was one of the original landowners. In 1688, William Evans became the first white man to settle in what would become Evesham Township. He dug a cave in the side of Mount Laurel to live in while building a cabin. His son Thomas claimed a 1,000-acre tract in newly formed Evesham. (Courtesy Connie Evans.)

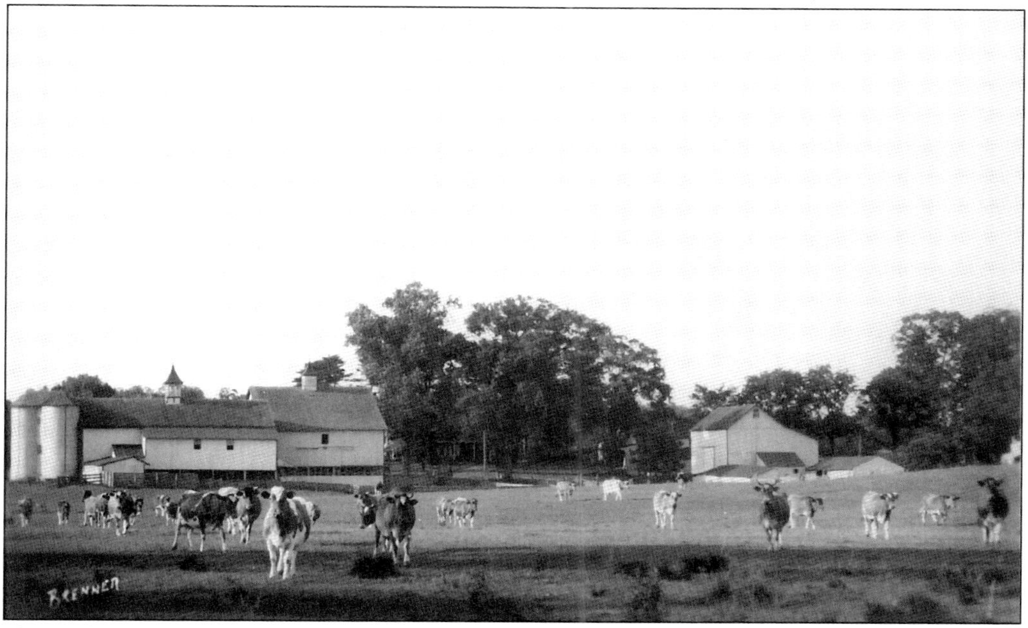

Shown here is the Evans family's Hillside Dairy Farms. Pictured at left is the cow barn. The building at right is a horse barn. The herd was predominantly Holstein; each cow received a name, and its unique markings were recorded. This portion of the farm is presently the Evesham Schools Transportation Center. (Courtesy Connie Evans.)

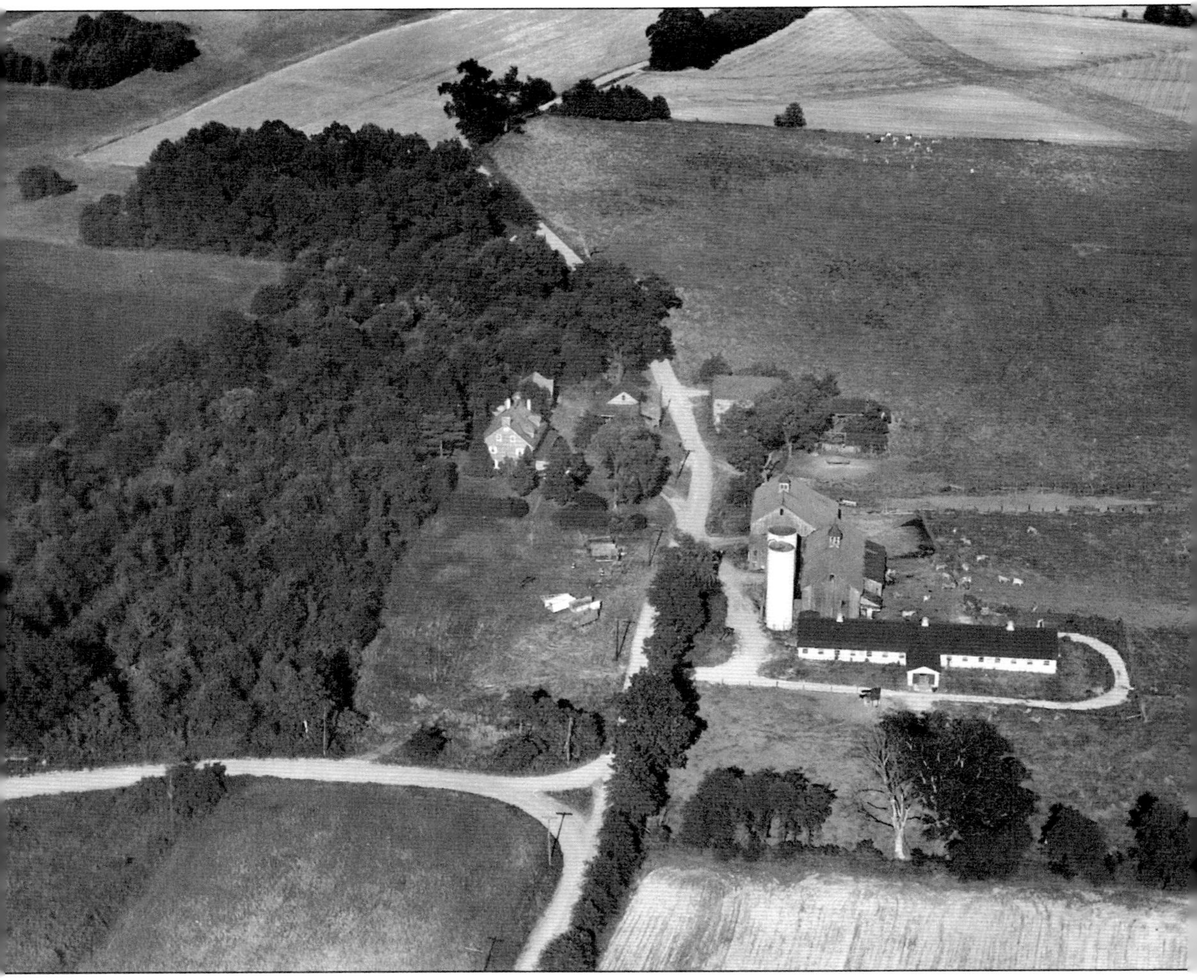

In this aerial view of Hillside Farms, Westcott Road is in the foreground. The farm at this time comprised 360 acres. The land was later developed into a portion of Brush Hollow, Cherokee High School, and Marlton Middle School. The farmhouse, the last of the Evans family farmhouses, still stands. The decline in milk prices caused farming operations to end here in 1969. (Courtesy Connie Evans.)

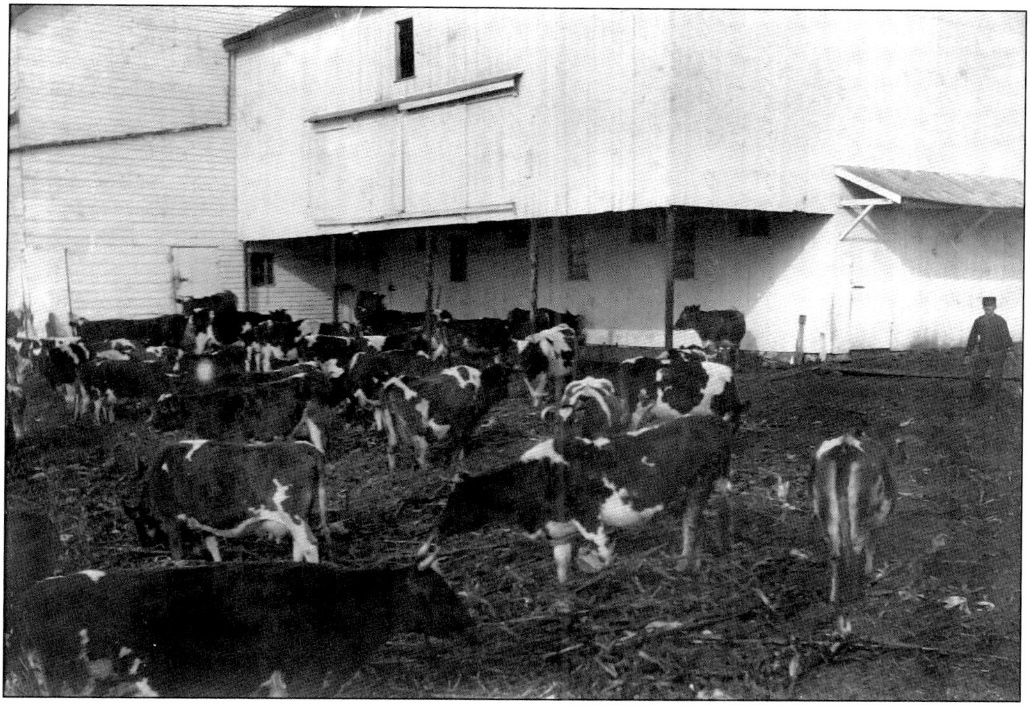

A herd of cows grazes at Hillside Dairy Farm. (Courtesy Connie Evans.)

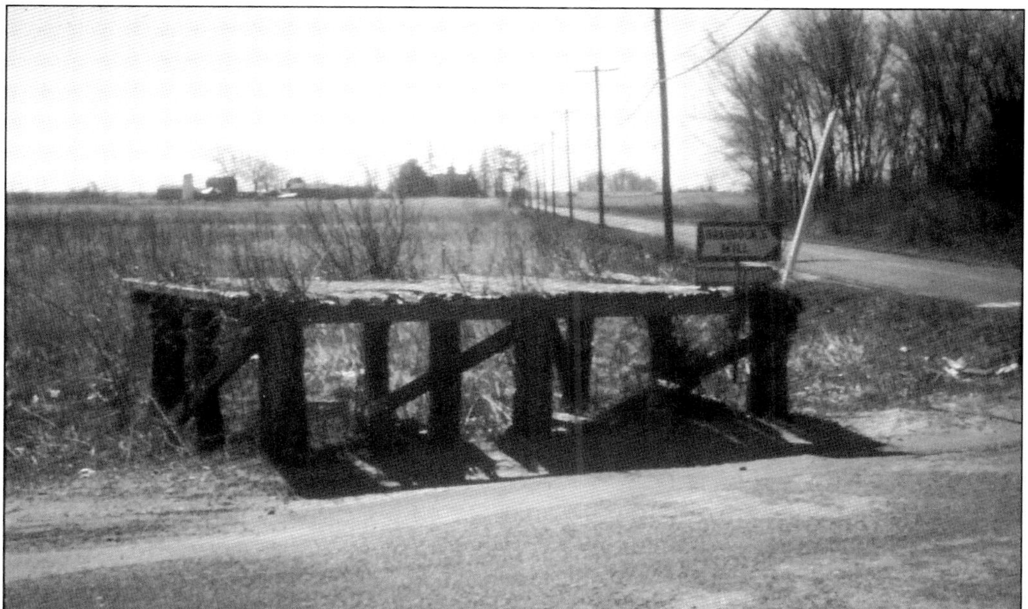

Local dairy farmers used this wooden platform. They left milk cans on the platform to be picked up for processing. The driver then returned the cans, and farmers identified theirs by the farm number. Farmers discontinued use of the platform after tank trucks came into service. Old Marlton Pike is in the foreground; the farmland in the background became Brush Hollow. (Courtesy Connie Evans.)

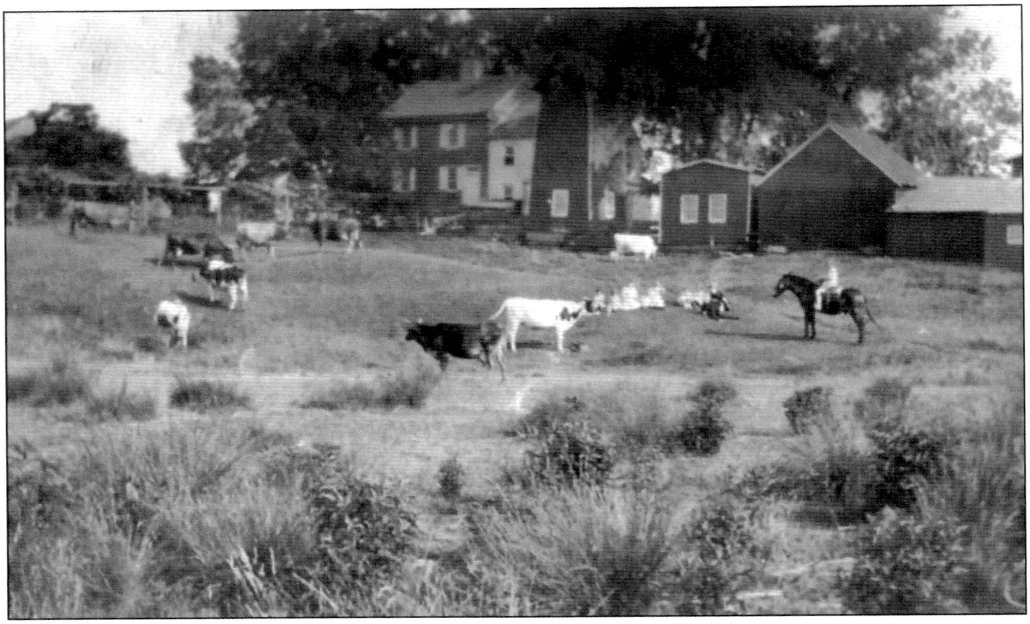

Shown here is the Maggie Olt farm in 1928. (Courtesy Edna Wirth.)

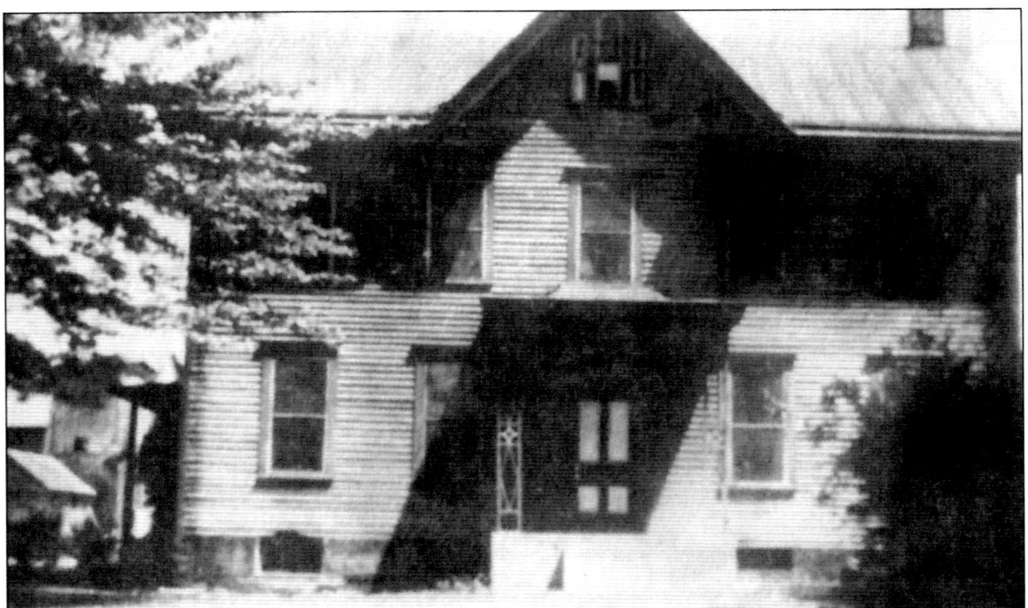

This was the Warrington farmhouse on Brick Road. In 1918, the Warrington family purchased the farmland that stood on both sides of Brick Road and stretched across Route 73. They had apple, peach, and cherry orchards as well as vegetable crops on 145 acres. The Warringtons sold their farm in 1953 to a group of five individuals who formed a corporation and sold off portions over a period of years. In the early 1970s, seven acres were used for the construction of Garden State Community Hospital. The farmhouse, which was demolished about 1962, stood on this parcel.

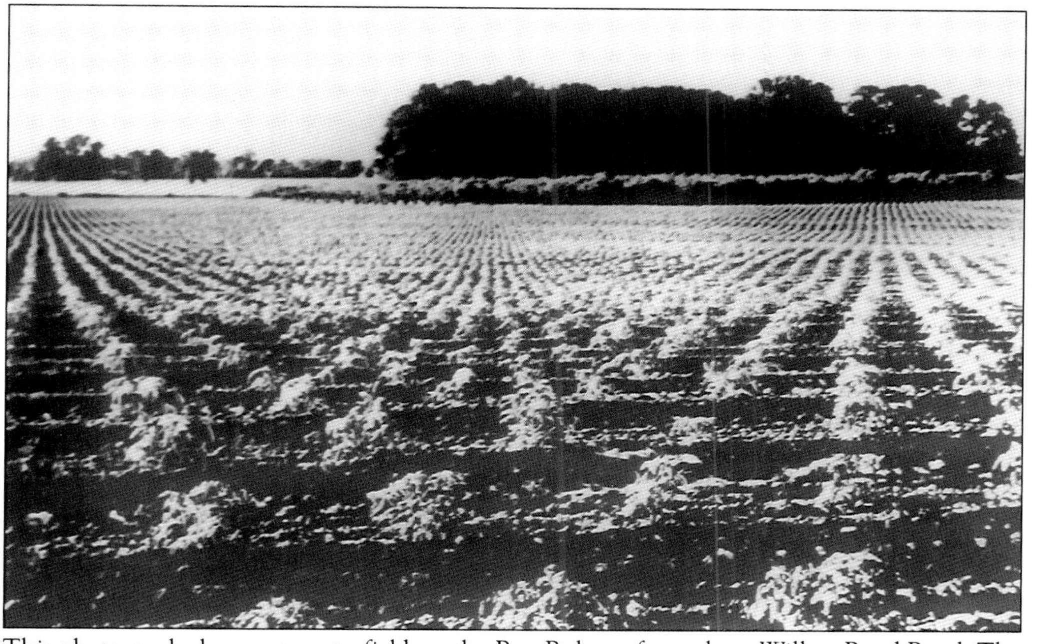

This photograph shows a tomato field on the Ben Roberts farm along Willow Bend Road. The area became Brush Hollow in the early 1970s. (Courtesy Edna Wirth.)

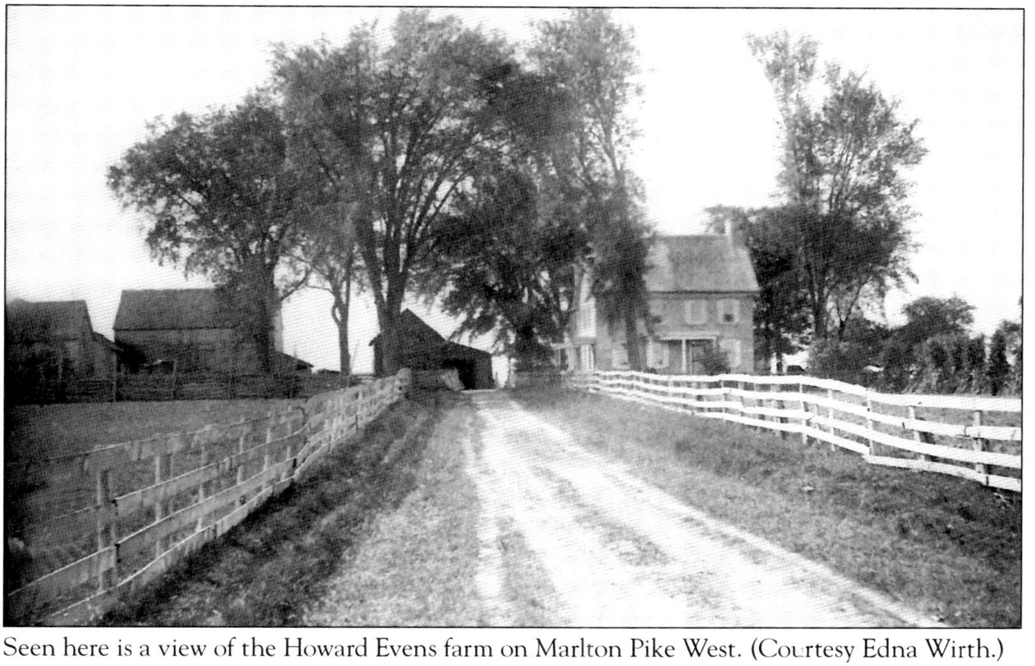

Seen here is a view of the Howard Evens farm on Marlton Pike West. (Courtesy Edna Wirth.)

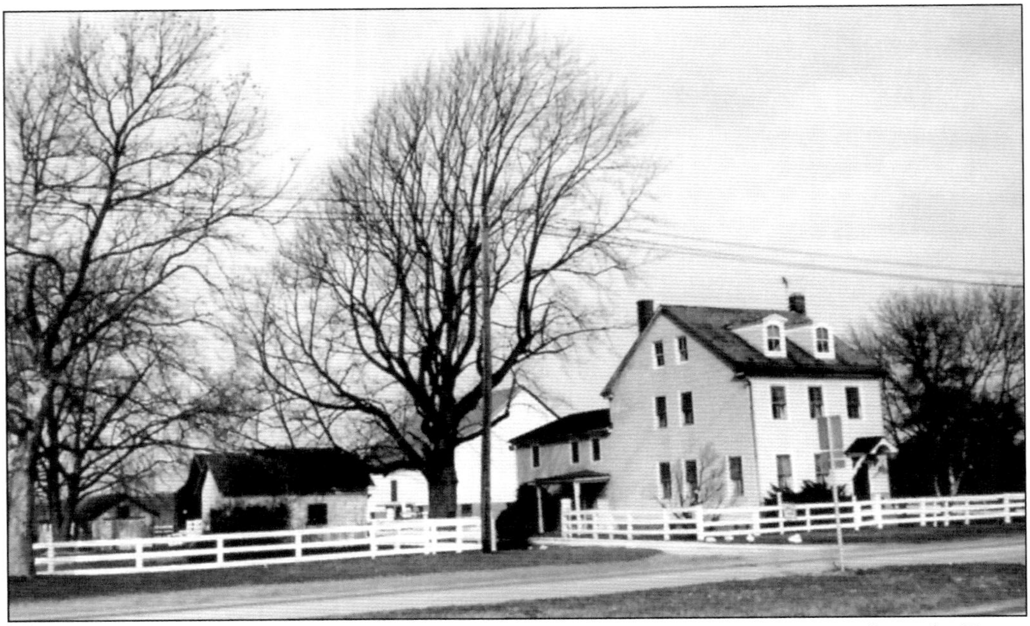

Pictured is the Gohagan farm in 1975. This farm stretched along Route 73 across from the Evans School. It contained a track for training harness-racing horses. (Photograph by Miriam Wurst, courtesy Edna Wirth.)

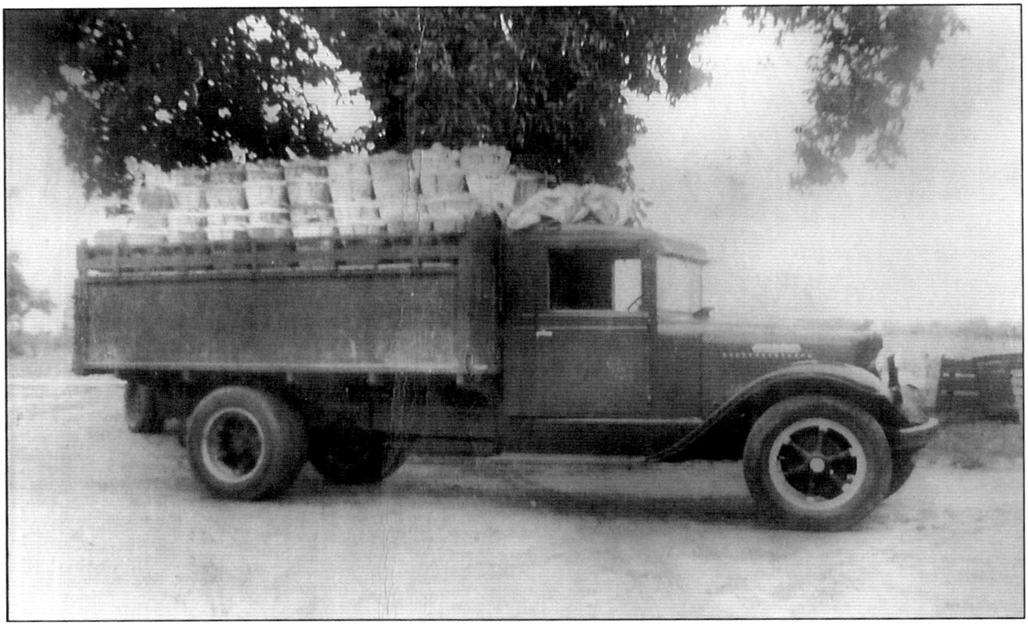

This photograph shows a truck at the Powell farm in the area of Greentree Road and Route 73. It is loaded with tomatoes to be hauled to the Campbell Soup Company plant in Camden. It could carry 124 baskets. Byron Roberts purchased the Powell farm in the 1940s. (Courtesy Bruce Powell.)

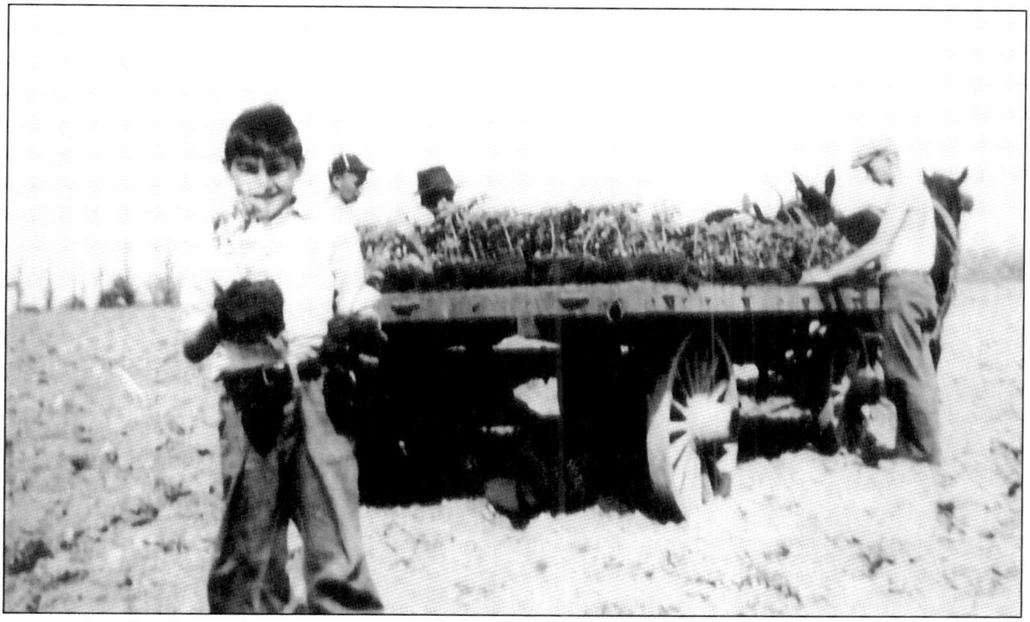

Pictured with a horse-drawn wagon on the Powell farm are, from left to right, Raymond, Harold, Elwood, and Robert Powell. A moment after this photograph was taken, the horses jumped and ran over Raymond with the wagon; he survived with no harm. A few years later, Elwood and Robert would serve in World War II, perhaps eating soup made from their tomatoes. (Courtesy Bruce Powell.)

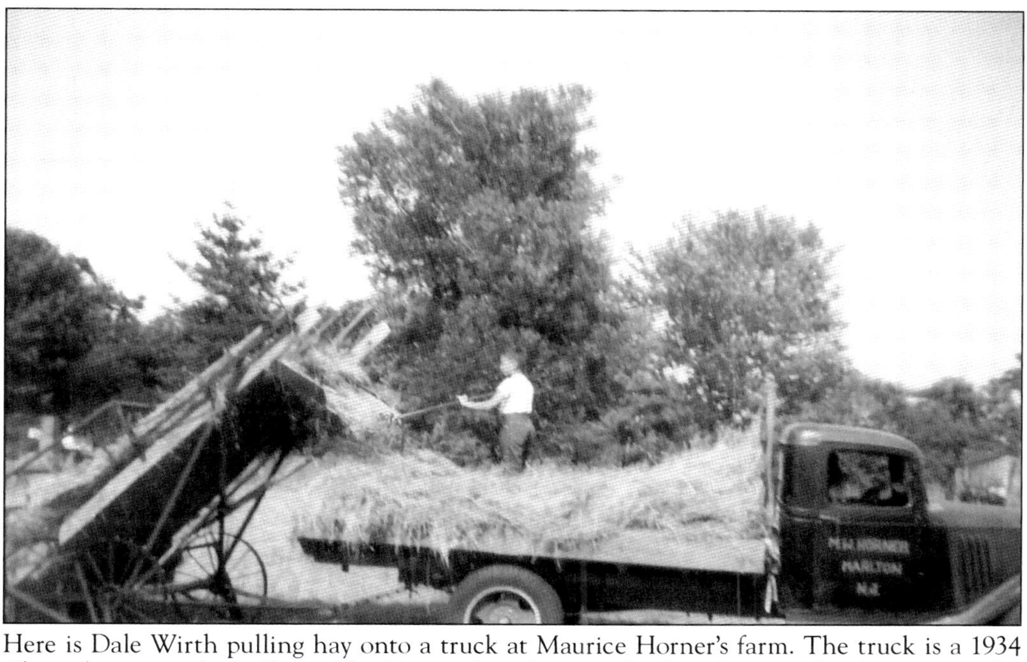

Here is Dale Wirth pulling hay onto a truck at Maurice Horner's farm. The truck is a 1934 Chevrolet one-and-a-half-ton. The Horner farm became the Tara housing development in the mid-1970s. (Courtesy Bruce Powell.)

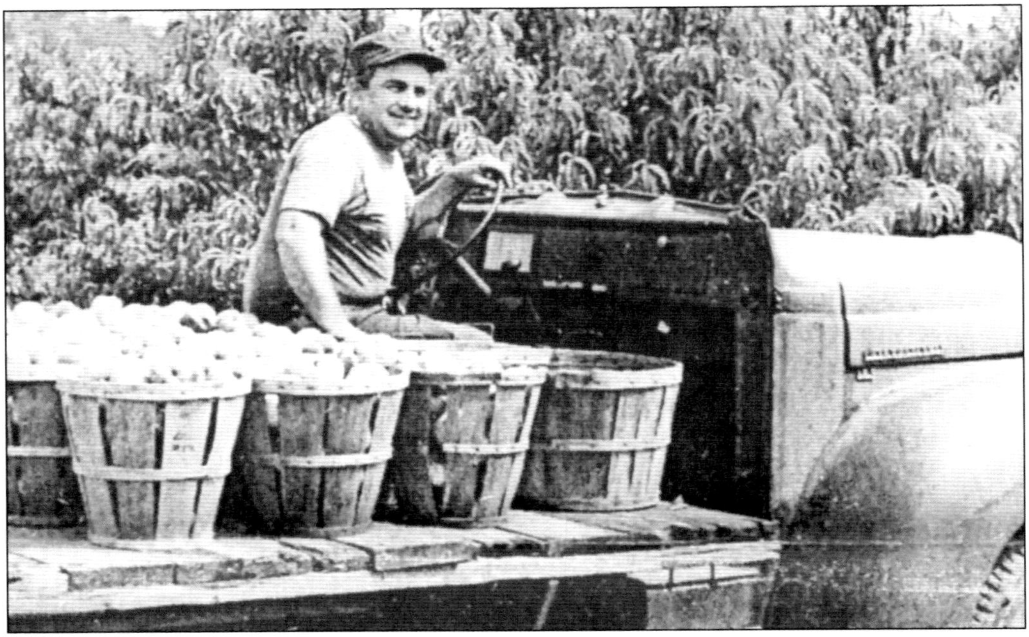

Phil Traino is pictured with a load of peaches from his 100-acre farm along Greentree Road between Route 73 and Church Road. The Traino farm operated a produce stand on Greentree Road, selling crops grown on the farm. It also had a wholesale produce business that began in 1906.

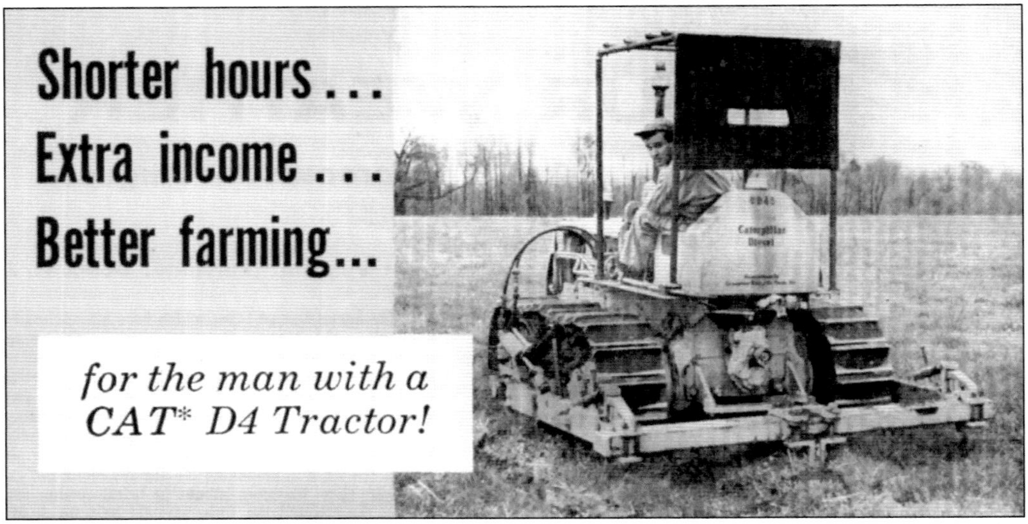

Nick Savich was featured in an ad for Caterpillar Tractor Company and is shown demonstrating his CAT D4 tractor. The Savich farm was a dairy farm on Old Marlton Pike east of Heritage Village. Milan Savich purchased the farm in 1939 from Earl Powers. The Savich family operated a dairy here as Home Dairy Farm and offered home delivery of dairy products. A dairy bar opened here in the 1960s, featuring homemade ice cream. An Indian burial ground that dates to 2500 B.C. was discovered on the farm. The Savich family moved from here in 1975, and Evesham Township acquired the property under the Green Acres program. The house burned down in 1985.

Shown is the icehouse at the Savich farm. Farms used these to store ice during warm weather. (Courtesy Edna Wirth.)

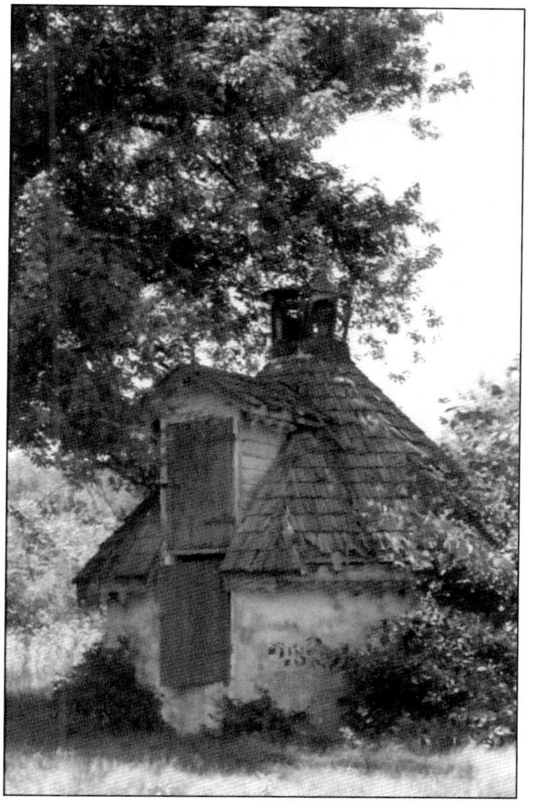

Horace Roberts bought the 150-acre William Garwood farm in 1912. His son Byron took over the farm in the 1920s and operated it until his death in 1966. This farm stood along the northwest border of Evesham Township centered on Route 73 and Greentree Road. Roberts purchased the Harvey Lippincott farm on Cropwell Road in the 1930s. In the 1940s, he purchased the Powell farm on the south side of Greentree Road. The acquisitions of these farms expanded the Roberts farm to 300 acres. Here is the Garwood farmhouse in 1975 shortly before its demolition. (Photograph by Miriam Wurst, courtesy Edna Wirth.)

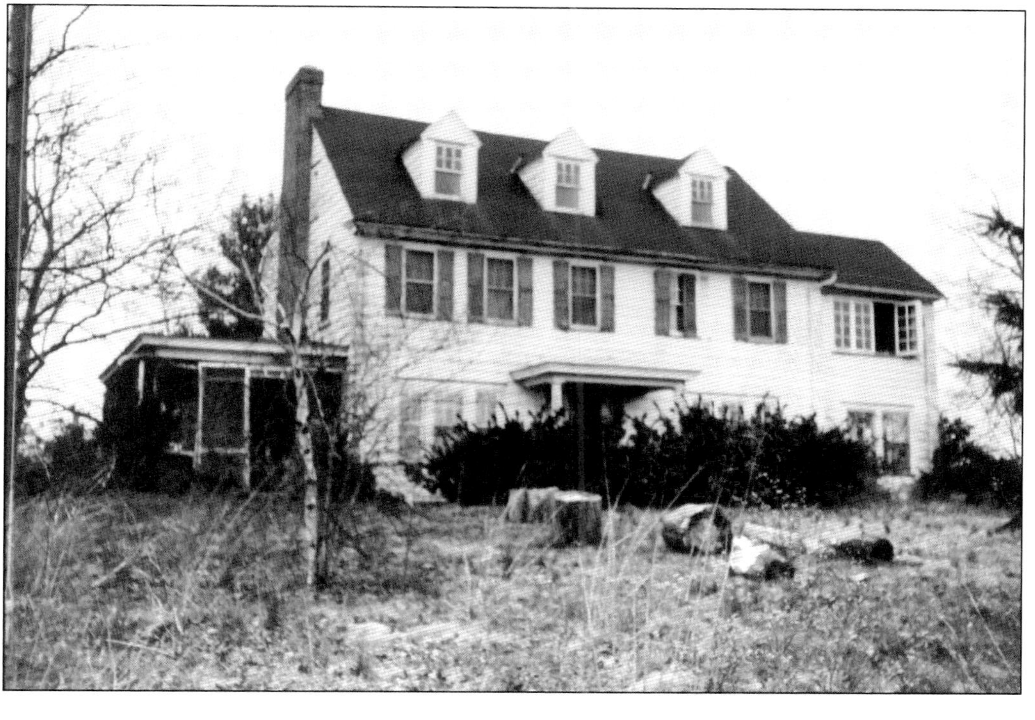

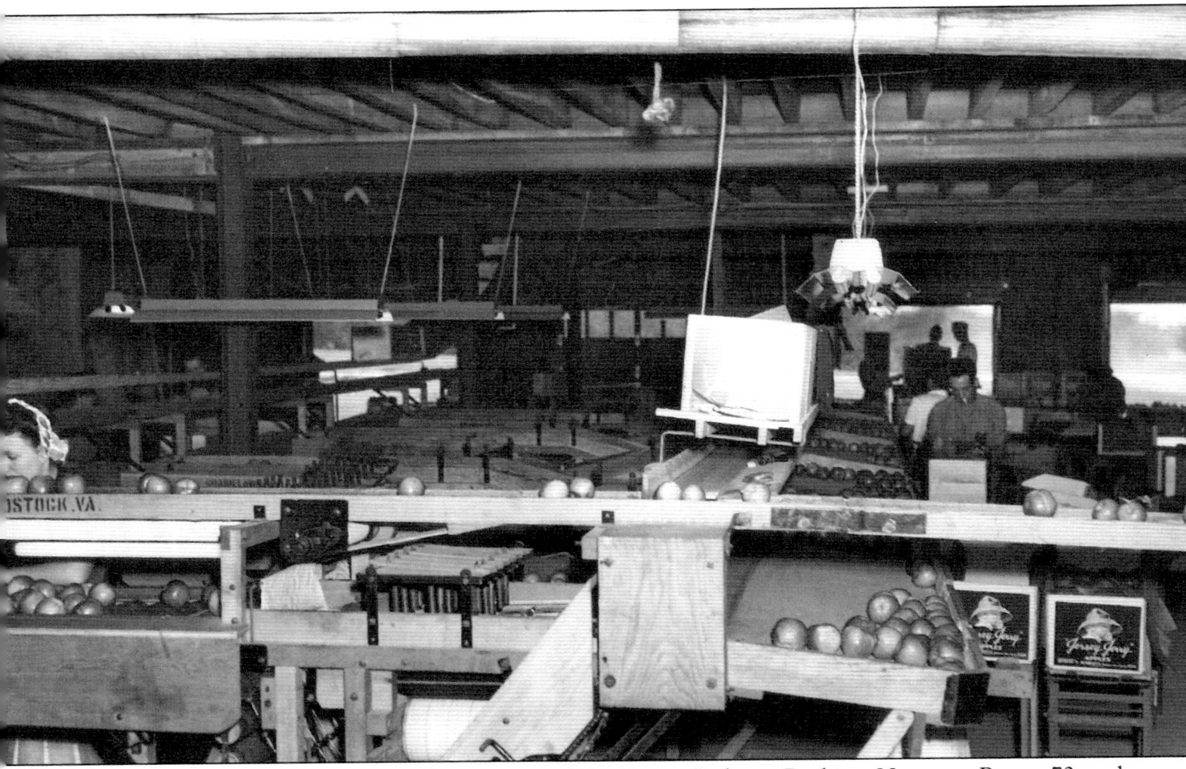

This 1946 photograph shows the interior of the Byron Roberts Packing House at Route 73 and Greentree Road, with Cropwell Road running behind it. The building was demolished in 1979 to make way for Greentree Shopping Center. Roberts was a member of the Jersey Fruit Cooperative Association, which packed fruit under the Jersey Jerry label. (Courtesy New Jersey State Archives, Department of State.)

Shown is North Cropwell Road in 1967 as it passes through the Roberts farm leading to Route 73. On the left is part of a peach orchard, with an apple orchard on the right. North Cropwell Road ends at this point today and joins West Lincoln Drive.

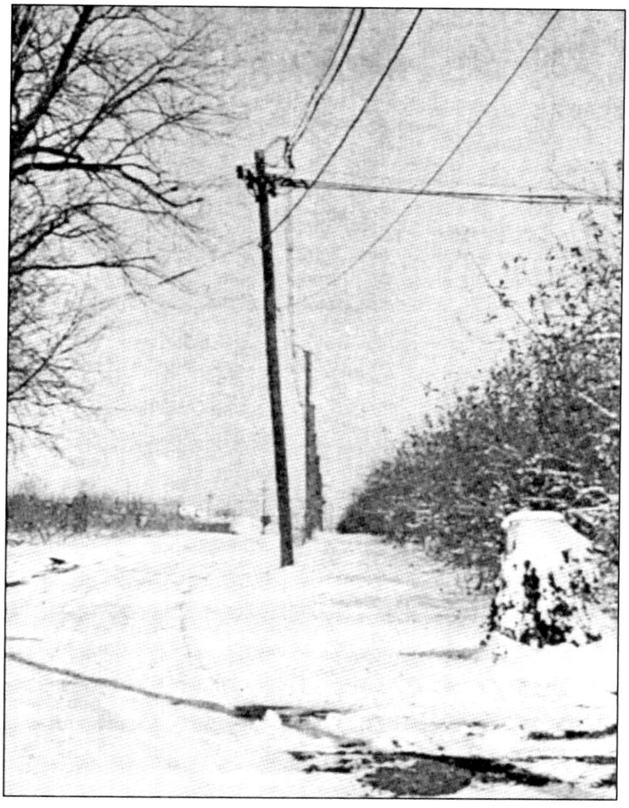

The Roberts farm contained several houses that tenants rented. The Powell family leased this house, which was at Greentree and Cropwell Road behind the Roberts fruit packinghouse. The Roberts Christmas tree plantation can be seen in the left background and an apple orchard on the right, which sat next to Cropwell Road. (Photograph by Miriam Wurst, courtesy Edna Wirth.)

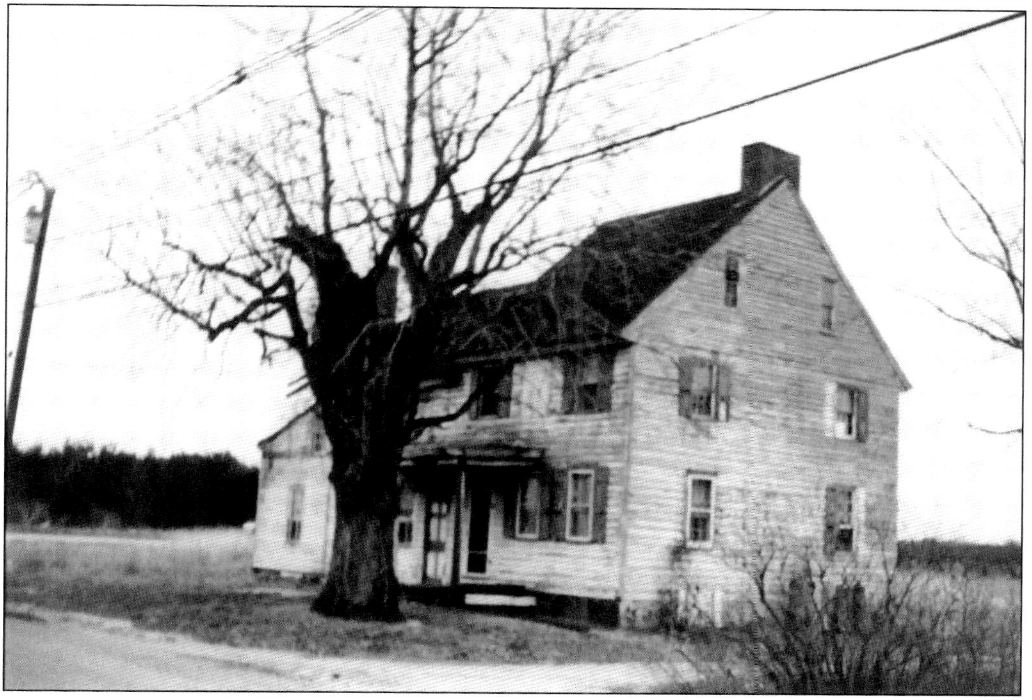

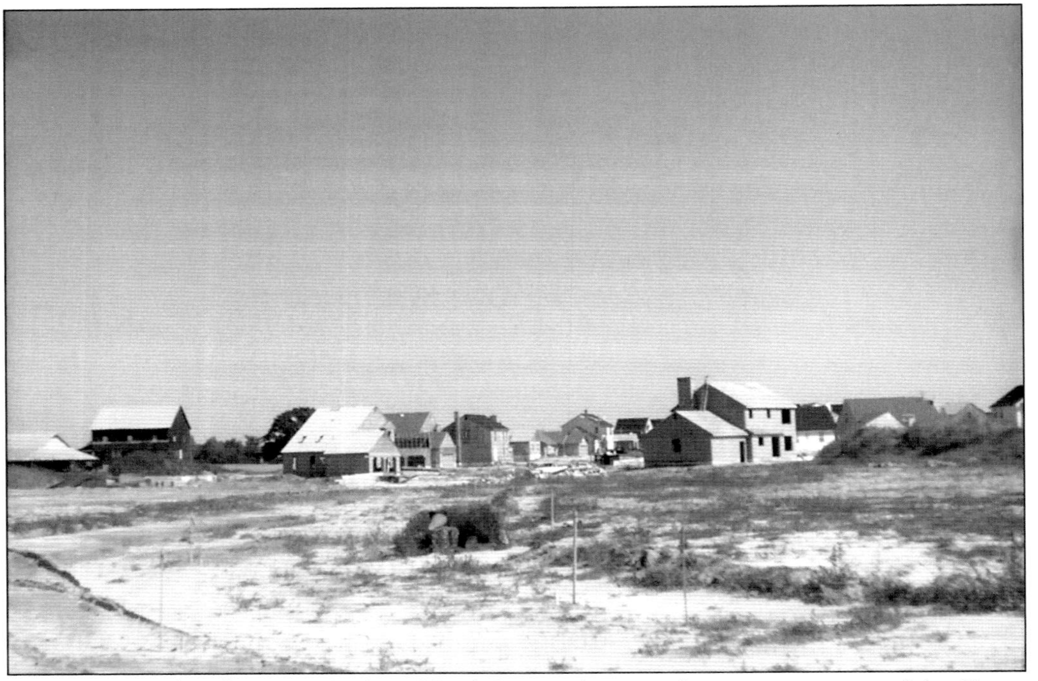

This photograph, taken in 1986 from North Locust Avenue, shows construction of the Green Lane Farms development, built on 53 acres of the John Hines farm. The barn can be seen on the left. The Hines farm totaled 90 acres and stretched across Maple Avenue, where the Vineyards of Greentree development was built. The family operated a farm market on Maple Avenue. (Photograph by the author.)

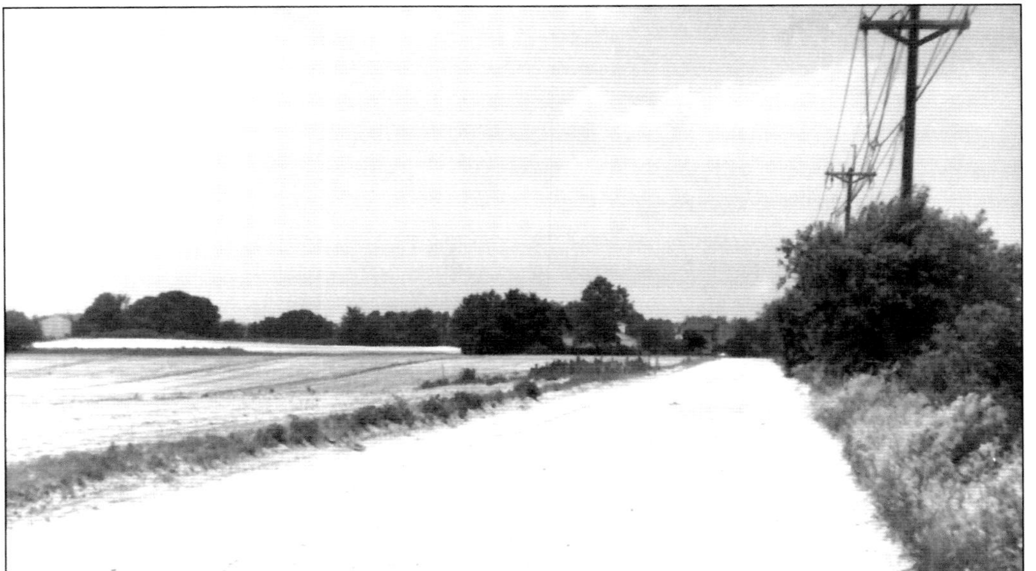

Shown here is North Locust Avenue in 1987 before the road was paved and widened. The farmland in this scene would soon be developed into the Quail Run residential community. (Photograph by the author.)

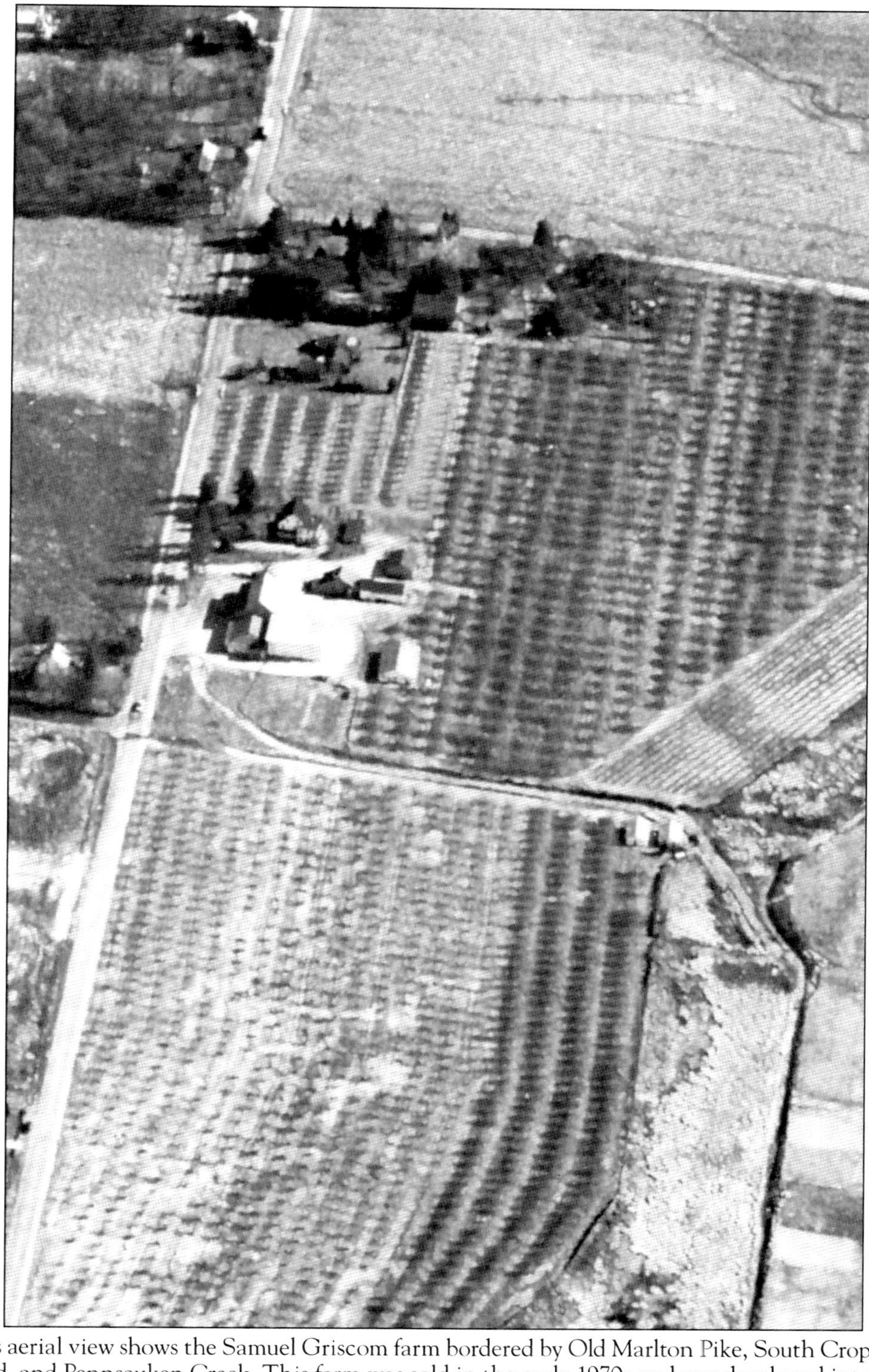

This aerial view shows the Samuel Griscom farm bordered by Old Marlton Pike, South Cropwell Road, and Pennsauken Creek. This farm was sold in the early 1970s and was developed into the Marlton Village community.

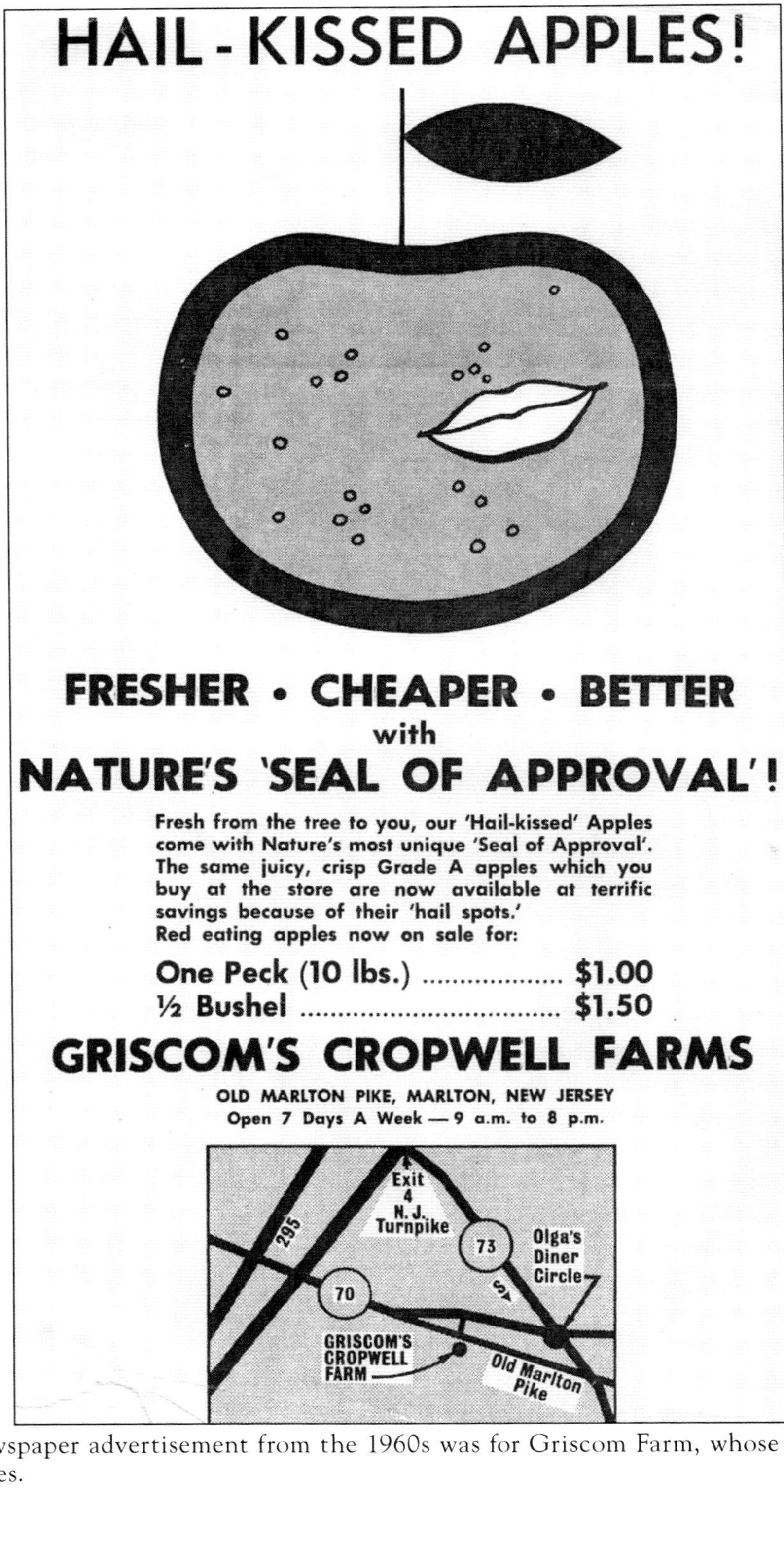

This newspaper advertisement from the 1960s was for Griscom Farm, whose main crop was apples.

Four

Schools

Evesham Township's first schools were private, operated by the Quakers. The Friends were pioneers in education, establishing schools even before building a meetinghouse. In Evesham, they established two schools before opening the Cropwell Friends Meeting House in 1809. These two schools, at Cropwell and Pine Grove, were the only schools in Evesham until 1840. At that time, the Friends accepted the new idea of free schools. This led to the building of the Old Union Schoolhouse on the west side of South Maple Avenue. It remained in use until 1876, when a new two-room school was built across South Maple.

At this time, villages developed, increasing the need for schools. In Evesham, five districts were formed. Besides Marlton, included were Pine Grove, Jacques Bridge, Greentree (sometimes called London Grove), and Milford, which had two schools: one for African American students and another for white students. In 1905, the Marlton School was converted to three rooms. In 1918, the township voted for consolidation. The outlying schools were closed except for Jacques Bridge, which finally shut its doors in 1928.

Until 1914, high school grades 9 and 10 were held at Marlton, while students in grades 11 and 12 were transferred to Haddonfield High School. After 1914, students in all four high school grades were at Haddonfield. In 1918, the school board appended a six-room addition to the Marlton School, and in 1930 it became a 12-room school with a basement and office. In 1925, a full-time lunchroom opened to serve hot foods. This established Marlton as a pioneering advocate of school lunch programs. This initial growth was only the beginning of what was to come.

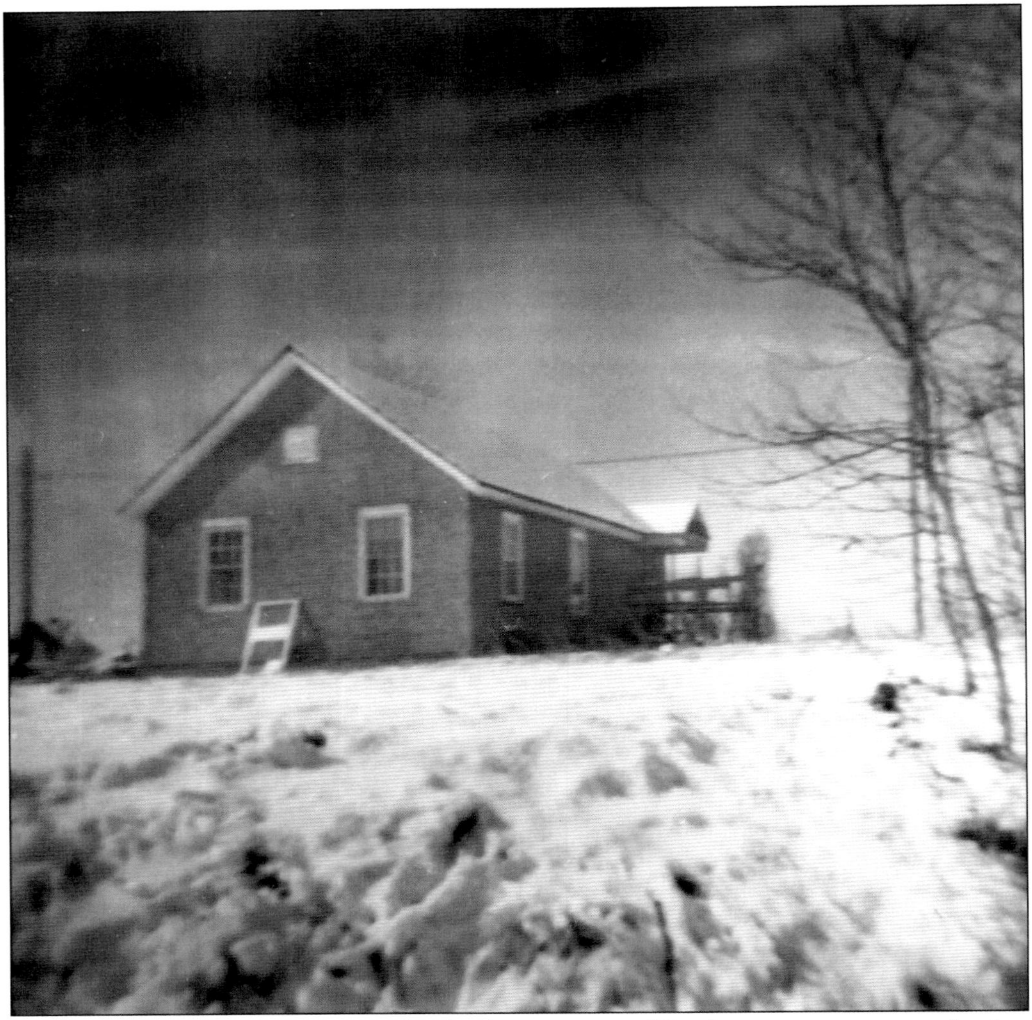

A schoolhouse opened in 1820 in the Evesboro section of Evesham as a one-room school at Greentree and Evesboro-Medford Roads. It was known variously as the London Grove, Greentree, or Evesboro School. It closed in 1918, along with the Pine Grove and Kresson schoolhouses. Classes were then held at the Marlton School, which had been expanded to accommodate the additional classes and became the central school in Evesham.

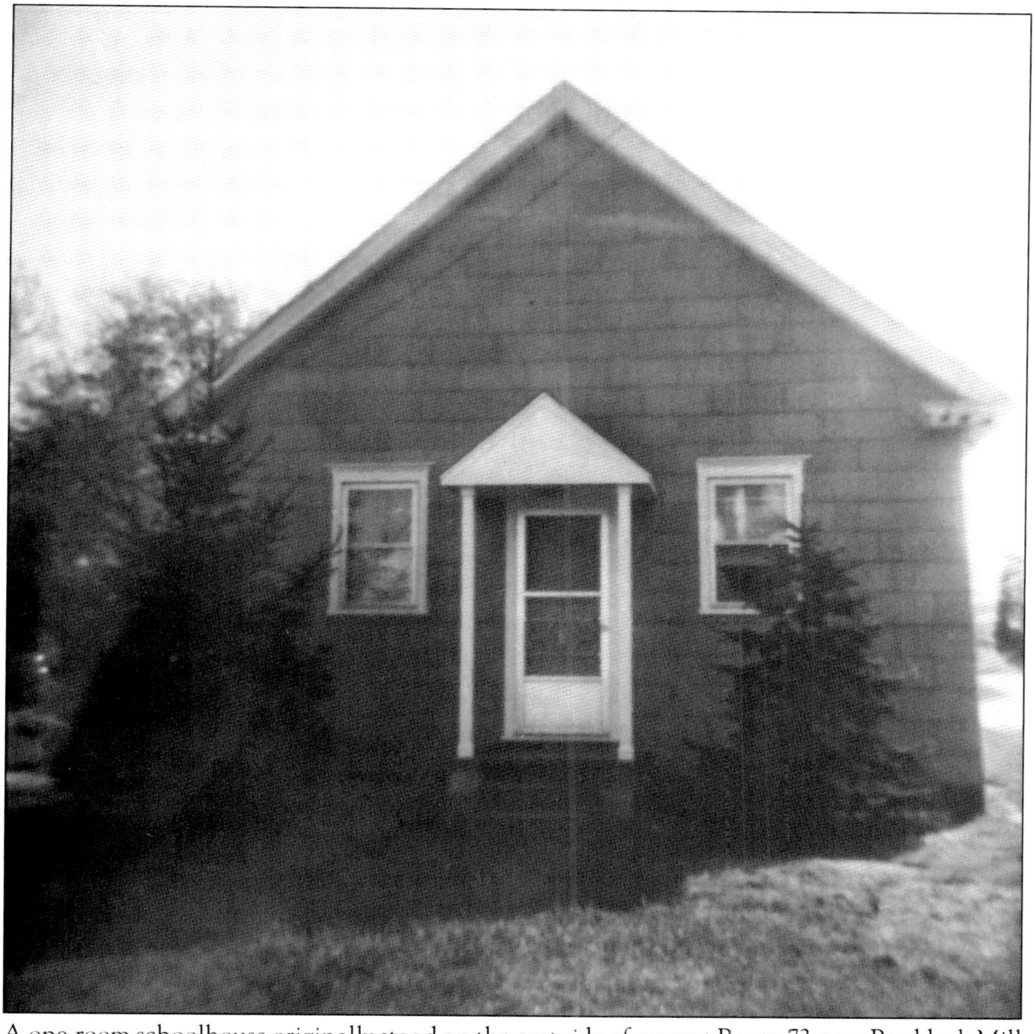

A one-room schoolhouse originally stood on the east side of present Route 73 near Braddock Mill Road. School officials later moved the building to the west side of Route 73 at the intersection of Kresson and Braddock Mill Roads. Kresson School closed in 1918, when the Marlton School became the central school for Evesham. A school for African American students in Evesham also operated near Kresson in an area called Pine Parlour. It closed when Evesham integrated its schools about 1900. (Courtesy Edna Wirth.)

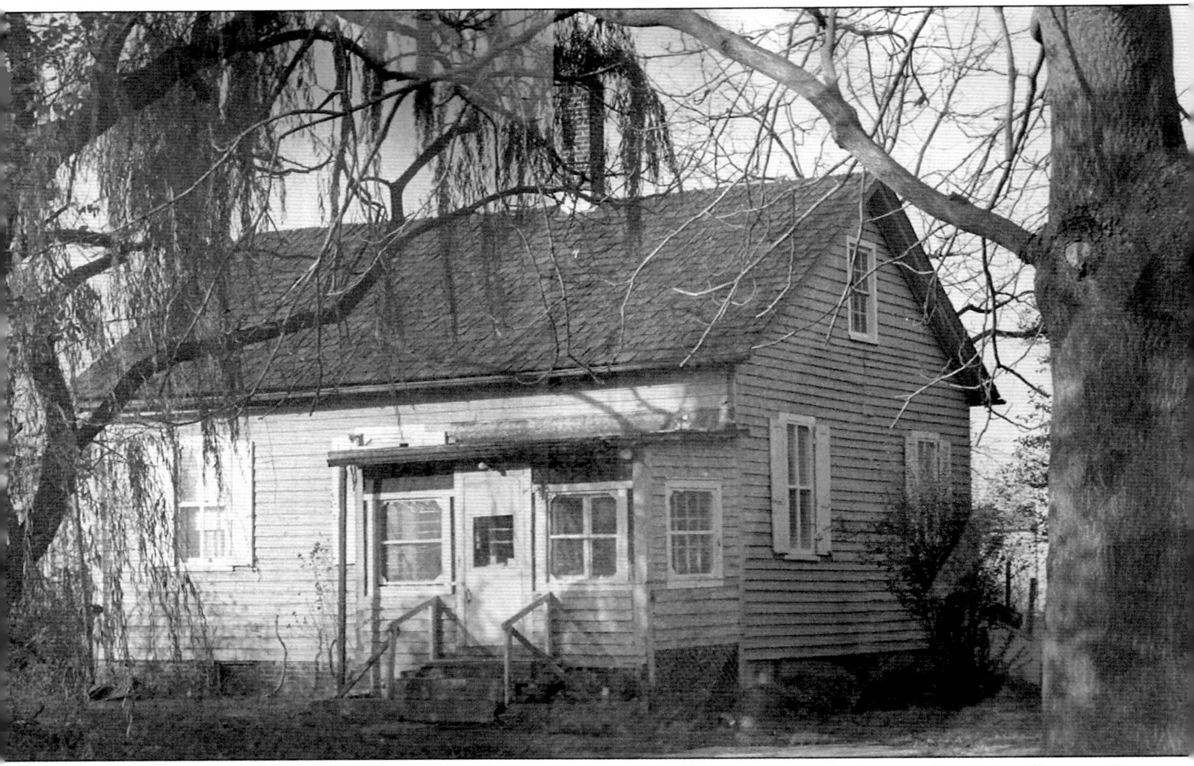

This mid-1970s photograph shows the former Cropwell School on the grounds of the Cropwell Friends Meeting House. It was built to replace an older schoolhouse constructed along Pennsauken Creek and moved around 1815 to behind the present-day meetinghouse on Old Marlton Pike. The building served as a school until 1877. (Courtesy Edna Wirth.)

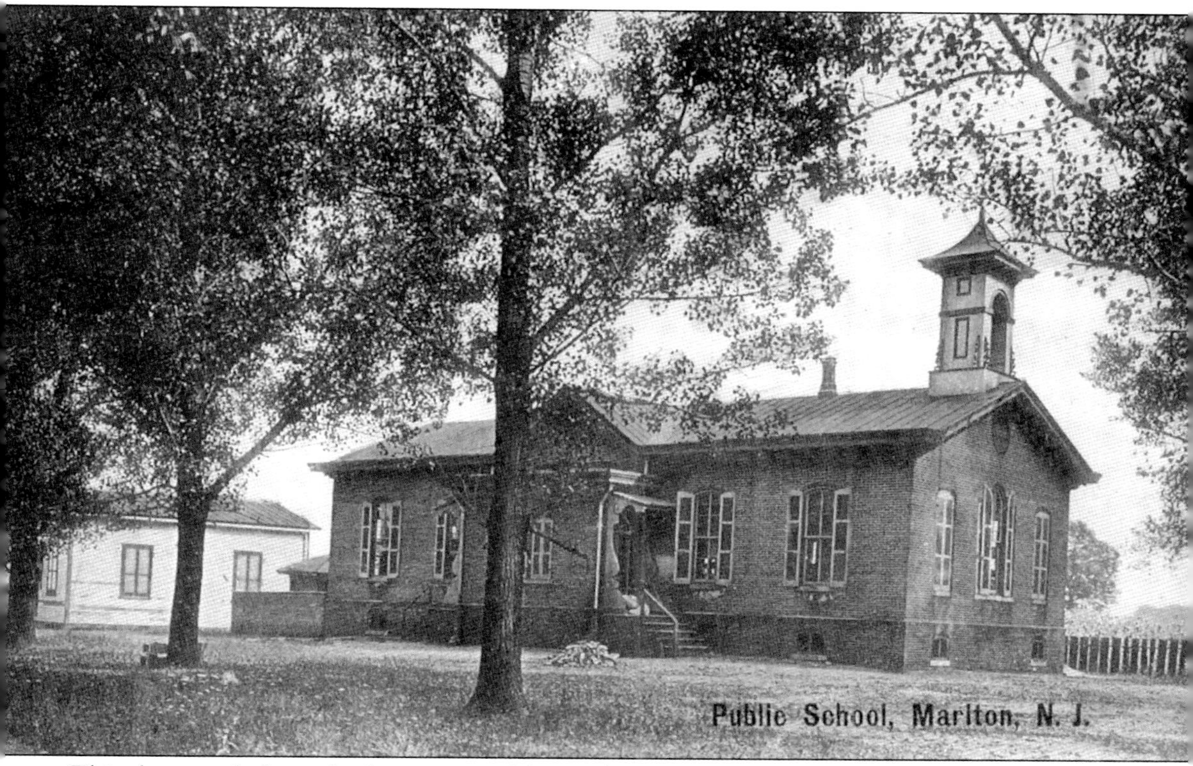

This photograph shows the first section of the Marlton School, built in 1876, facing Oak Avenue. It replaced a building across Maple Avenue called the Old Union Schoolhouse. School officials then expanded it to a three-room building in 1905. It last served as a school in 1976, after which it became the Evesham School District Administration Building. (Courtesy Evesham Historical Society.)

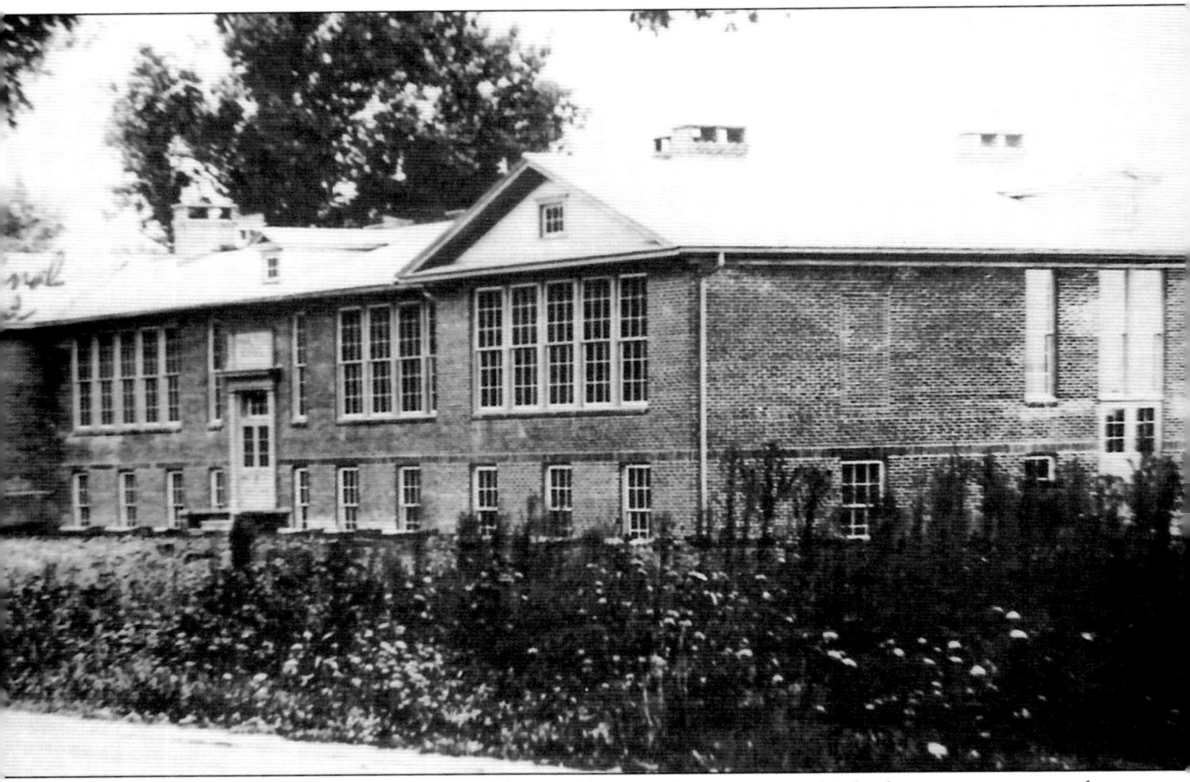

In 1918, the Marlton School received an addition of six rooms, which the voters approved in 1916. This view from Maple Avenue shows the 1918 addition with the original two-room school on the far left. When this wing opened, the one-room schoolhouses at Evesboro, Kresson, and Pine Grove consolidated into the newly expanded building. (Courtesy Edna Wirth.)

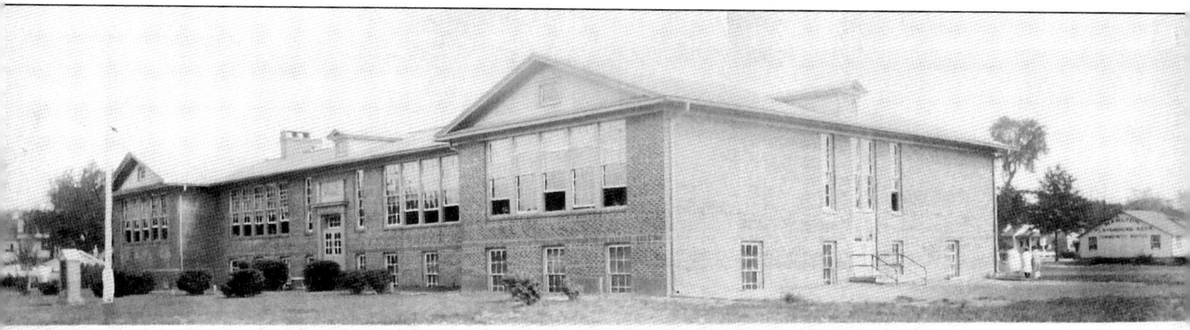

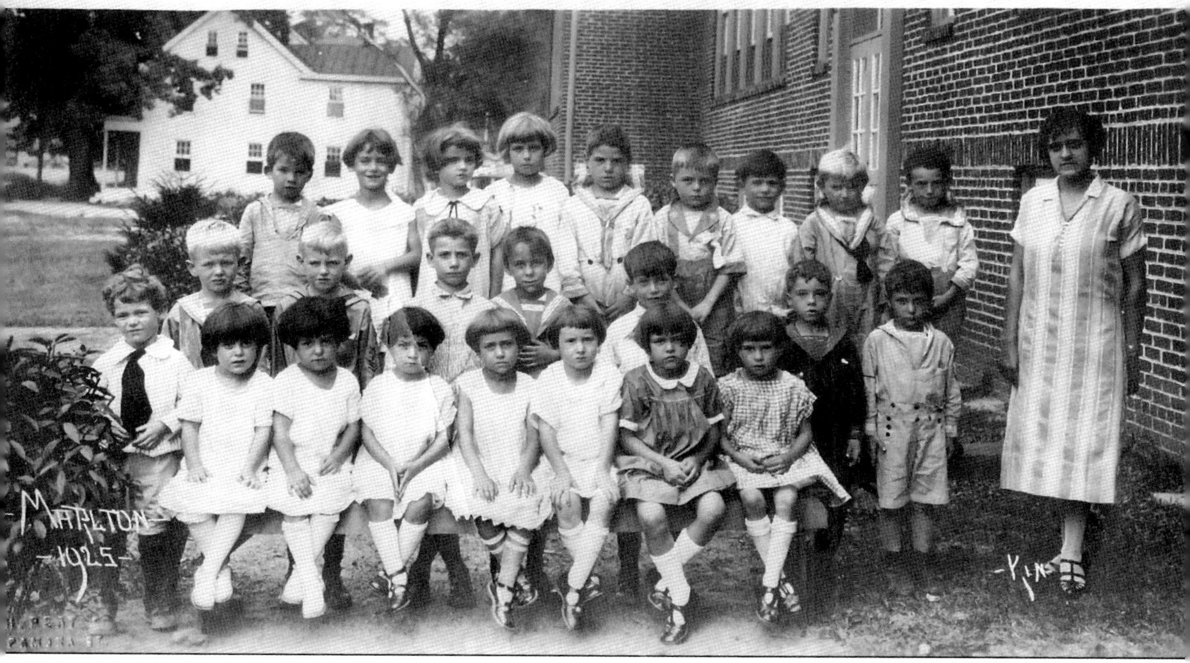

This 1925 class photograph from the Marlton School includes an exterior view of the front of the building from Maple Avenue. In 1925, officials installed a cafeteria in the basement of the school. Evesham was one of the pioneering districts to offer students a hot lunch. The 1930 expansion would be built to the right of this scene. (Courtesy Edna Wirth.)

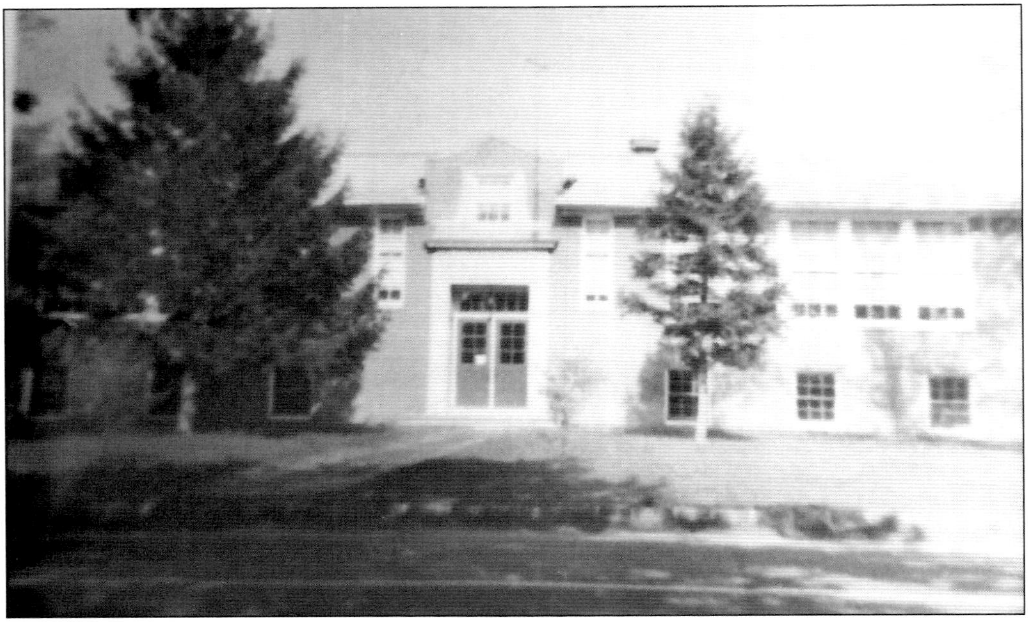

The Marlton School expanded for the final time in 1930, with the addition of four rooms, as the size of the property did not permit any further expansion. By this time, the schoolhouse in Jacques Bridge had closed, and its students transferred here. (Courtesy Edna Wirth.)

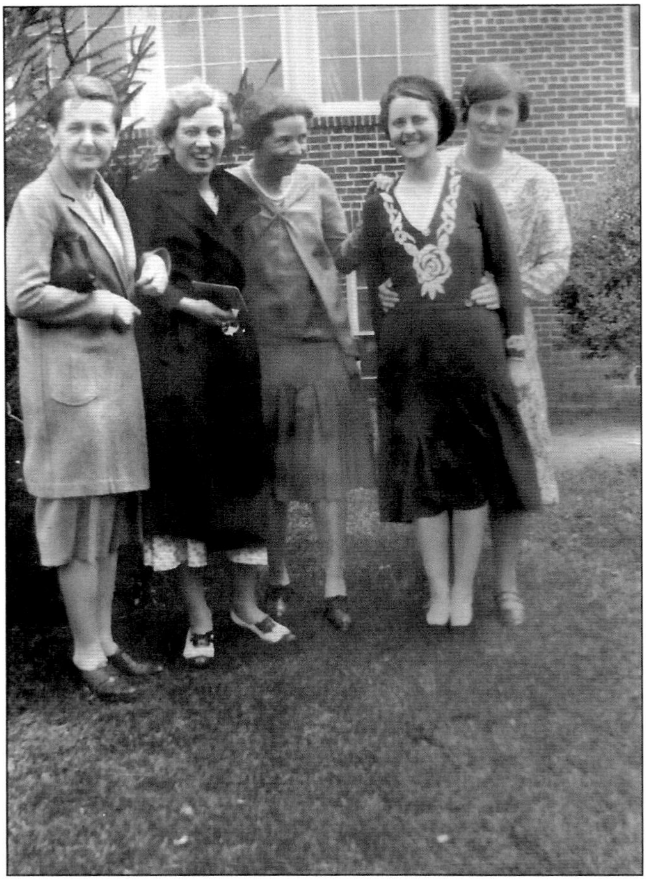

Featured in this group shot of teachers at the Marlton School in 1931 are, from left to right, Miss Williams, Miss Herr, Mrs. Larson, unidentified, and Miss Windel. (Courtesy Edna Wirth.)

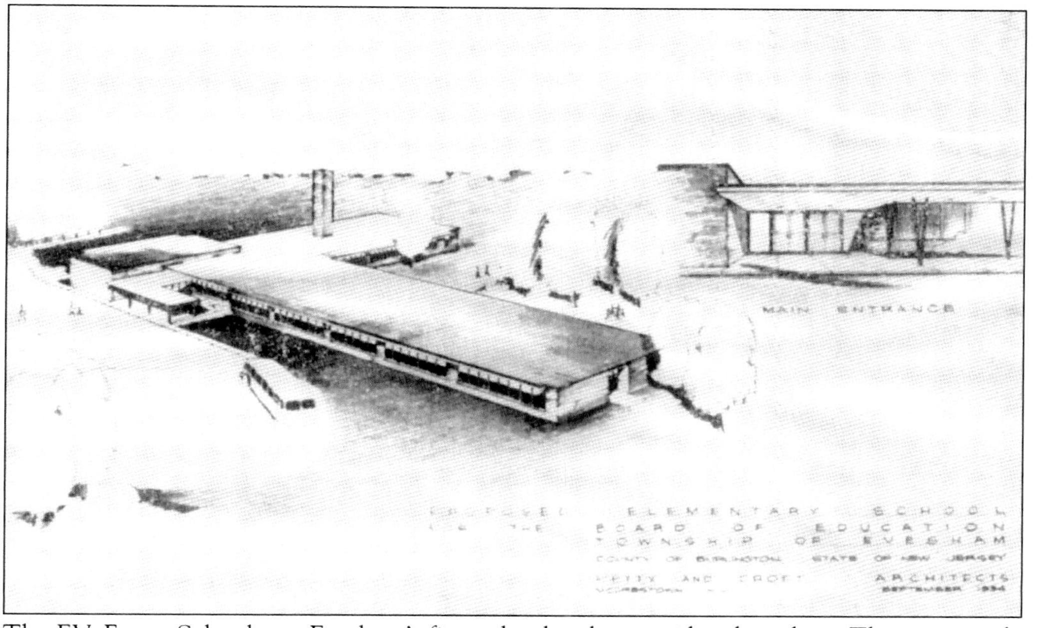

The F.V. Evans School was Evesham's first school to be considered modern. This is an early architectural rendering prepared while it was in the planning stage, and the actual building is very similar to this drawing. The school opened with 10 rooms and then expanded over the years. Grades five through eight and kindergarten attended here when it first opened. (Courtesy Evesham Historical Society.)

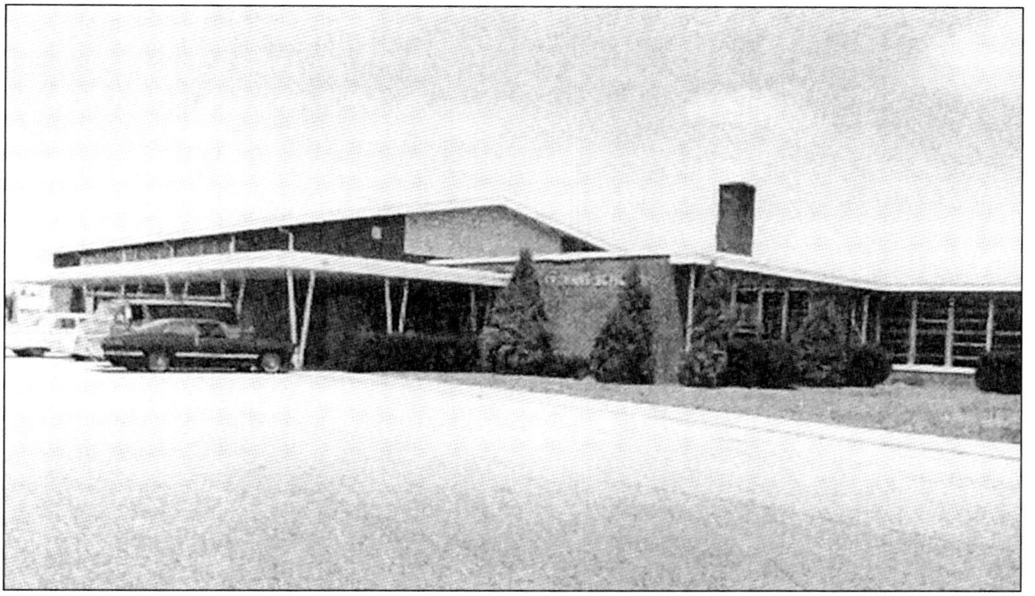

The Evans School opened in 1956 at Route 73 and Maple Avenue, housing the Evesham district's upper grades. The school was named in honor of Florence V. Evans, who taught and served as principal at the Marlton School. It was expanded in 1962 and again in 1966 to accommodate growth in student enrollment and to make the building more usable as a middle school. In 1976, it became an elementary school with the opening of Marlton Middle School.

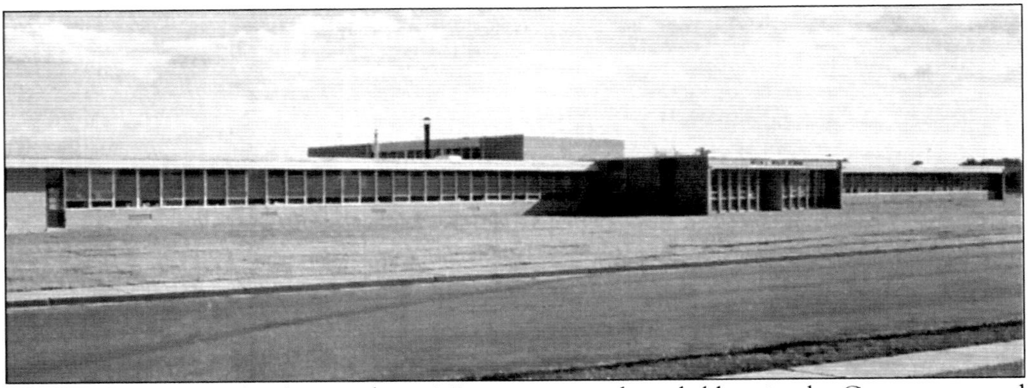

Beeler Elementary School opened in 1962 to accommodate children in the Georgetown and Heritage Village area. The school was named in honor of Helen L. Beeler, who began as a teacher at the Jacques Bridge schoolhouse in 1917. She later taught at the Marlton School and Evans School, where she became principal.

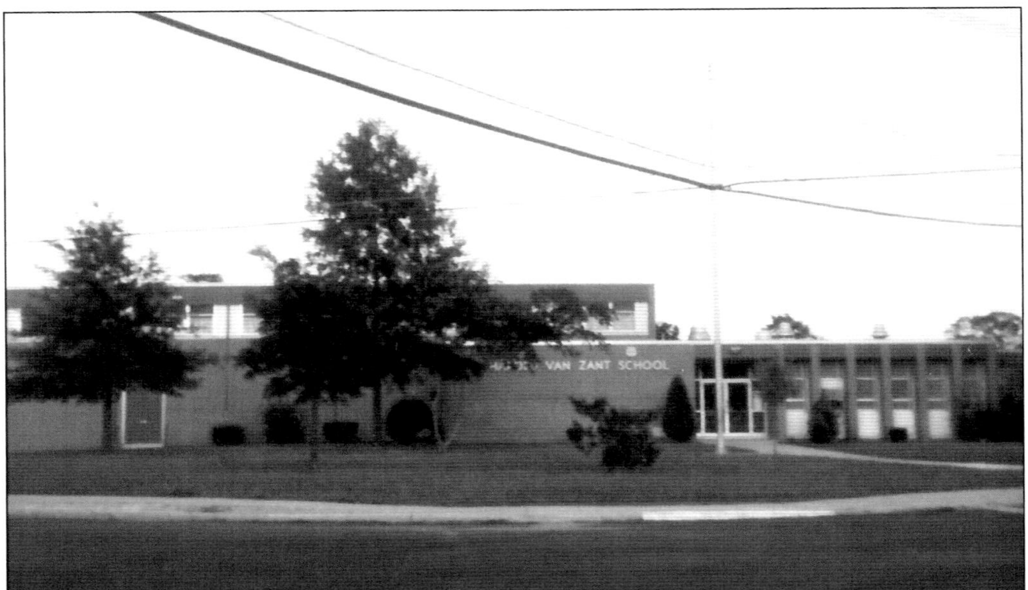

In 1968, the Van Zant Elementary School opened in the Woodstream development. Planning for the school began in 1964, but the voters rejected a bond issue, which later passed in 1966. A resolution approved on July 11, 1967, named it the J. Harold Van Zant School. Van Zant was a former school board member and president and was active in civic functions. (Photograph by the author.)

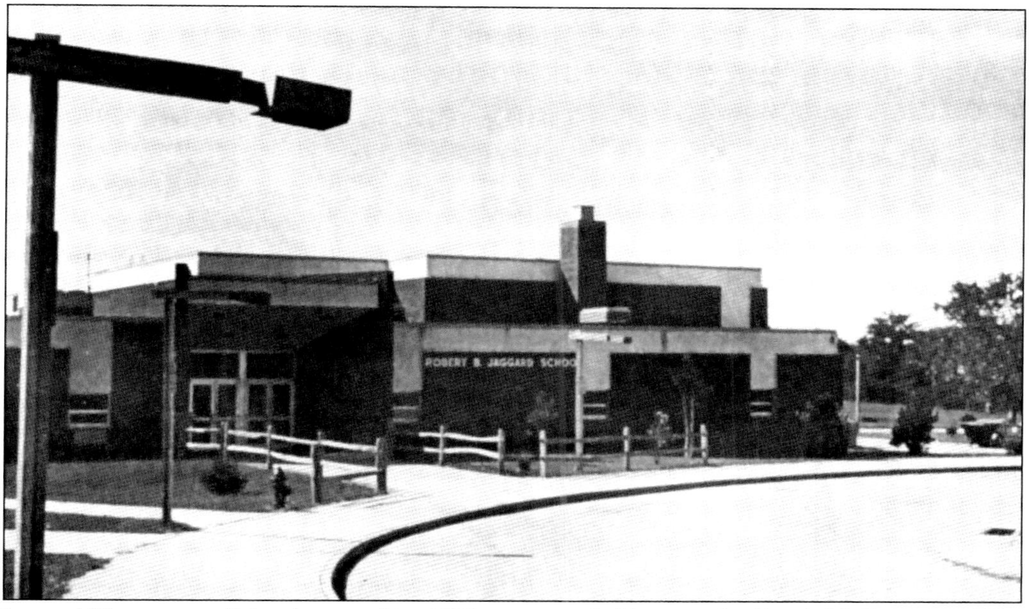

Jaggard Elementary School opened in 1972, serving children in the Brush Hollow area. The school was named for Robert B. Jaggard, a longtime resident of Evesham. He was an engineer and a member of the board of education. Jaggard served as chairman of the building committee and oversaw construction of the Beeler and Van Zant Schools.

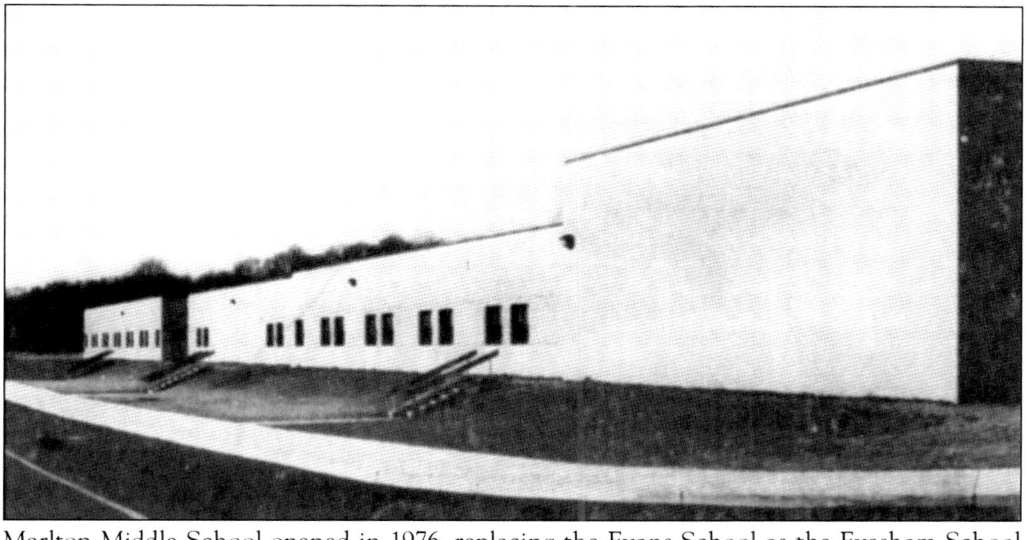

Marlton Middle School opened in 1976, replacing the Evans School as the Evesham School District's middle school. It was built with the concept of three small schools within one large building. These three schools, or houses as they are called, have their own administrative offices and share a library, gymnasium, and cafeteria.

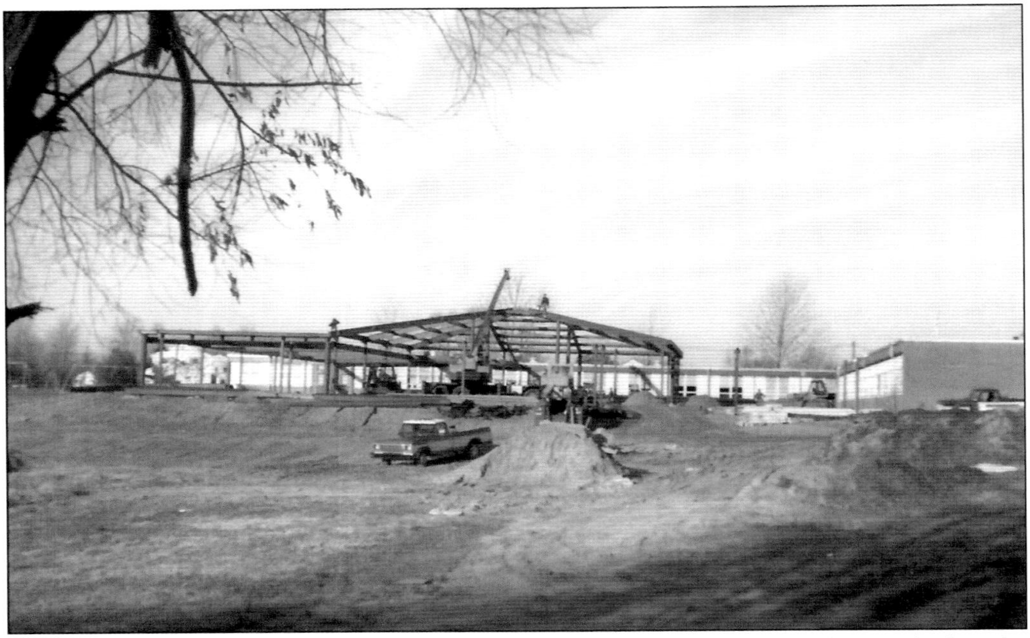

In 1988, Evesham School District underwent a major building program, with additions built at the Evans, Beeler, and Van Zant Schools to relieve space crunches caused by increased enrollment. The district completed the projects in 1989. This photograph was taken during the construction of the 1988 expansion at Van Zant School. (Photograph by the author.)

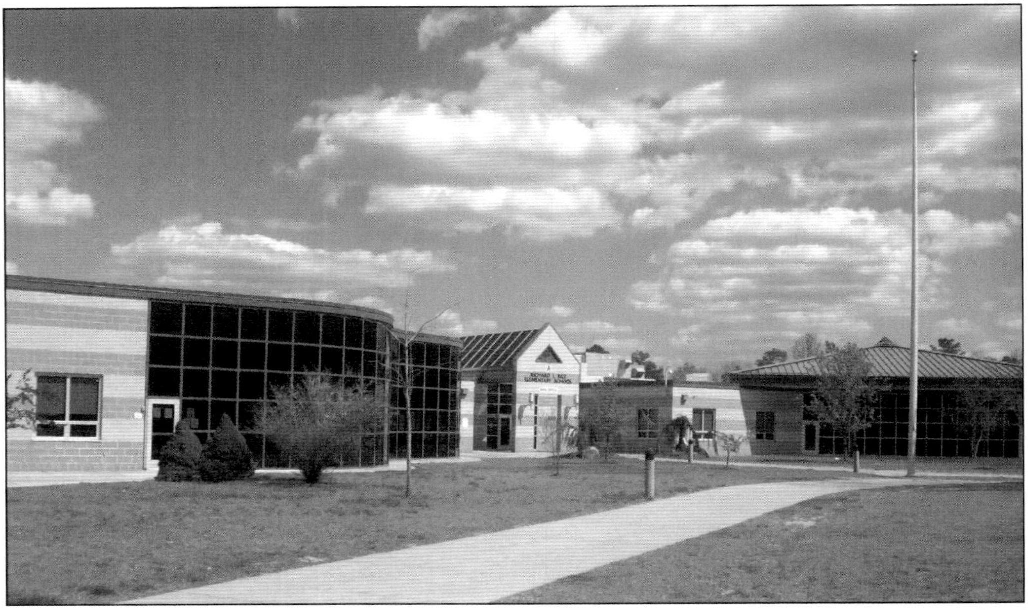

Shown here is Rice Elementary School in the Kings Grant section. Opened in 1989, the school was named in honor of Richard L. Rice, a member of the Evesham School Board from 1957 to 1977. He served terms as board vice president and was involved with the transportation, personnel, and negotiation committees. He also served as secretary for the Marlton Lions Club. (Photograph by the author.)

Dr. Leroy Meland became superintendent of the Evesham School District in 1969. He served in this position during a period of transition for the district. He oversaw the construction of new school facilities and the expansion of existing ones. He retired in 1992. The district named its administration building in his honor.

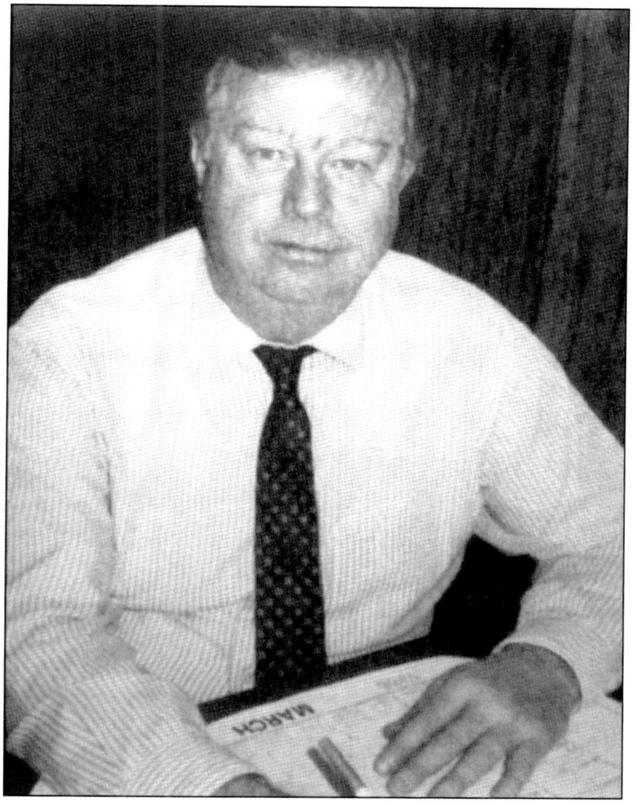

Pictured is DeMasi Elementary and Middle School on Evesboro-Medford Road. Frances S. DeMasi began teaching sixth grade at the Evans School in 1958. She was promoted to elementary supervisor in 1968, a position she held until her retirement from the Evesham School District in 1990. The district honored her in 1993 by naming this school for her. DeMasi spent time as a volunteer in Evesham schools after she retired. She died at age 88 in 2011. (Photograph by the author.)

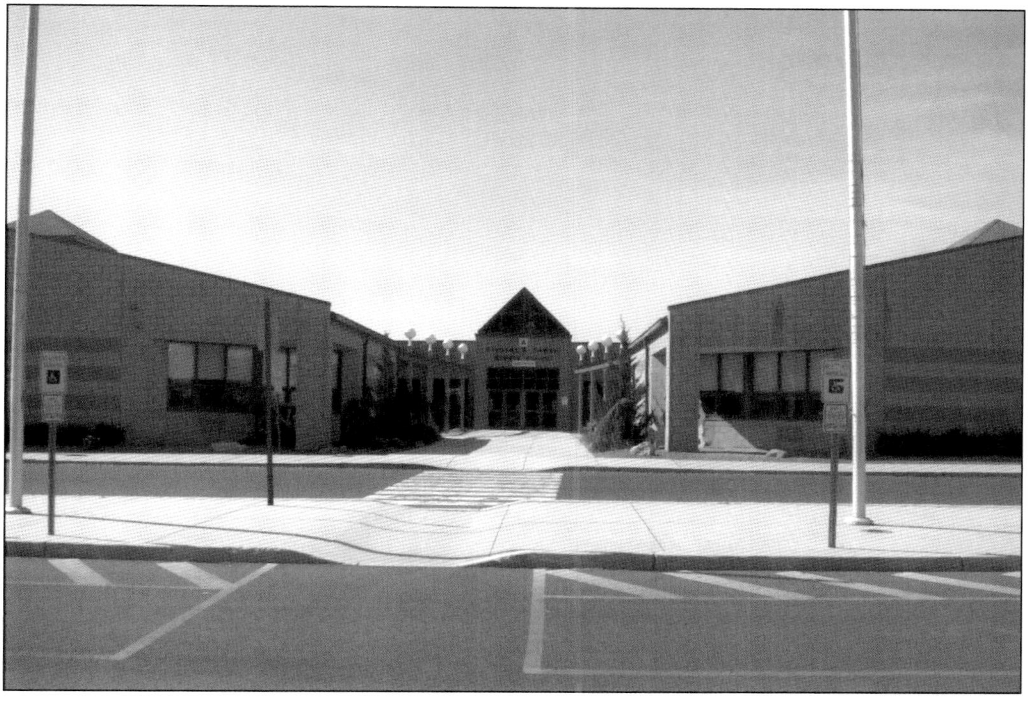

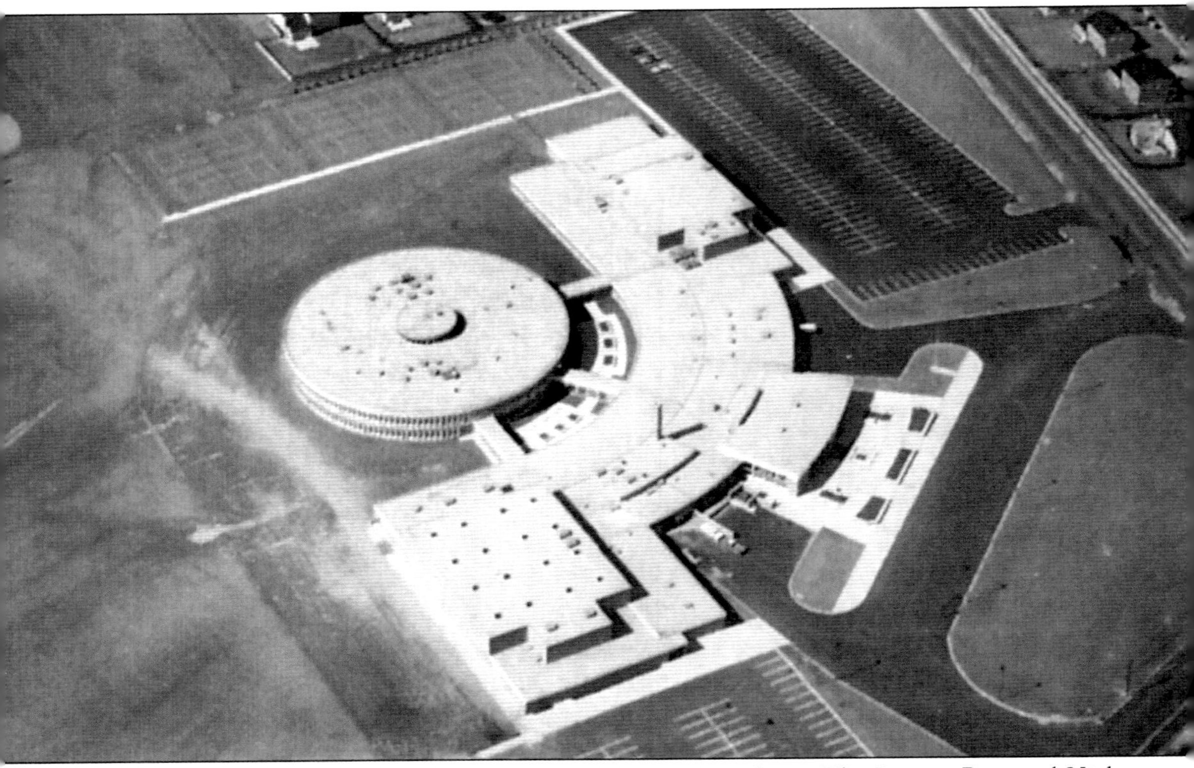

This aerial view of Cherokee High School shows its original size. The Lenape Regional High School District opened Cherokee in 1975 with grades 9 and 10. A wing was added to Cherokee in 2001, known as Cherokee South; the original section was then named Cherokee North. Also, in 2001, the Lenape Performing Arts Center was opened here. Before Cherokee opened, high school students attended Lenape High School in Medford, which opened in 1958. Prior to this, high school students were transferred to other districts. In 1971, the Lenape District opened Shawnee High School in the southeastern portion of Medford. Some high school students in Evesham then attended here.

Five

Community Services

Evesham has always provided its residents with the services needed for day-to-day life. As the township's population grew, the need for these services greatly increased. The building boom, which began in the 1950s, ushered in the need for more roads and residences needing trash collection, water and sewer connections, and fire and police protection. An early organization was the Marlton Fire Company, founded in 1898. Over the years, new fire equipment has been added to keep pace with the types of buildings being constructed in the township. A publicly elected fire commission was established in 1968 to oversee the operations of fire protection in Evesham Township. The addition of a first-aid squad in the early 1940s added a vital service to Evesham. Police protection in Evesham began with a constable and then was organized into a volunteer group in the 1950s before becoming a full-time paid force in 1966.

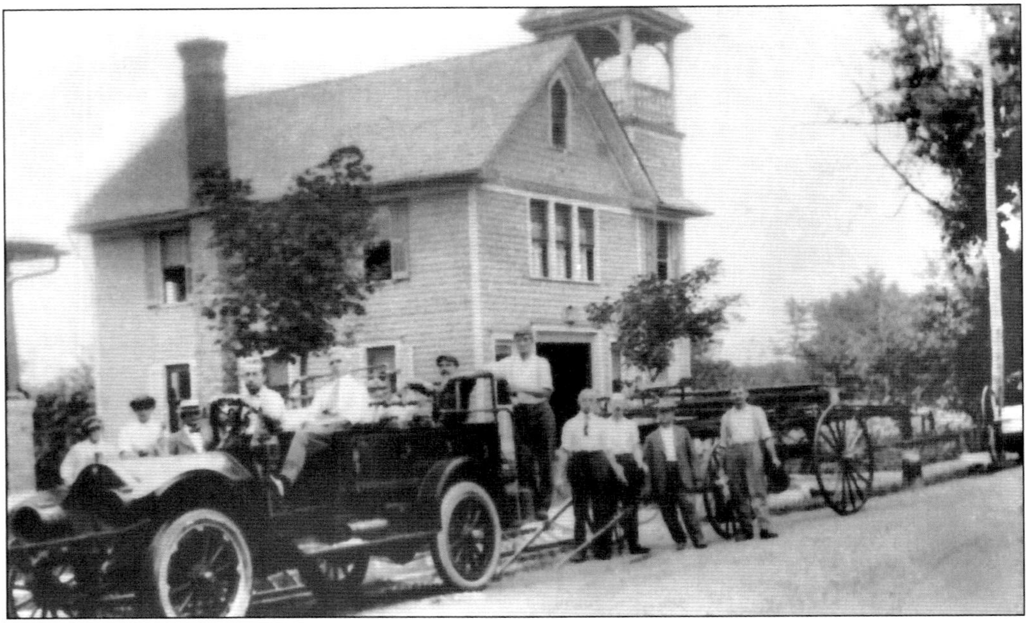

Shown is the original Marlton Firehouse at 26 East Main Street. This site was purchased in December 1900, and the firehouse was completed in January 1903. When founded in 1898, the Marlton Fire Company was first housed at the rear of Brick's General Store warehouse at Main Street and Maple Avenue. (Courtesy Edna Wirth.)

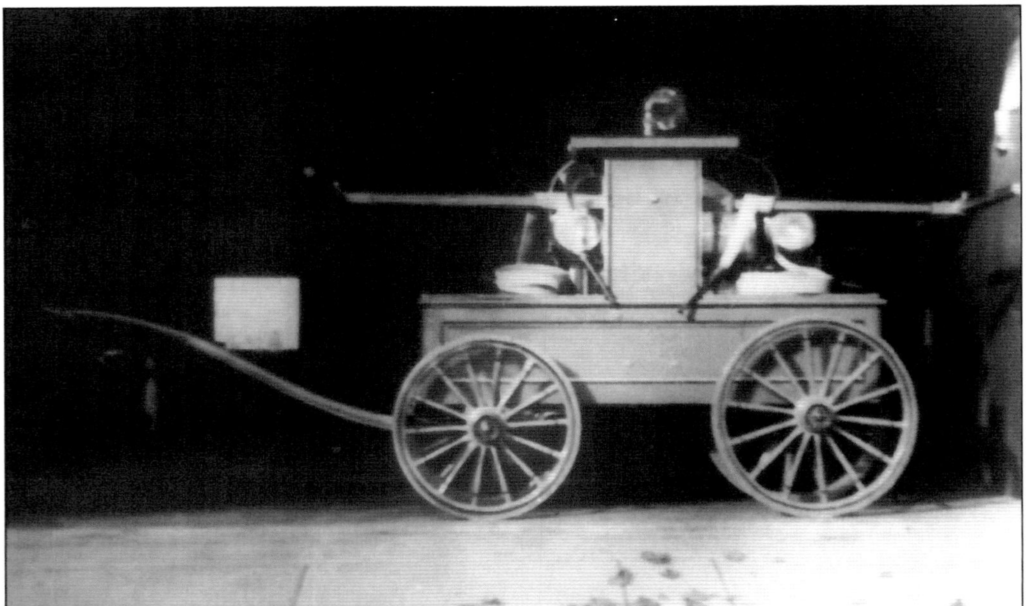

Shown is the c. 1743 hand-drawn pumper used by the Marlton Fire Company in its early years. (Courtesy Edna Wirth.)

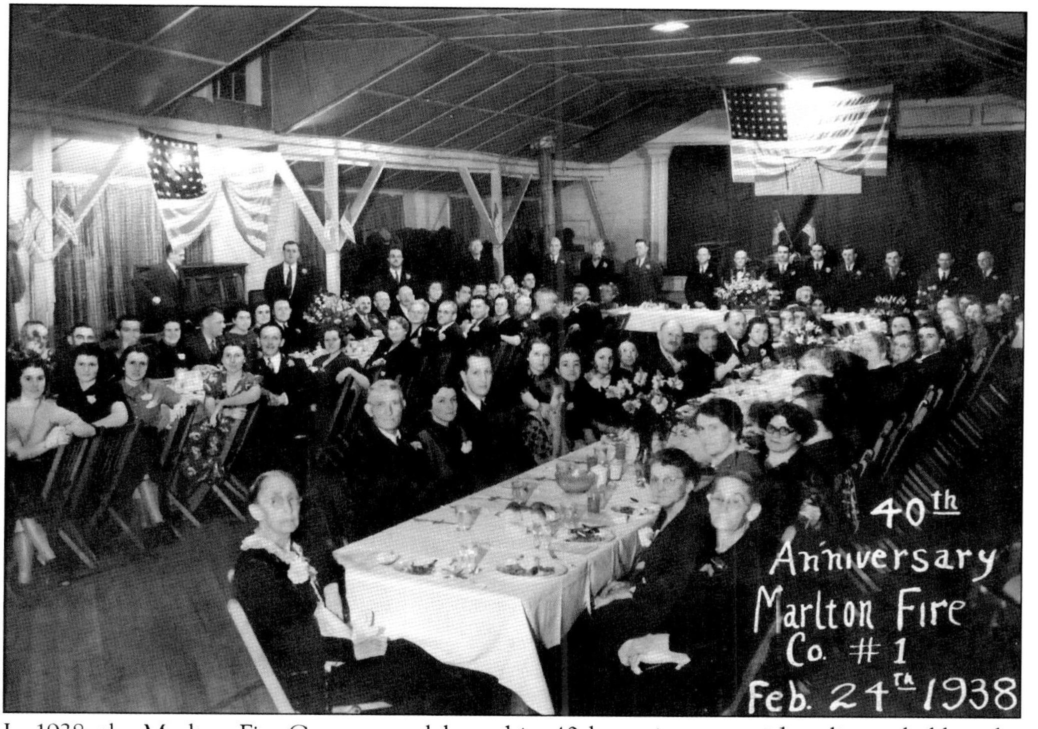

In 1938, the Marlton Fire Company celebrated its 40th anniversary with a dinner held at the Community House on Oak Avenue. About 100 people attended the affair, where a roast ham supper was served. The guests joined in group singing between courses and were entertained by a group of tap-dancing young girls. (Courtesy Evesham Historical Society.)

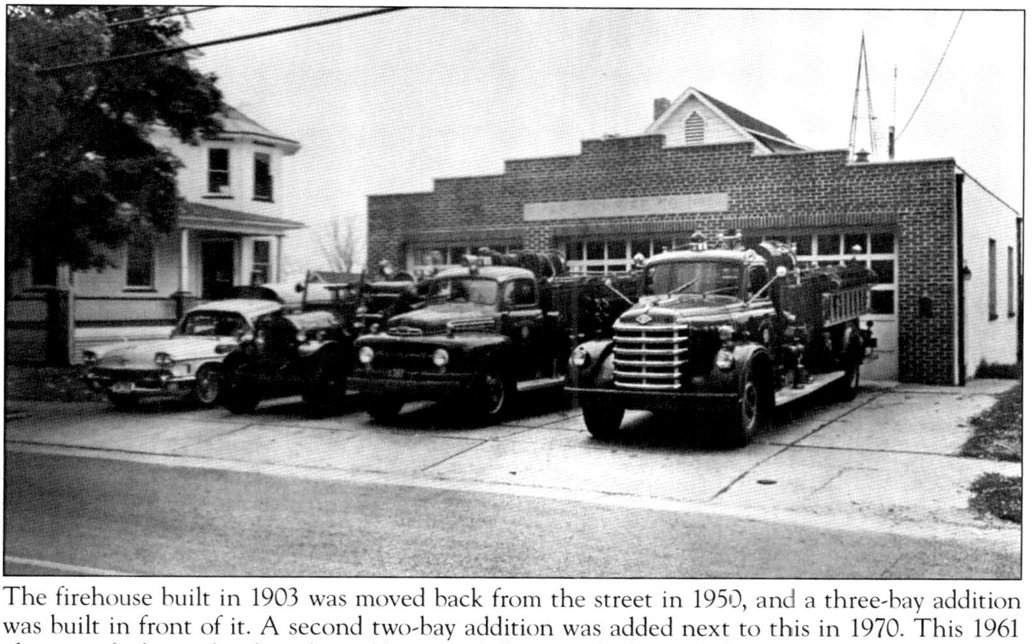

The firehouse built in 1903 was moved back from the street in 1950, and a three-bay addition was built in front of it. A second two-bay addition was added next to this in 1970. This 1961 photograph shows the three-bay addition and the 1903 firehouse behind it.

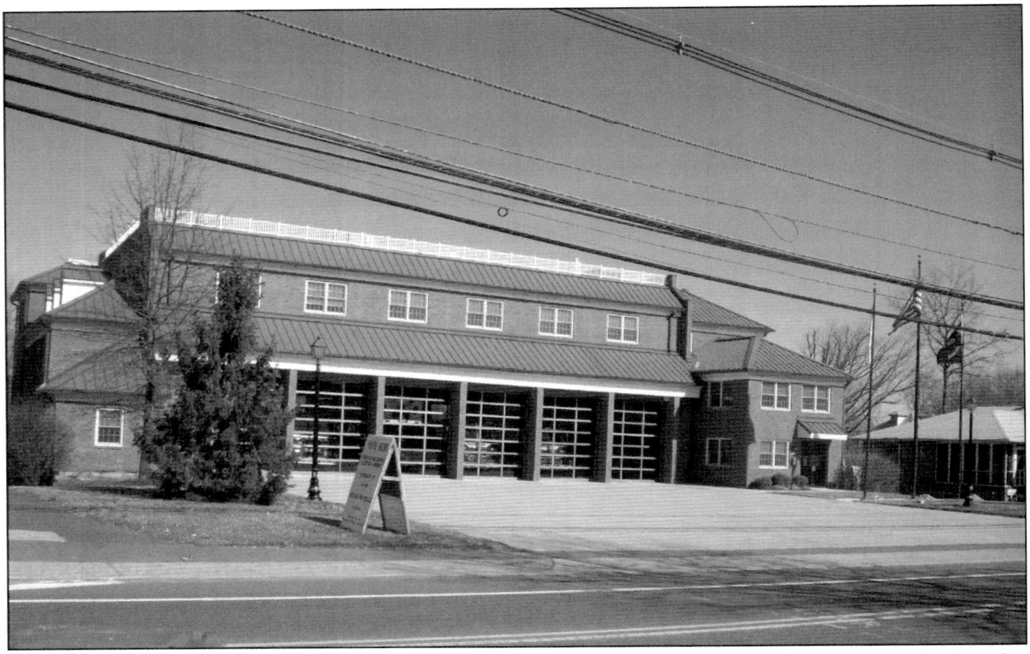

In 1997, the 1950 and 1970 additions made to the Marlton firehouse were demolished and a replacement firehouse built on the site. The 1903 firehouse was moved to the rear of the property and became a museum. By this time, the Evesham Fire District evolved into a service with volunteer and paid personnel operating three stations providing fire, rescue, and emergency medical service. (Photograph by the author.)

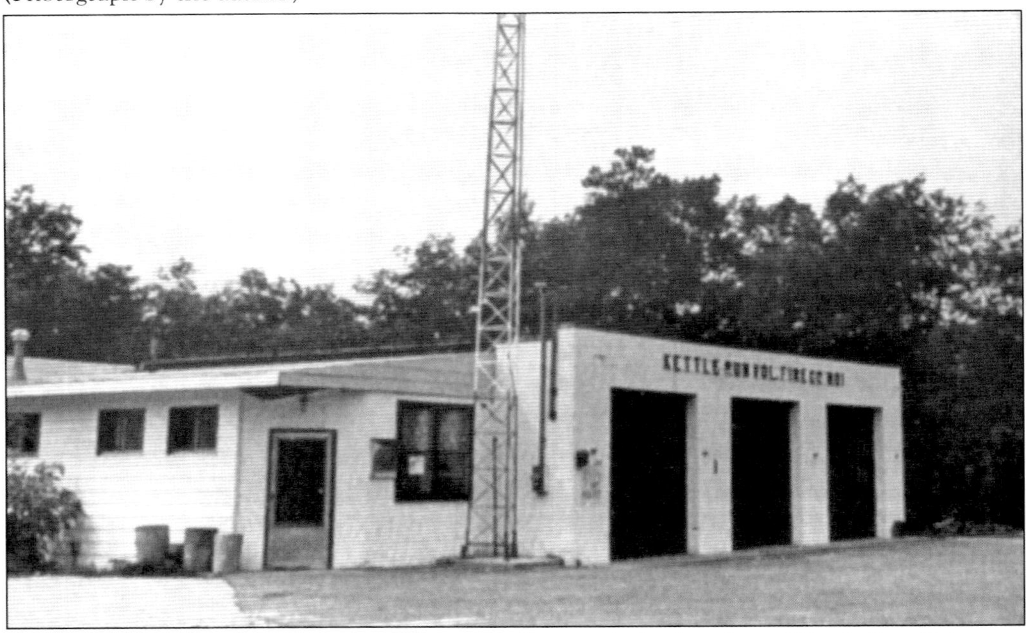

Firefighting came to the southern portion of Evesham with the founding of Kettle Run Volunteer Fire Company in 1957. Shown is the original station at Hopewell Road and Chestnut Avenue. In 1992, a third firehouse was dedicated in the Kings Grant section.

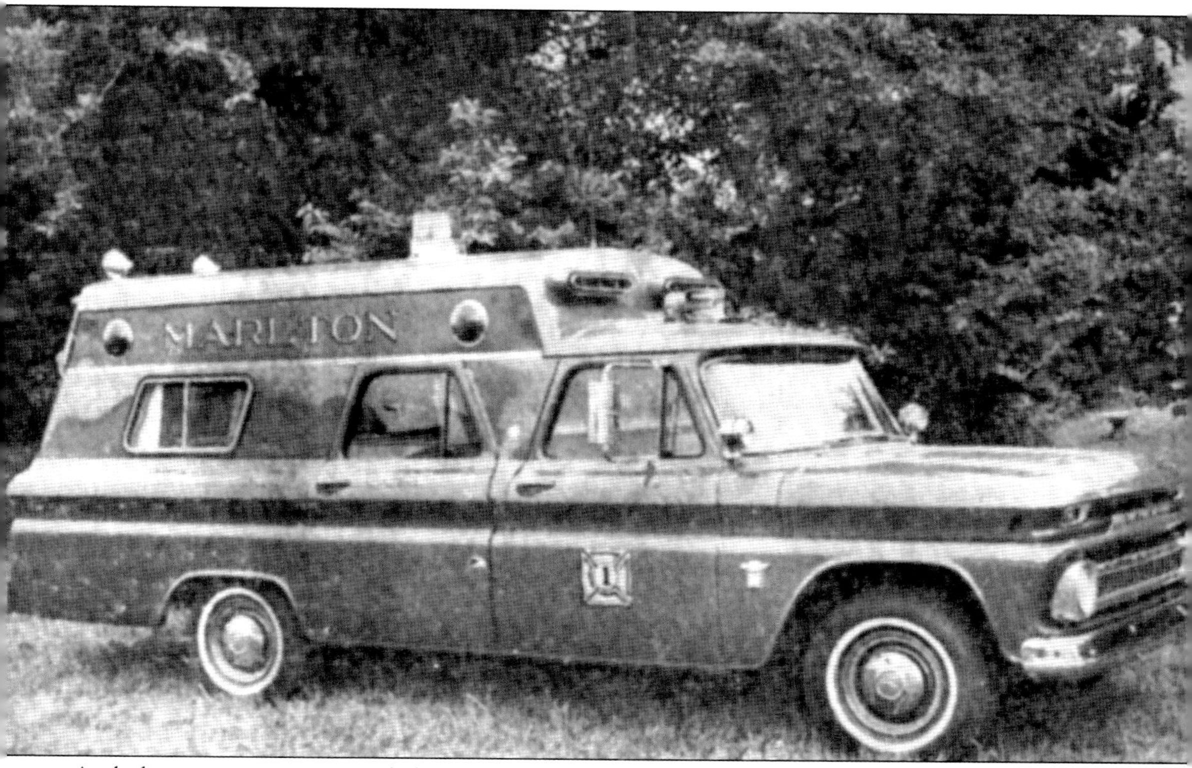

Ambulance service was provided to Evesham beginning in 1942 with the creation of the Marlton Community Ambulance Association. In 1952, at the request of the association, the Marlton Fire Company assumed responsibility for the service. The name was then changed to the Marlton First Aid Squad. Shown is the squad's first new vehicle, purchased in 1964, a Chevrolet Challenger ambulance. (Courtesy Evesham Historical Society.)

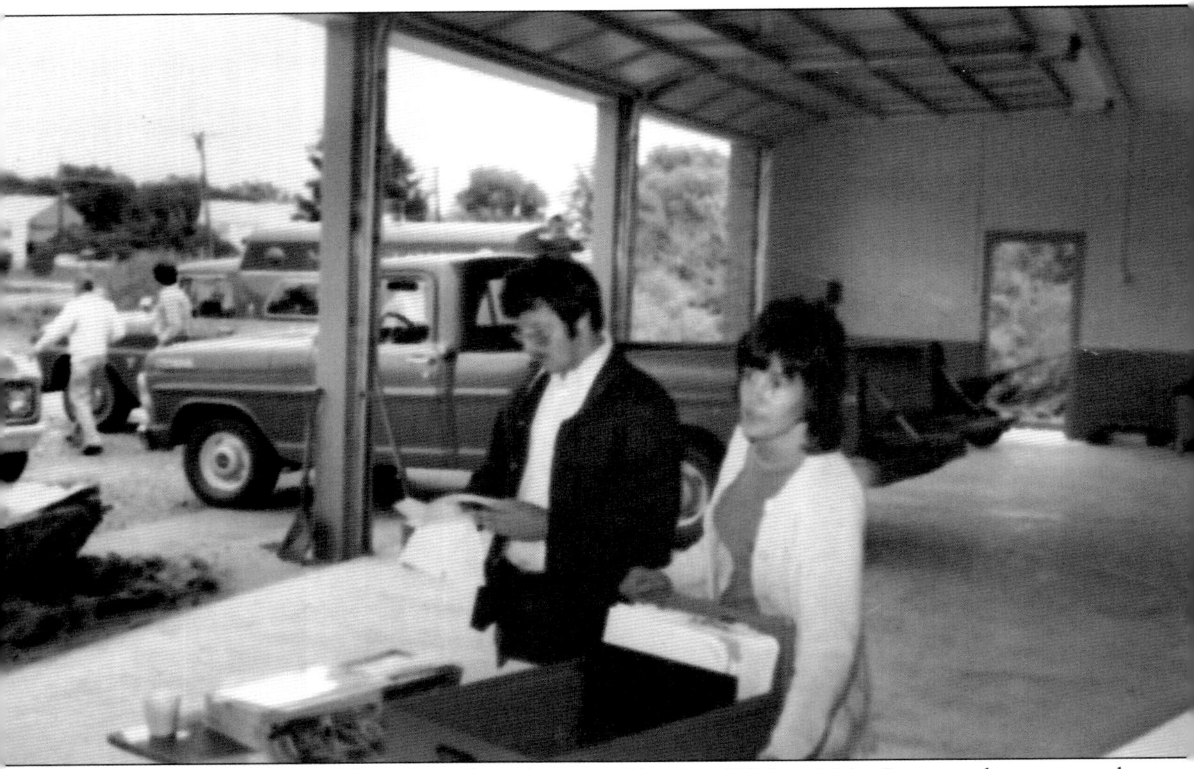

The Marlton First Aid Squad purchased a tract of land at 129 East Main Street and constructed a building there in 1974. The squad relied on fund drives at this time, and nearly $10,000 was raised that year and applied to the building's cost. Shown in this photograph is Assistant Captain Barbara Olt with an unidentified person inside the building during the final stages of construction. (Courtesy Stephen Pritti.)

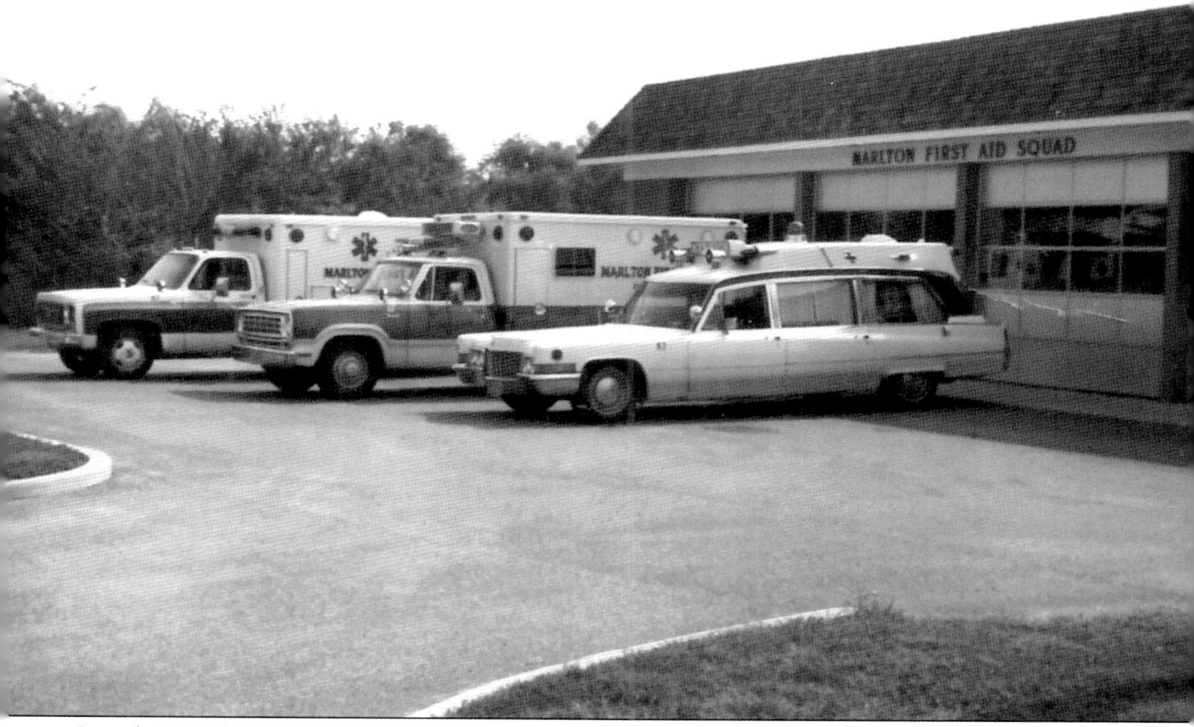

Seen here is the Marlton First Aid Squad headquarters at 129 East Main Street. This building gave the squad more space to operate and was later expanded. The squad returned its operations to the Evesham Fire Department in 1990 and became Evesham EMS. In 1998, Evesham EMS moved into the Marlton Firehouse at 26 East Main Street. This building then became Evesham School District's operations division headquarters. (Courtesy Stephen Pritti.)

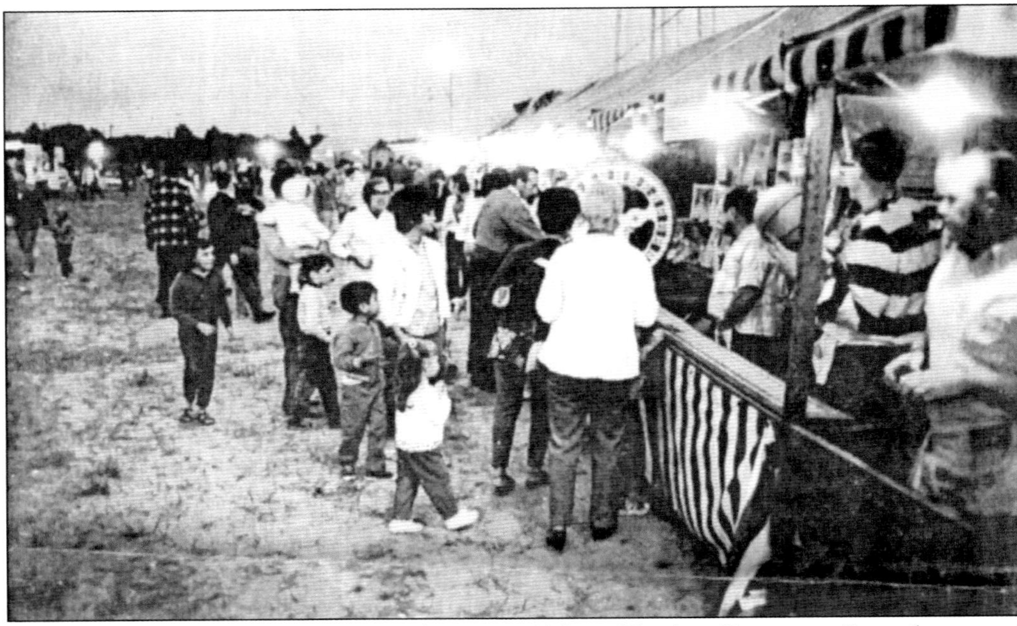

For many years, the Evesham Jaycees, Marlton Lions Club, and Evesham Recreation Council sponsored a carnival during the summer. This photograph is from the 1969 carnival held at the site of present-day Tri-Town Plaza at Route 70 and Plymouth Drive. The carnival ended during the 1980s.

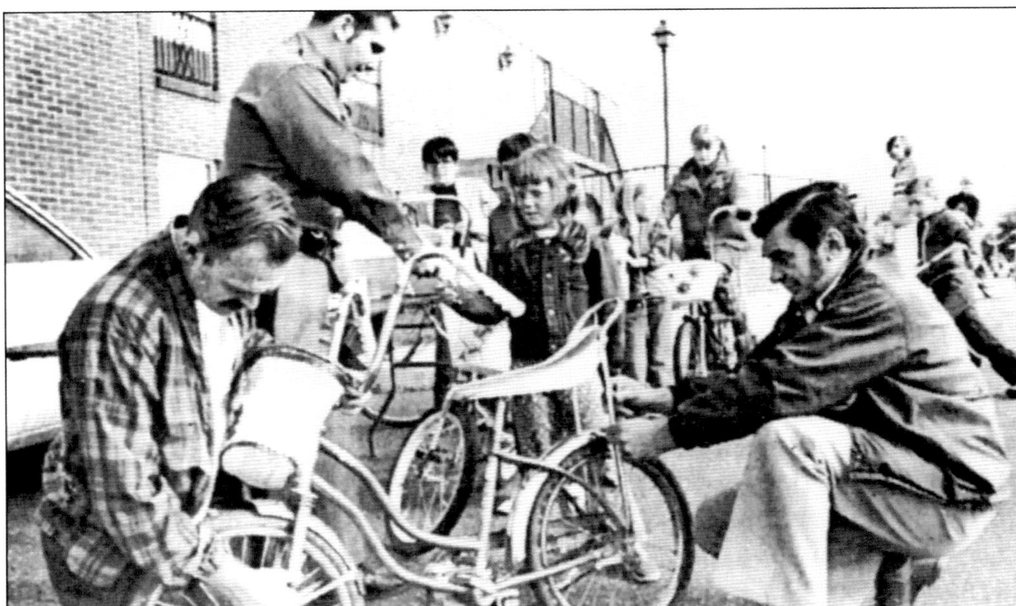

Evesham Police conducted yearly bicycle inspections with the assistance of the Evesham Jaycees and VFW Post 6295. This photograph from the 1972 inspection at the Municipal Building shows, from left to right, Don McDermott, Patrolman Richard Halaseck, and Nick Rumbos checking a bicycle. Bikes were also registered with the police department by stamping a number into the frame, which could identify the owner if recovered.

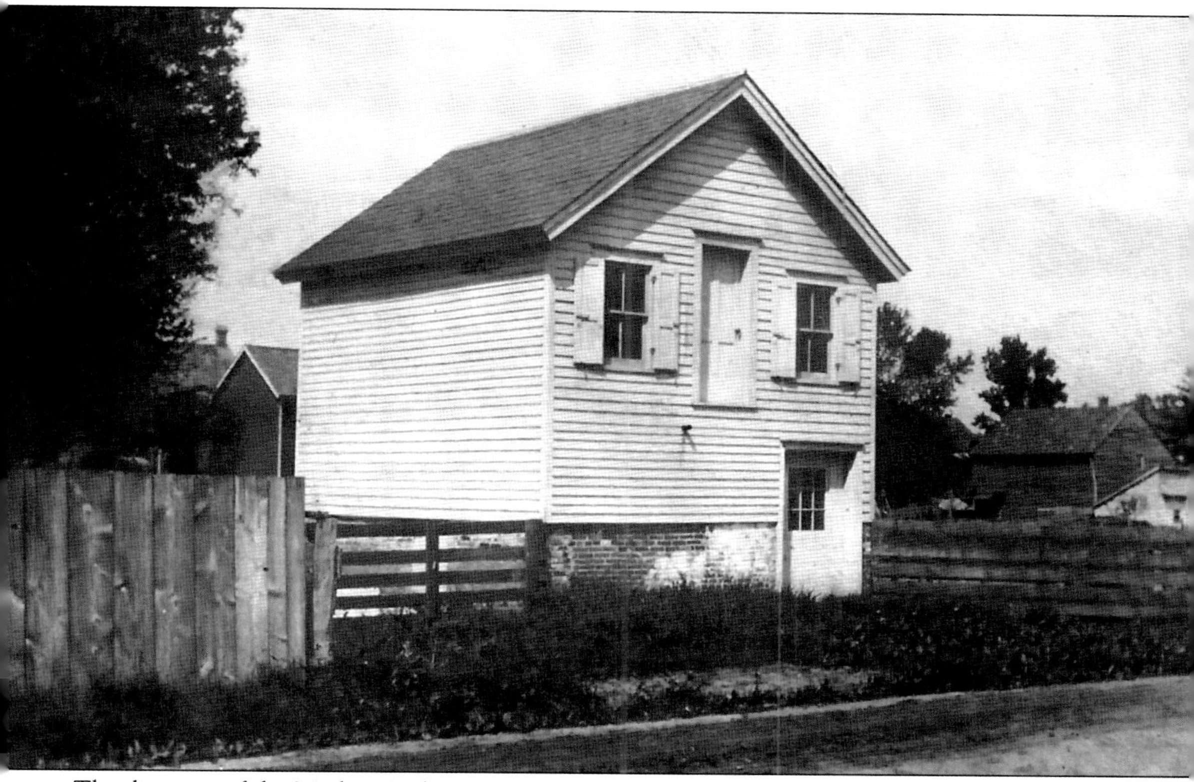

The directors of the Marlton Light, Heat, and Power Company purchased a lot on Oak Avenue from Charles Chew across from the Marlton School in 1903 for a gashouse. There was a lime pit behind the fence on the left. Gas streetlights were then installed along Main Street, Maple Avenue, Locust Avenue, and Cooper Street. They were lit each evening by a gas lighter and extinguished in the morning. These lamplighters were young boys who were paid $15 a month. The company was dissolved in 1926. (Courtesy Evesham Historical Society.)

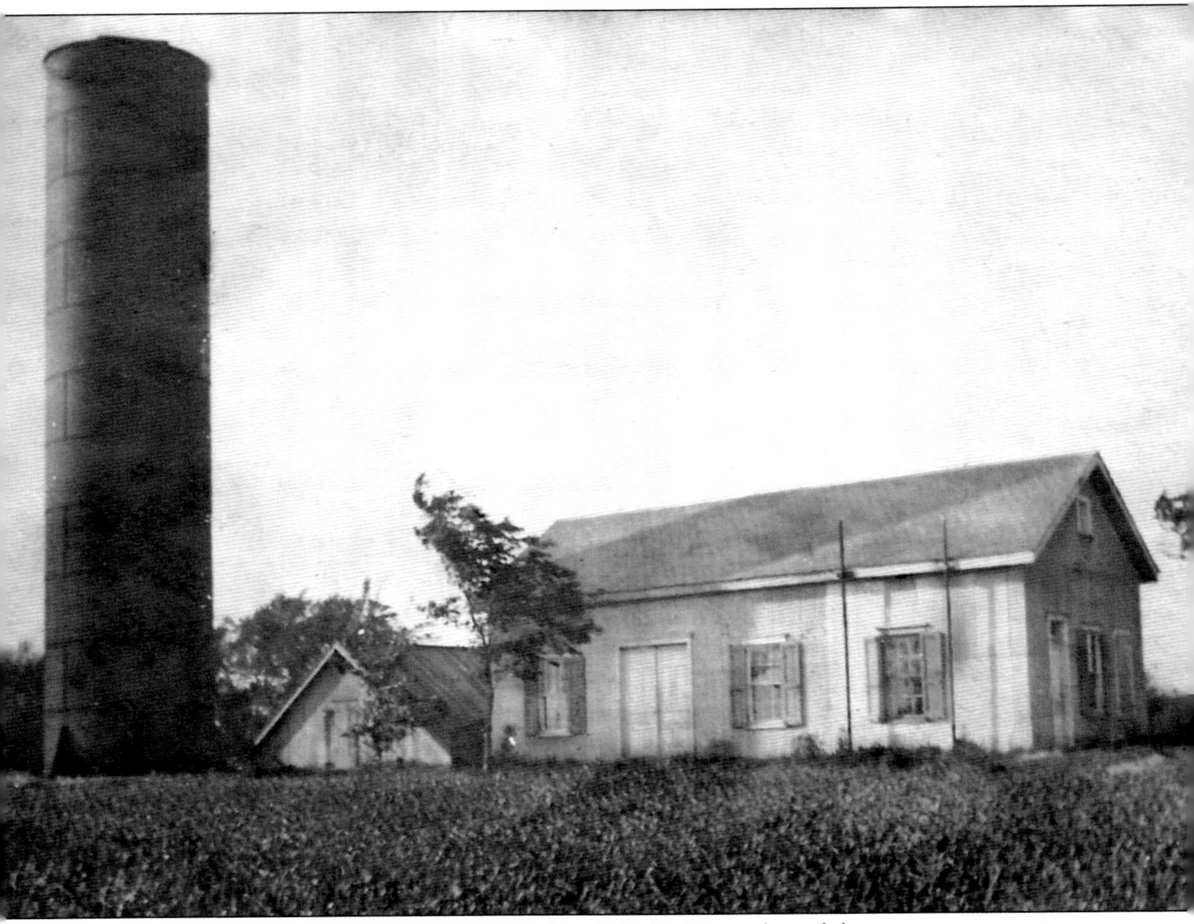

The Marlton Water Company was formed in 1897. By December of that year, water mains were run through the village of Marlton, and a standpipe and pump house were completed on Evesham Avenue. The company was purchased by Evesham Township in the late 1950s. This facility was acquired by Evesham Municipal Utilities Authority in 1960. The plant was dismantled in 1963 with the opening of wells and a 500,000-gallon water tower on Plymouth Drive. (Courtesy Evesham Historical Society.)

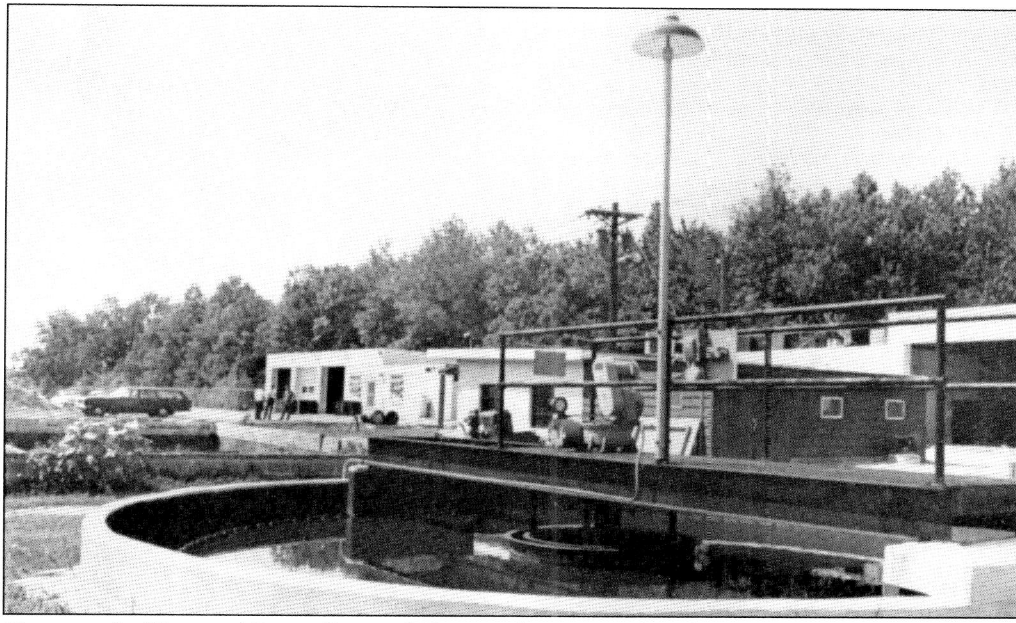

Shown is the Elmwood Sewer Disposal Plant in the 1970s. This plant was built by the developers of Georgetowne for that project. The Evesham Sewerage Authority was established by ordinance in 1955. The authority was given the right to acquire sewer and water facilities in 1959 and was renamed Evesham Municipal Utilities Authority. The acquisition of the water facilities came around 1960 and the sewer facilities in 1961.

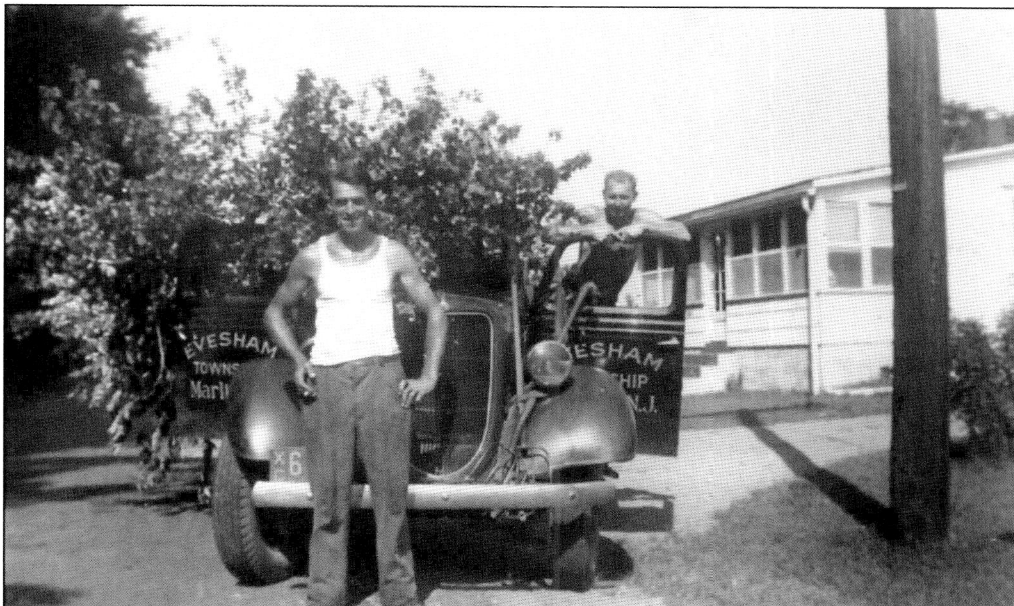

Posing with an Evesham Township truck in the 1950s are Harry Anderson (left) and Harvey Wirth. These two men made up the Evesham Township Public Works Department at that time. (Courtesy Dolores Wirth.)

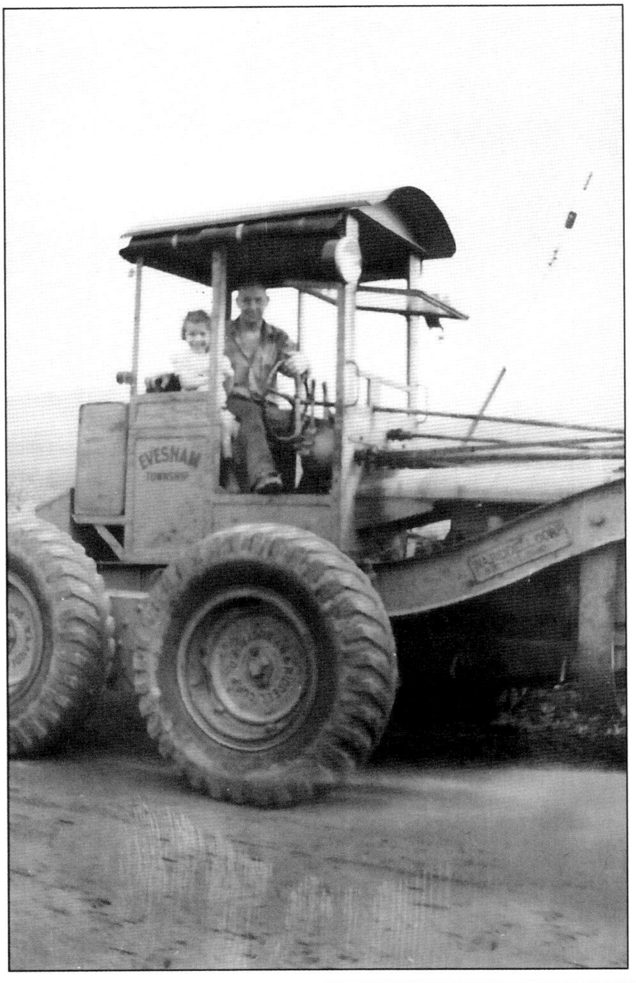

Dolores Wirth poses with her father, Harvey, on a grader used by Evesham Township for smoothing dirt roads and for snow removal. (Courtesy Dolores Wirth.)

A building used during World War I at Camp Dix was brought to Marlton for use as a community house. It was used for community events, most notably oyster and chicken suppers held to raise funds for the fire company. Lines for the suppers would reach more than a block long, and sometimes over 2,000 suppers were served. In March 1958, a snowstorm caused the roof of the structure to collapse, and it was not rebuilt. (Courtesy Dolores Wirth.)

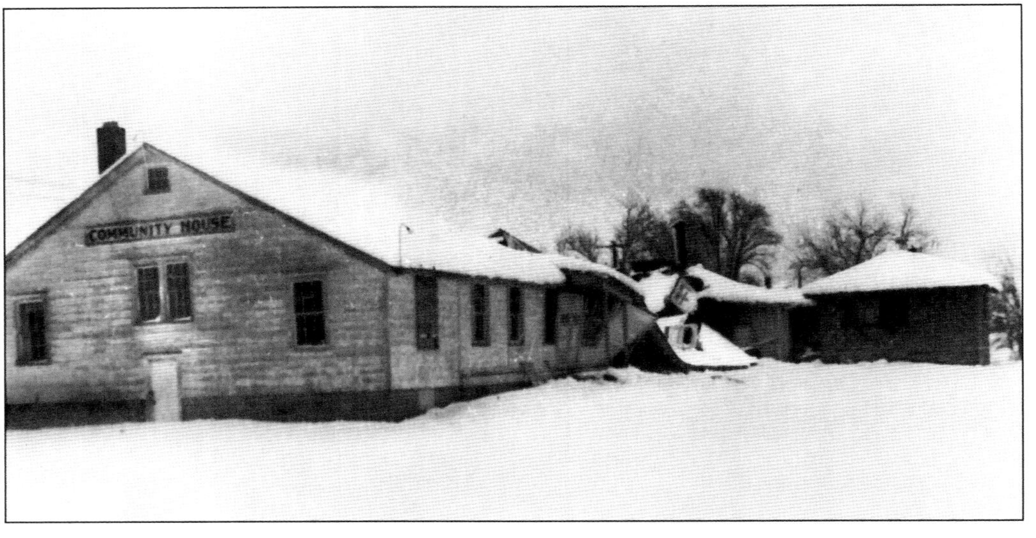

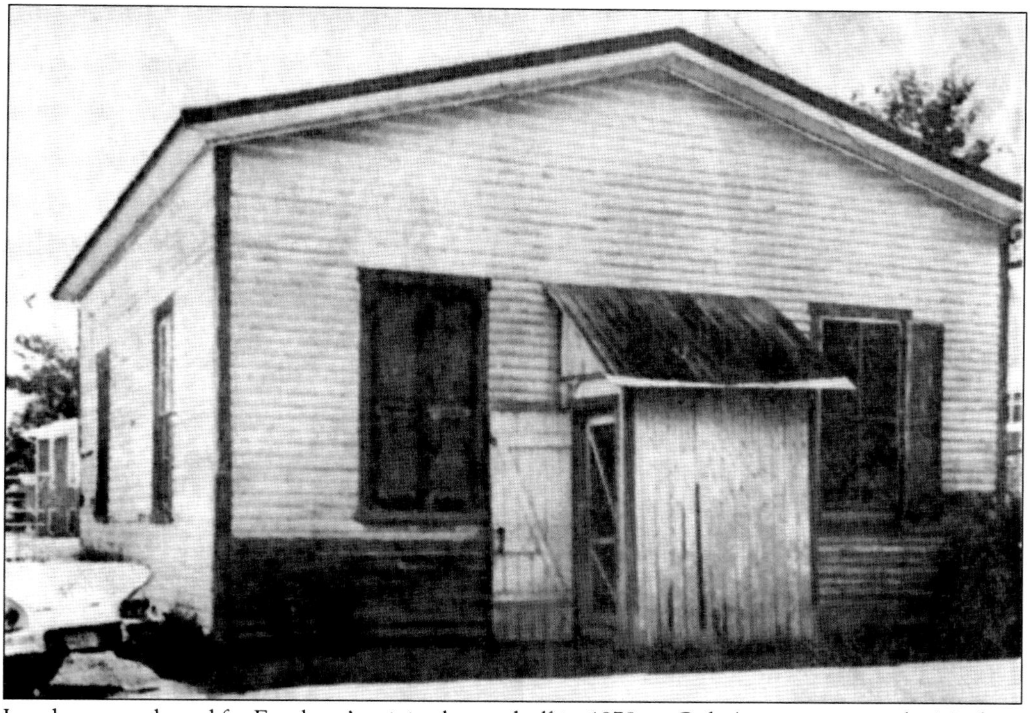

Land was purchased for Evesham's original town hall in 1878 on Oak Avenue next to the Marlton School. This building was last used for township meetings in 1957. It contained a jail cell and was also used as a spare classroom. It was demolished in the mid-1960s after falling into a dilapidated condition. (Courtesy Evesham Historical Society.)

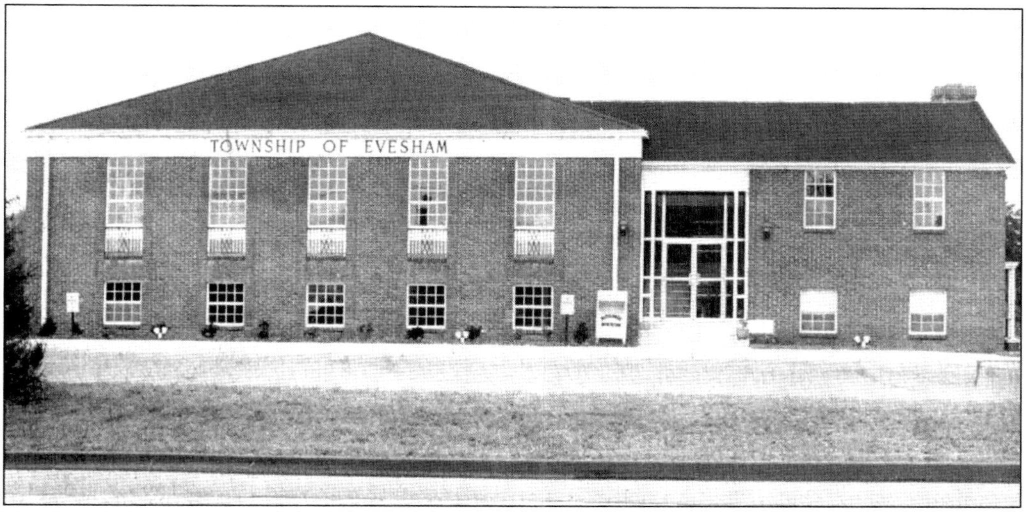

Evesham's first municipal building with township services and offices in a central location was constructed at 125 East Main Street in 1966. A cornerstone-laying ceremony was held on December 31, 1966. The building originally contained the Evesham library, police department, tax collector, office of the assessor, township clerk, and manager. The facility also contained a large hall that was used as a courtroom and for township meetings. This building was used until 1998 and demolished in June 2012.

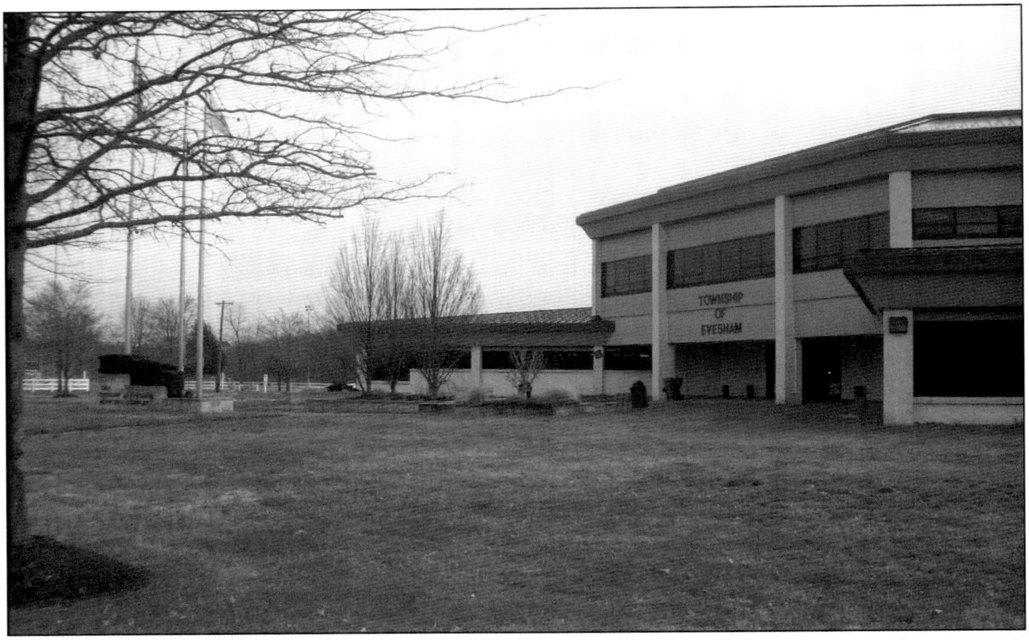

Evesham Township's current Municipal Building at 984 Tuckerton Road was opened in 1998. A dedication ceremony was held in July of that year that included the burying of a time capsule to be opened in December 2096.

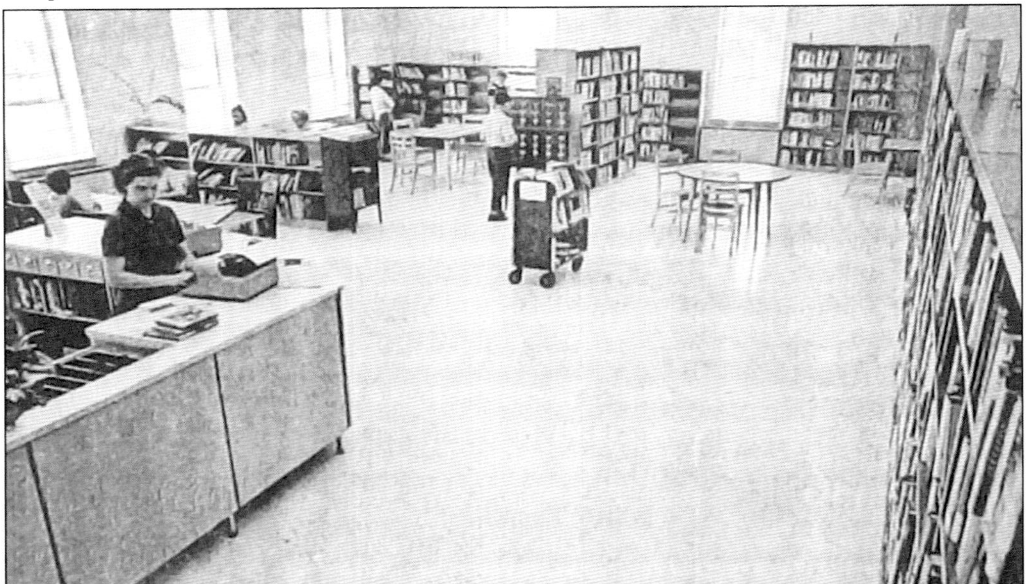

The Friends of the Evesham Township Public Library Inc. was founded in January 1963. The association raised money, joined the Burlington County Library System, and opened a library at Marlton School No. 1 on Maple Avenue in August 1963. In 1964, the library occupied space at 27 East Main Street. It relocated in 1967 to the then recently opened Municipal Building at 125 East Main Street, shown here. In 1976, the Evesham Library moved into rented space at Tri-Towne Plaza on Route 70, and in 1998 it moved to its current location at the Evesham Municipal Complex.

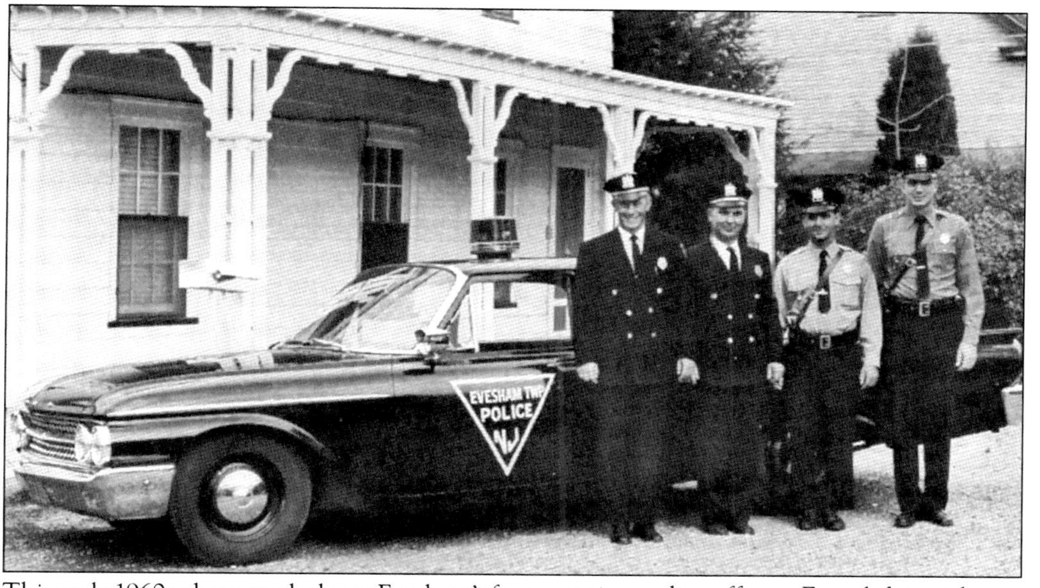

This early-1960s photograph shows Evesham's four part-time police officers. From left to right are Chief William Bradley, Sgt. Wilbur Ivins, and Patrolmen Webb Lingle and Robert McDaniels. Before these officers were hired in the late 1950s, Evesham had a constable. In 1960, Evesham formed a group of 32 volunteer police reserves. These officers were on duty at night along with the part-time officers. New Jersey State Police patrolled Evesham during the day.

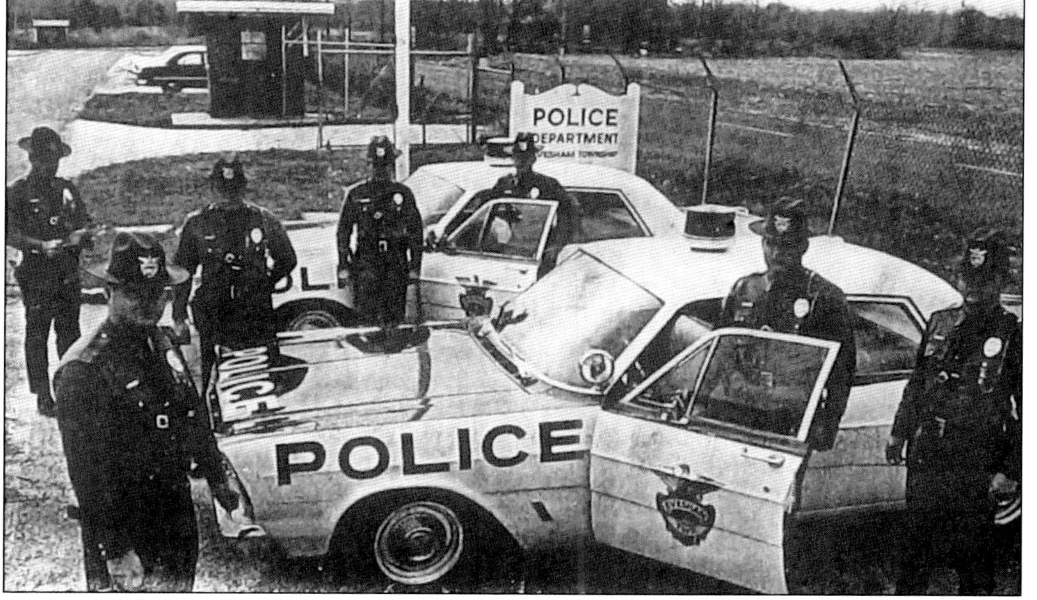

Evesham's full-time police department was established in July 1966. This November 1966 photograph shows the seven-man force. From left to right are (first row) Patrolmen Walter Ward, Nicholas Matteo, and Joseph Leedom; (second row) Chief Andrew Janssen and Patrolmen Edward Brown, Walter Morrell, and Neil Forte. The image was taken at the former Nike missile base on Tomlinson Mill Road, which housed the first headquarters for the force. Evesham Police Department then moved in early 1967 to the recently completed Municipal Building on Main Street.

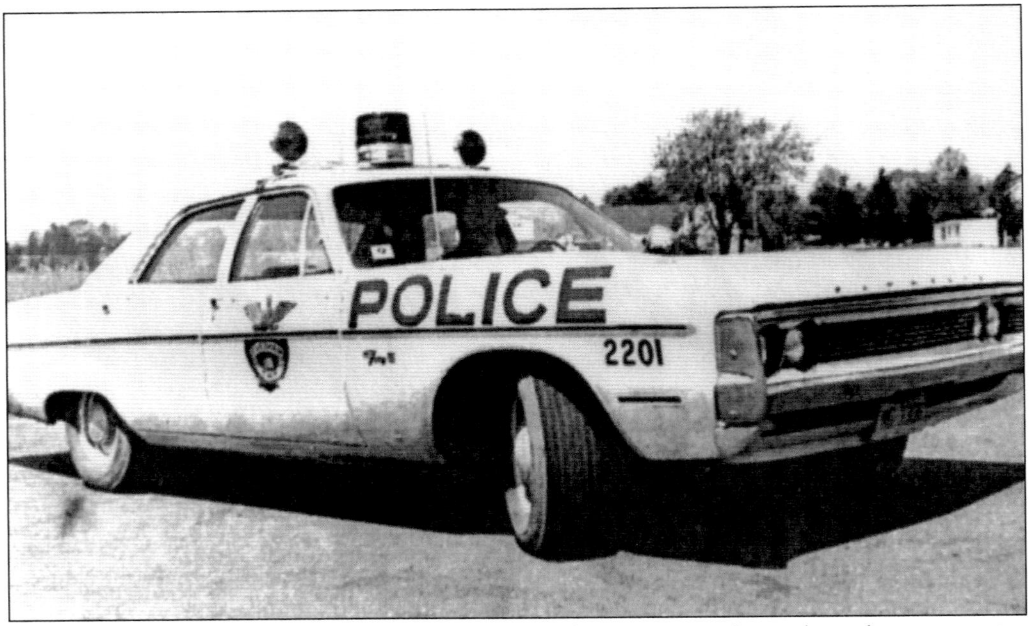

In 1970, Evesham Township purchased three Plymouth Fury III patrol cars through a cooperative state plan. One of these vehicles is shown here.

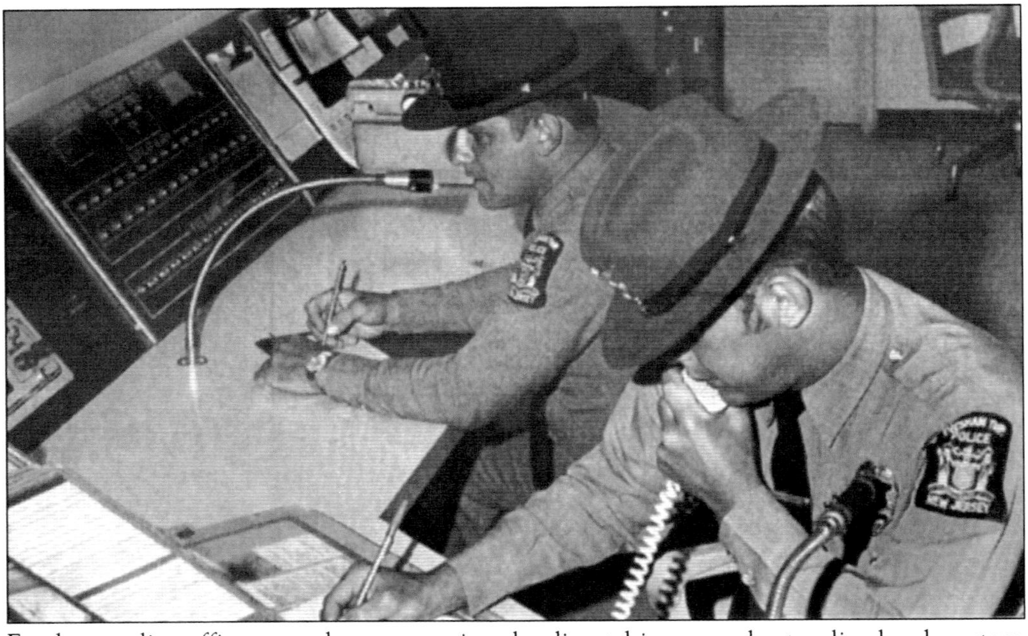

Evesham police officers are shown manning the dispatching console at police headquarters. Calls for police, fire, and ambulance were answered here and the appropriate service dispatched. A Plectron radio alert system was installed in 1971 for dispatching fire and ambulance calls. In 1978, emergency dispatching for Evesham was transferred to Burlington County Central Communications in Westampton, which was started earlier that year.

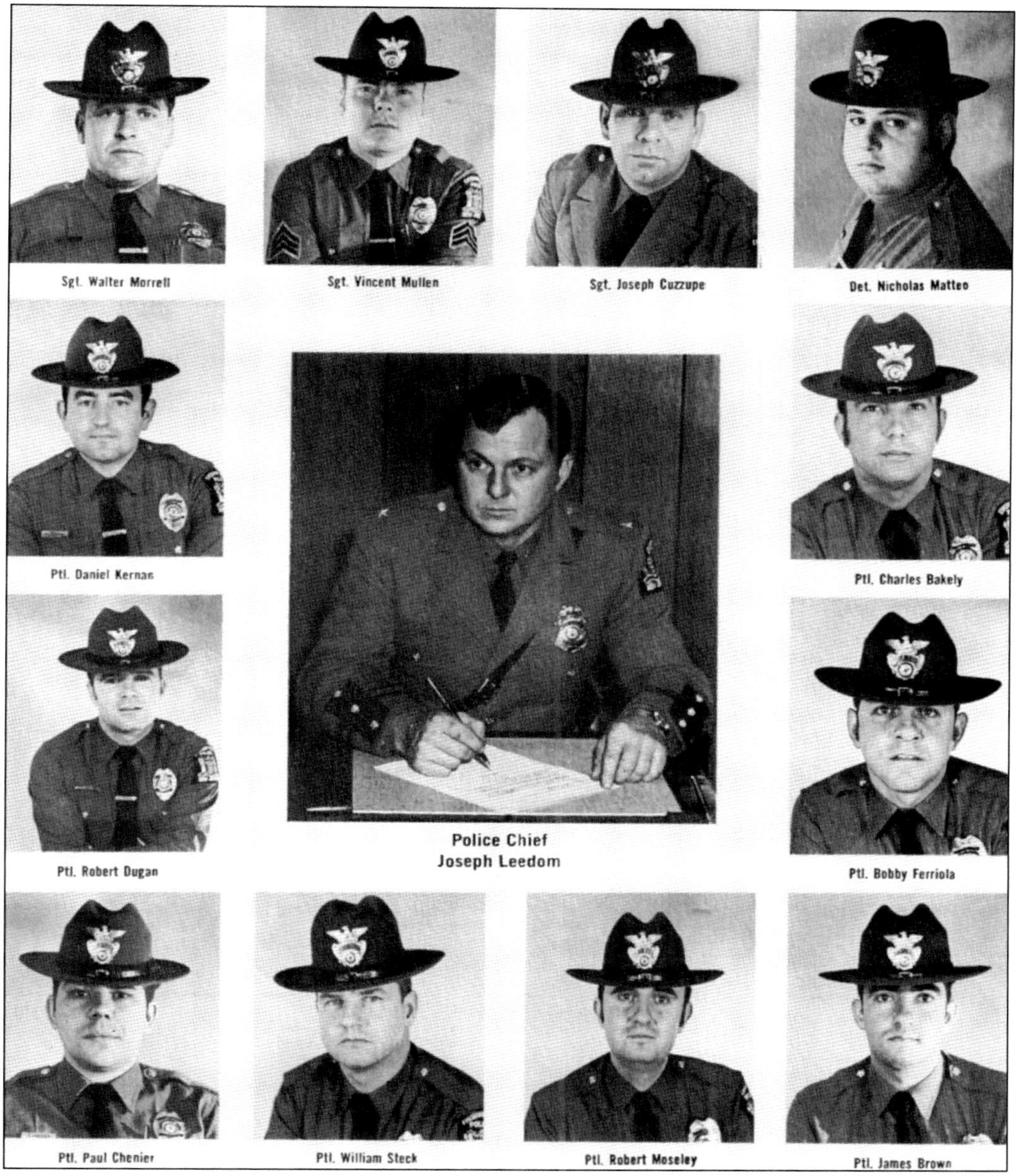

The Evesham Police Department grew to 13 members in 1971, as shown in this image. Joseph Leedom became the department's second chief in 1970. The original uniform worn by the department consisted of a grey blouse and pants with a black side stripe and a ten-gallon hat. (Courtesy Evesham Historical Society.)

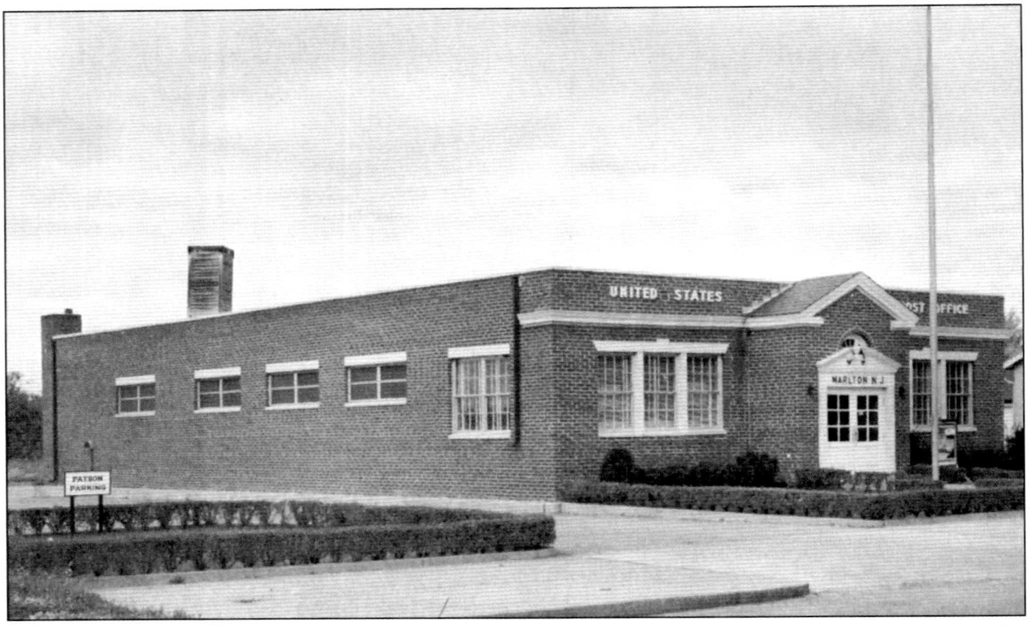

The Marlton Post Office moved into this building at 26 West Main Street in October 1957. The building contained 3,000 square feet of floor space and was obtained through a private financing program and leased by the federal government. Prior to opening this facility, the post office was located in nine different buildings over a span of 149 years in the village of Marlton.

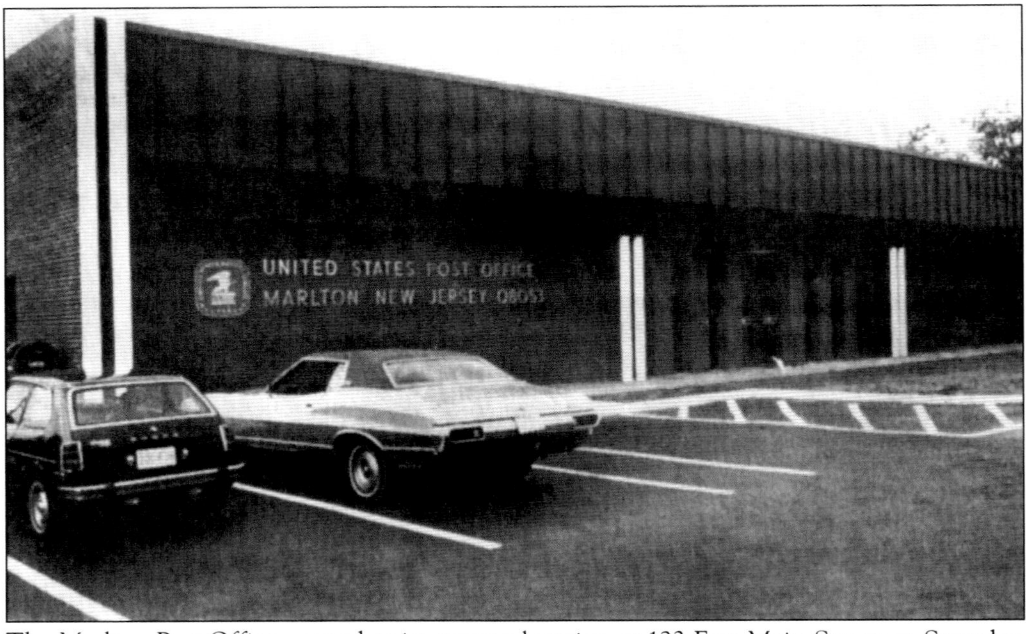

The Marlton Post Office opened at its present location at 123 East Main Street on Saturday, June 19, 1976. An open house was held on July 25, 1976, to show the public the new facility. (Courtesy Edna Wirth.)

Six

GROWTH YEARS

Evesham's early history ended in the mid-1950s, when farms were beginning to be sold to make way for residential developments. A planning board was founded in February 1955. This group formulated land use rules that created an orderly transformation of Evesham from a rural area to a suburban community. The population began to increase at a fast pace in the 1960s. Estimates place the increase at 250 percent between 1960 and 1970. This residential increase spurred commercial growth as well. Shopping centers sprang up to keep pace with the population growth. Township services also had to increase to keep up with the demand. In July 1969, Evesham's form of government changed from a committee to a council-manager. Even with this growth, the southern part of Evesham Township, which is protected by the Pinelands Preservation Act, is largely rural.

The unprecedented population increase brought growing pains, such as overcrowding in the schools, and township facilities quickly becoming inadequate. In the 1980s, the township embarked on a program to acquire open space to protect these areas from being developed. Also, in the 1980s, the township government formed a Historic Preservation Commission to preserve historic buildings in Evesham. By this time, a number of these buildings had already been lost. Development slowed in the 1990s, giving the township a chance to improve its facilities to accommodate the increase in population.

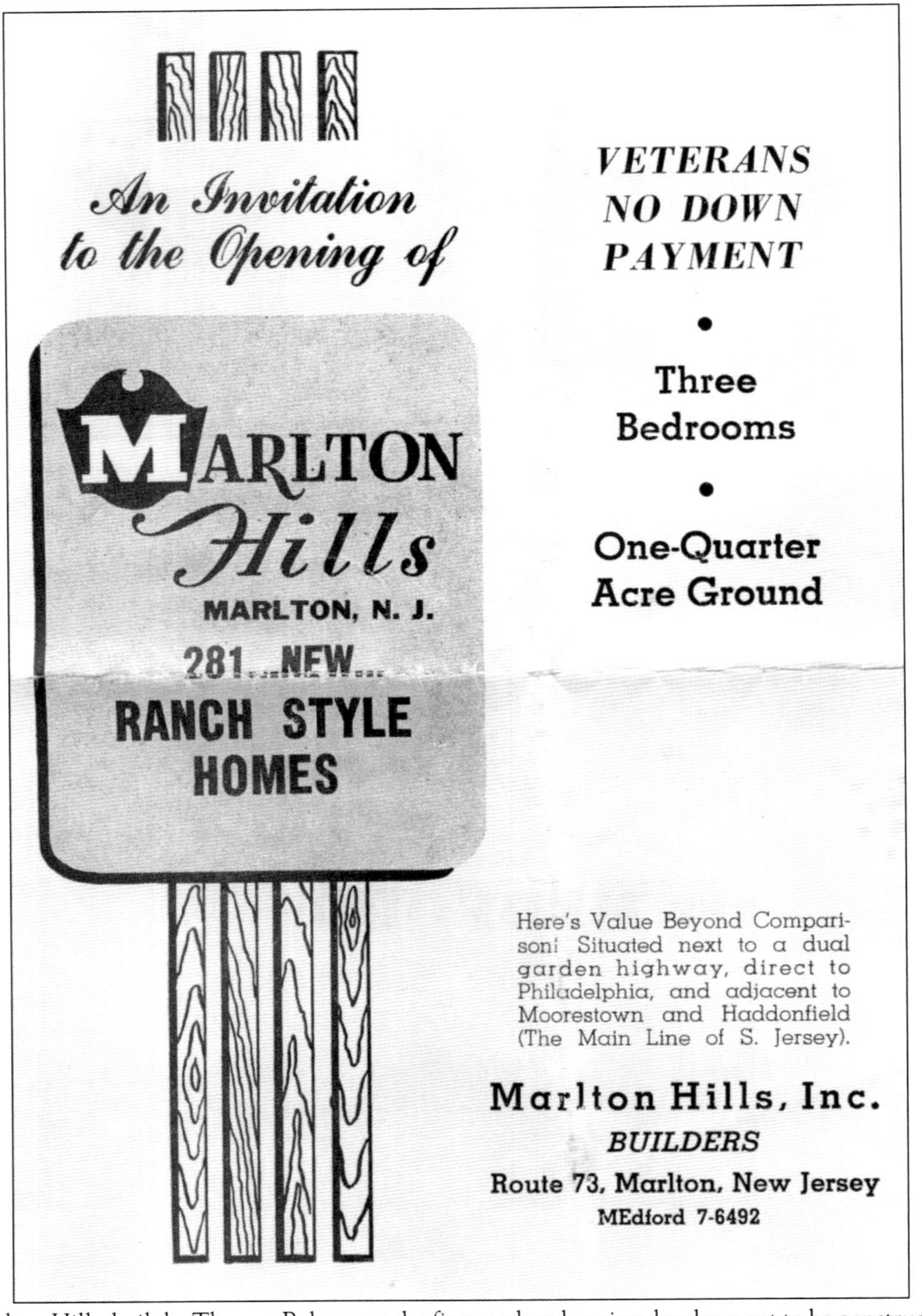

Marlton Hills, built by Thomas Baker, was the first modern housing development to be constructed in Evesham. Seventy-seven of the 281 homes originally planned were built between 1954 and 1955 on the development's west side off Route 73. Homes were built on the remaining lots by a different developer in the eastern portion near Maple Avenue between 1961 and 1962. The other remaining sections were built as the Evesboro West and London Square developments in the early 1960s. (Courtesy Guy Thompson.)

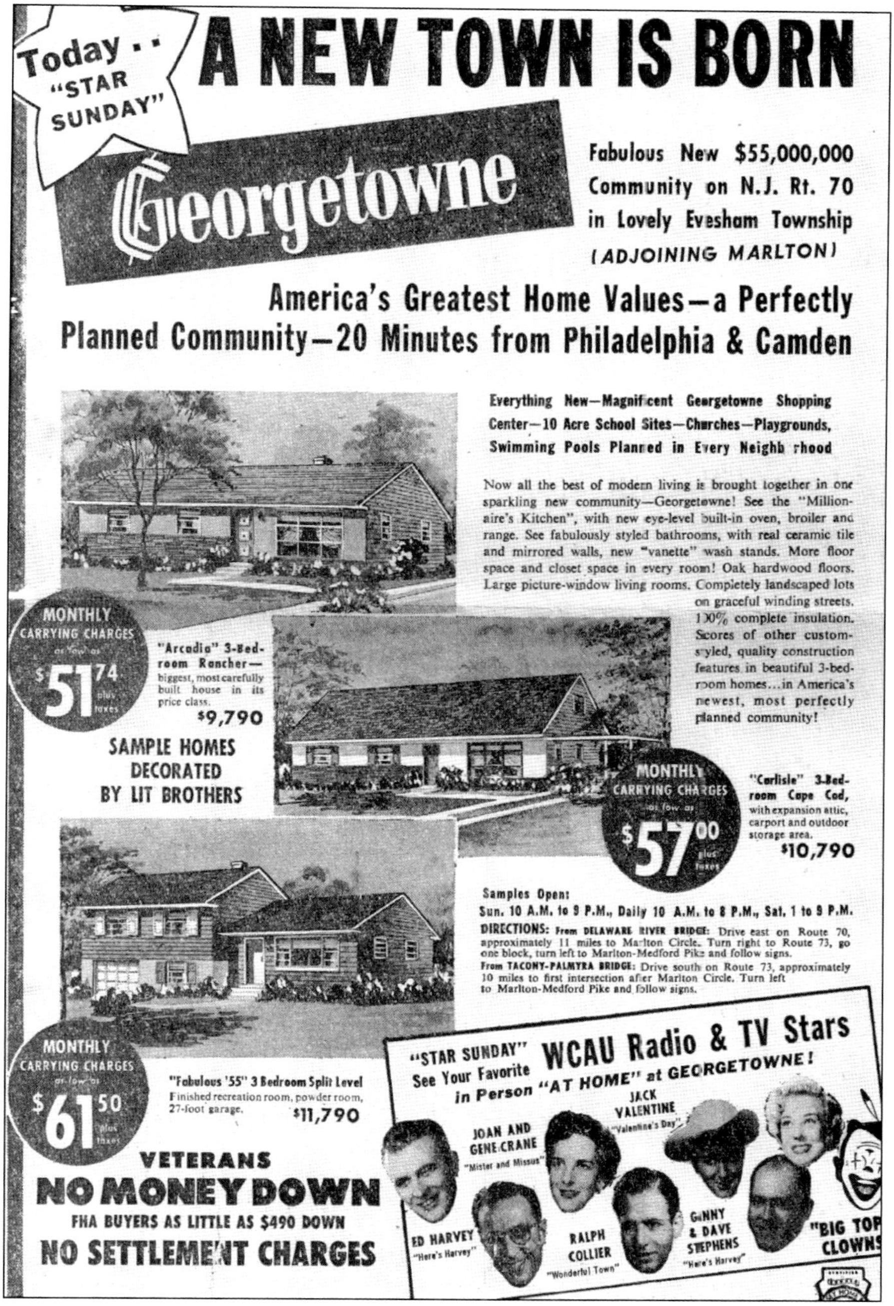

Construction began in March 1955 on what was to be a 4,000-home development called Georgetowne. On the day the model homes opened, an estimated crowd of 40,000 came to see them. While viewing the model homes, they were entertained by personalities from WCAU radio and television. With the Evesham constable overwhelmed by the traffic jam, state troopers had to be called in. Only a portion of Georgetown was actually built. Heritage Village was built on the remaining land between Main Street and Route 70, along with a small group of homes called Mayfair at Marlton. (Courtesy Edna Wirth.)

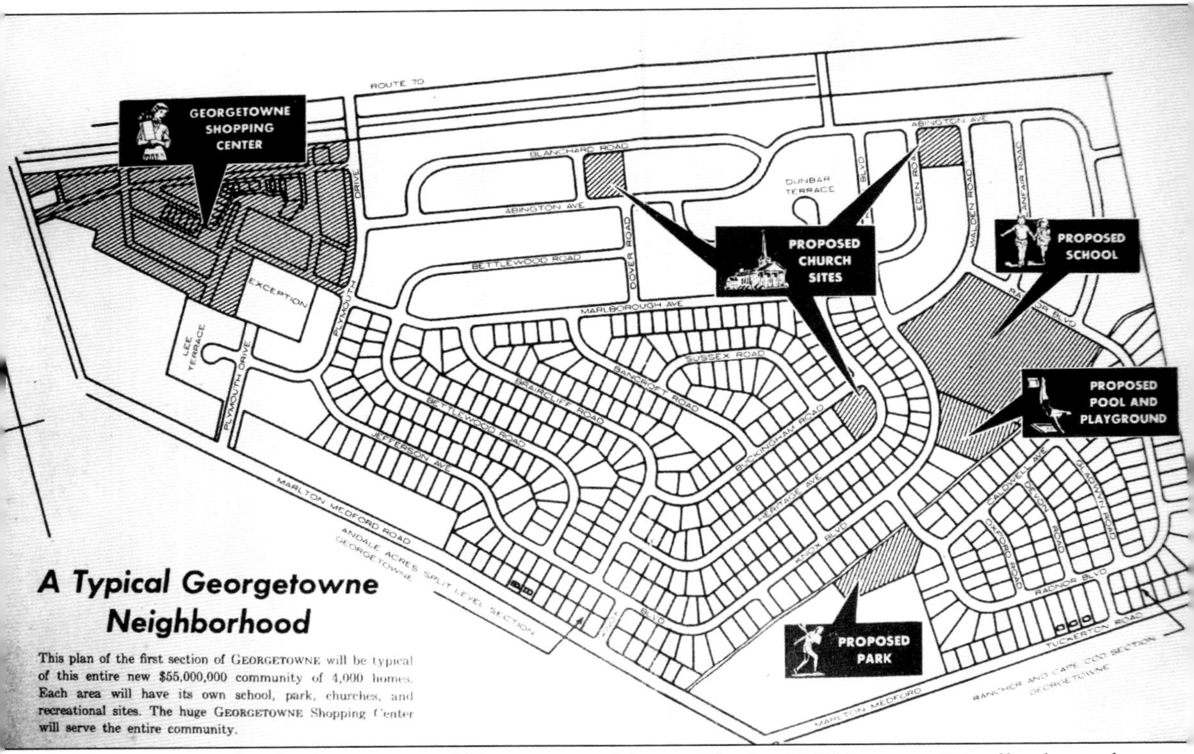

This was to be the first section of Georgetown. Along with the 4,000 homes originally planned, each section of the development was to contain a school, recreation areas, and swimming pools. A shopping center would serve the community, as well as churches. The developers built a sewage-disposal plant for the homes here. The development folded after 200 homes were built along Main Street and Tuckerton Road. A planned 1,500-home development called Mayfair at Marlton was begun here in 1957, but only a few of these homes were built. The remaining land was developed as Heritage Village from 1959 to 1964. (Courtesy Edna Wirth.)

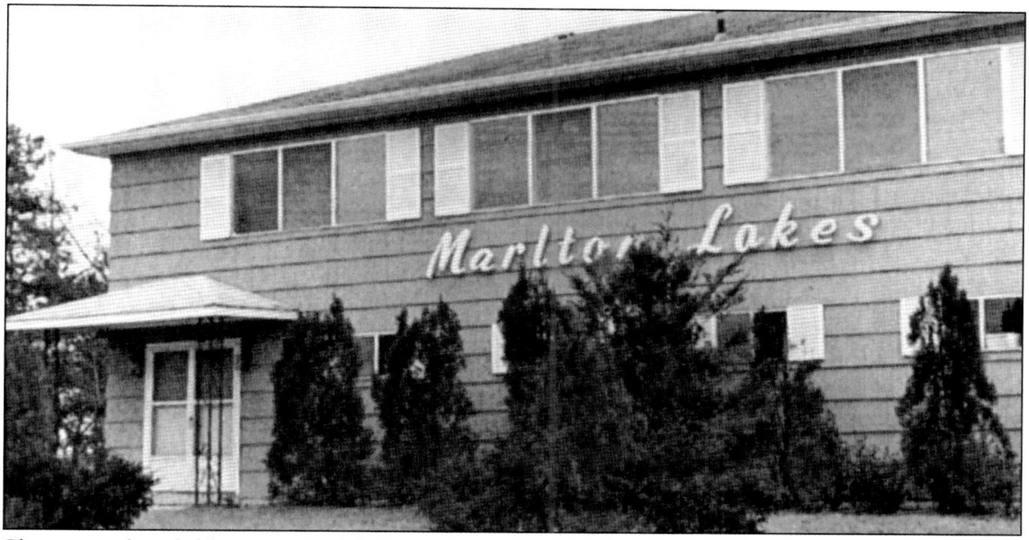

Shown is the clubhouse at Marlton Lakes in the 1970s. Marlton Lakes is a subdivision in Evesham's southern portion and consists of individual, custom-built homes. It was developed by US Development Corporation. The lakes that are the centerpiece of Marlton Lakes were once cranberry bogs. Also, in this area on Hopewell Road is a section of individual-built homes called Berlin Heights.

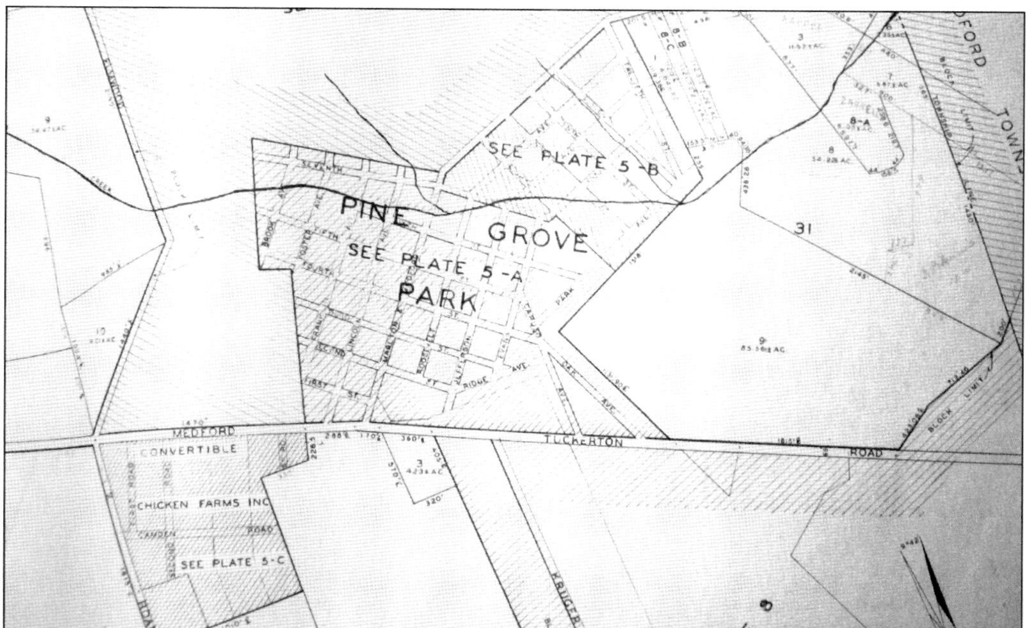

The New Jersey Bridge Development Company began a housing project called Pine Grove Park in the Pine Grove section in the mid-1920s. This was to contain about 1,400 building lots, which the developer was to lease to homeowners who would build a home there. Most of this development only existed on paper, as only small portions of the streets were built. In 1928, another development was laid out across Tuckerton Road by Convertible Chicken Farms Inc.; lots were sold in 1929. (Courtesy Edna Wirth.)

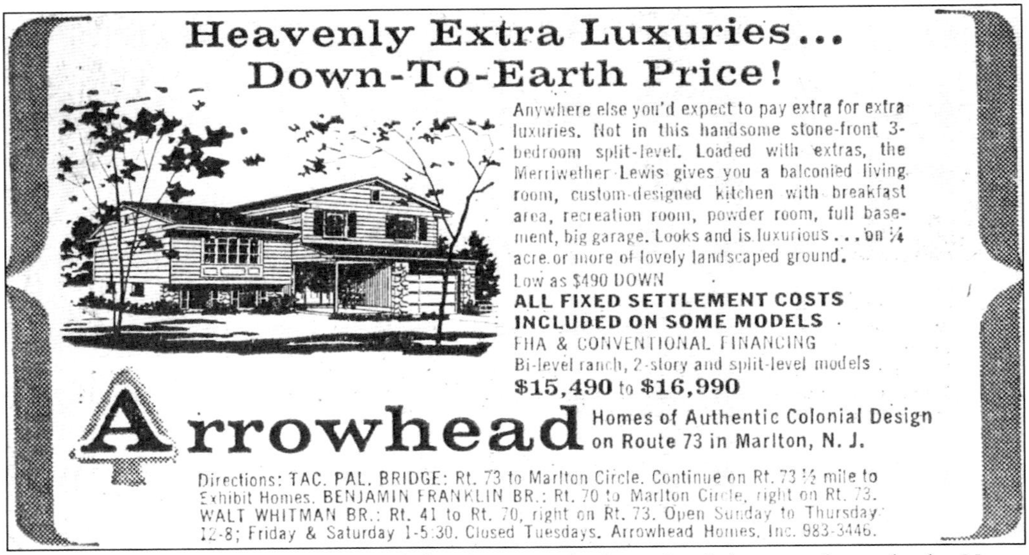

This 1964 ad was for the Arrowhead development, built on land that was formerly the Harry McElhone farm on Maple Avenue. The first developer in this section was Joseph Munger, who purchased 21 acres of farmland along Oak and Locust Avenues. He built homes along Locust, Florence, and Munger Avenues. Munger sold the remaining land to a developer who built Hickory Place between Munger and Oak Avenues.

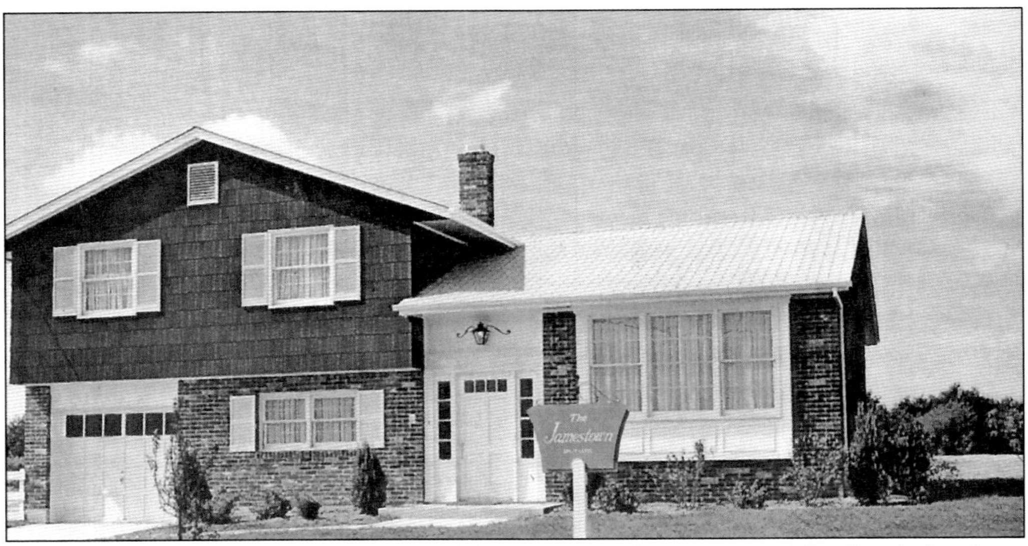

Shown is the Jamestown split-level model home at Woodstream, one of Evesham's first large residential developments. Chiusano Brothers Inc. purchased three farms extending from Route 70 across Greentree Road in the early 1960s and began building Woodstream in 1962. (Courtesy Jeffrey Auchter.)

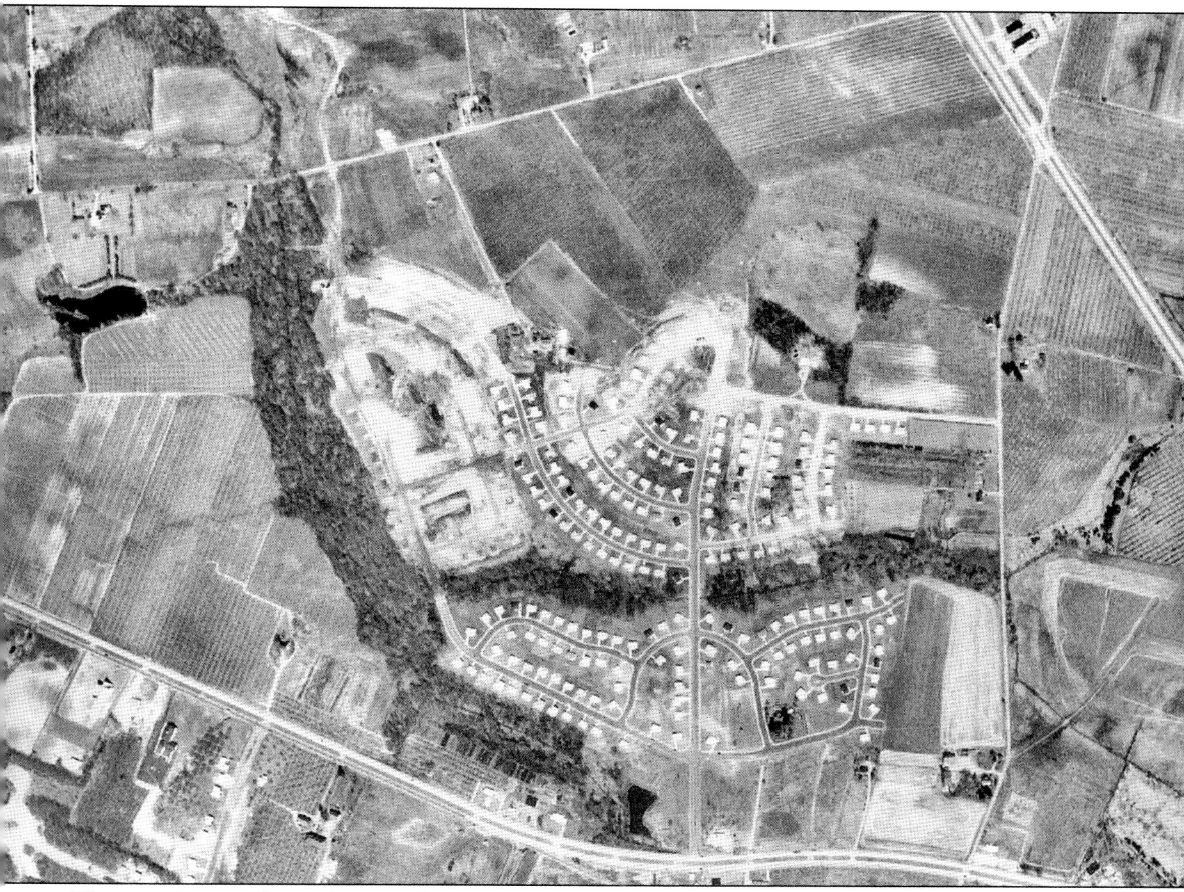

This aerial view of Woodstream from the spring of 1965 shows the progress of the development's construction. Woodstream was completed in 1968 with 650 homes, a swim club, elementary school, and an apartment complex. After Chiusano Brothers completed Woodstream in 1968, it continued to build in Evesham. Among its projects in the township are Brush Hollow, The Maples, Willow Ridge, and Briarwood.

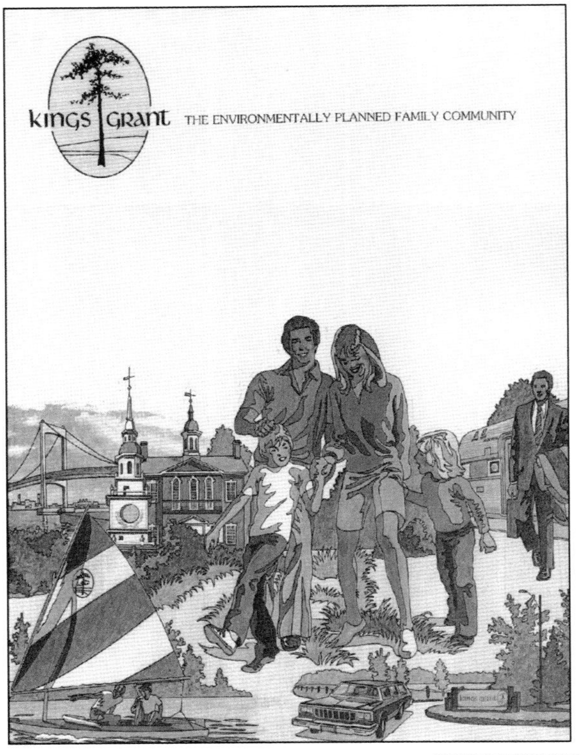

In 1967, William Seltzer, a Philadelphia developer and environmentalist, presented to Evesham officials his plan for Kings Grant (originally to be called King James Land Grant), then New Jersey's largest planned-unit development project. The project won approval in 1968, beginning years of planning by landscape architects, foresters, and naturalists. Construction began at Kings Grant in 1975 but was soon halted by a housing recession; construction resumed in 1980 under new management. Kings Grant is made up of different residential communities within the 1,800-acre site along Taunton Lake Road. (Courtesy Jeffrey Auchter.)

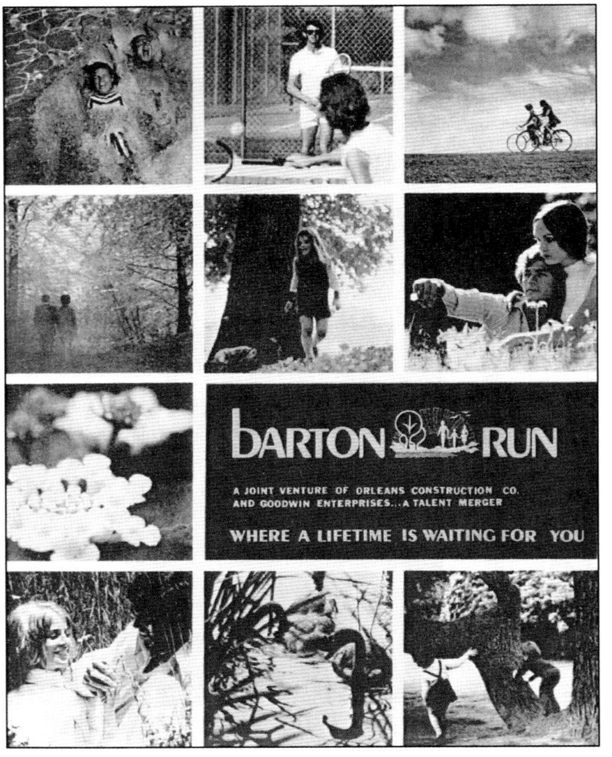

Barton Run was one of the planned-unit developments started in Evesham during the 1970s. This was a joint venture of A.P. Orleans Builders and Goodwin Enterprises. It was a nature-oriented development. Construction was halted in 1979 due to conflicts with the Pinelands Preservation Act. A compromise was reached and construction resumed in 1985. (Courtesy Jeffrey Auchter.)

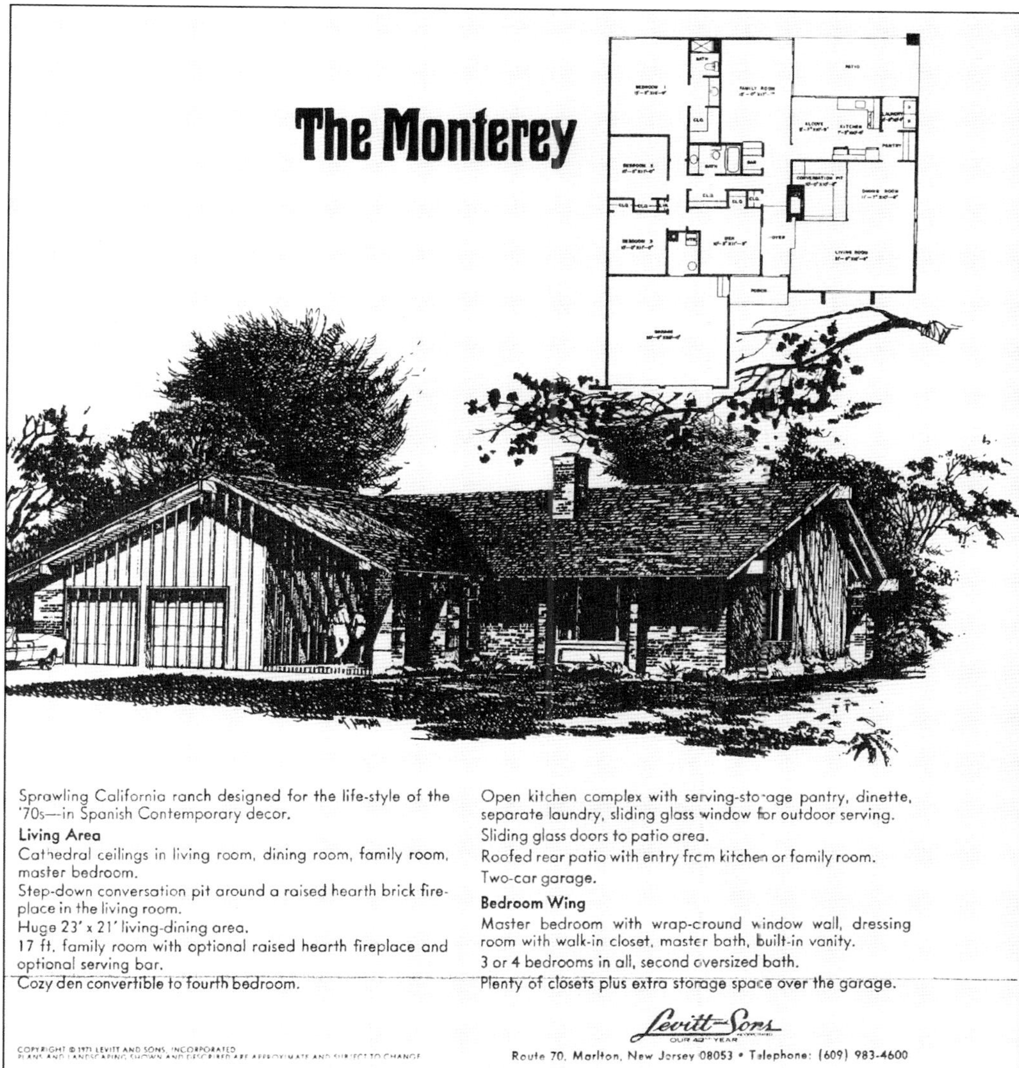

Levitt and Sons purchased ground for Cambridge Park in 1969 between Route 70 and Evesboro-Medford Road. This site was originally to be developed as South Crossing. The Monterey model was the top of the line. Levitt planned to build 1,200 homes in Cambridge Park; however, only about 300 were constructed when it pulled out in October 1972. The site later evolved into the Foxcroft, Heathrow, and Marlton Leas developments. (Courtesy Jeffrey Auchter.)

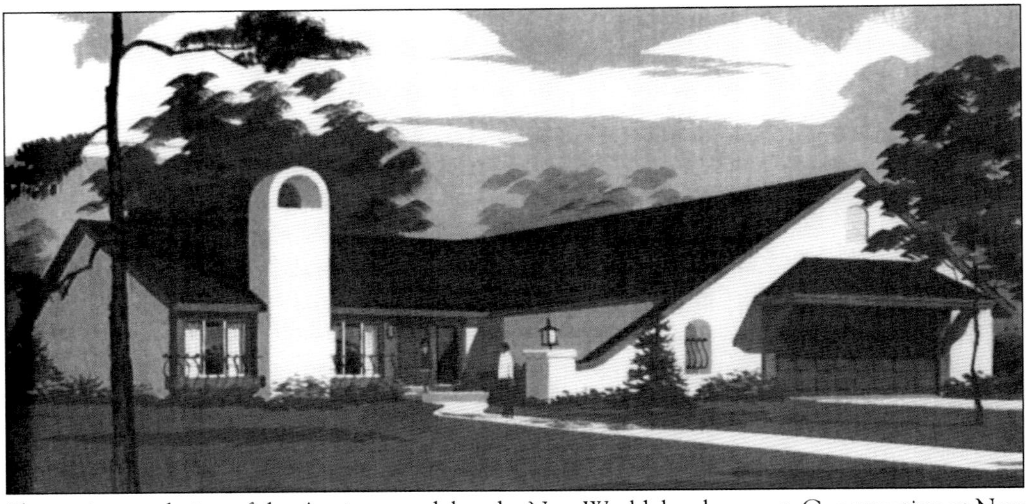

Shown is a rendering of the Antigua model at the New World development. Construction at New World began in 1973 at Route 73 and present-day Commonwealth Drive. In September 1973, the developer held an opening ceremony here. The culmination of the event was the delivery of a large structural globe by helicopter. High winds caused a cable to snap, and the globe rolled into a field nearby. After finally being mounted, it became the centerpiece of the model home display. (Courtesy Jeffrey Auchter.)

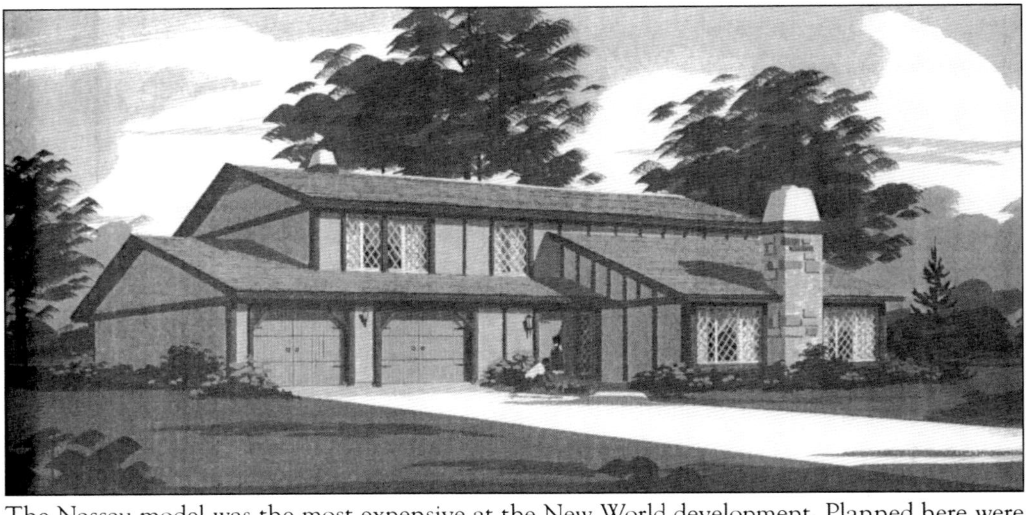

The Nassau model was the most expensive at the New World development. Planned here were 850 single-family homes along with 290 townhomes. In 1975, a lower-priced line of home models became available. Only about 65 single-family homes were actually built before a sewer moratorium forced an end to the development in 1975. (Courtesy Jeffrey Auchter.)

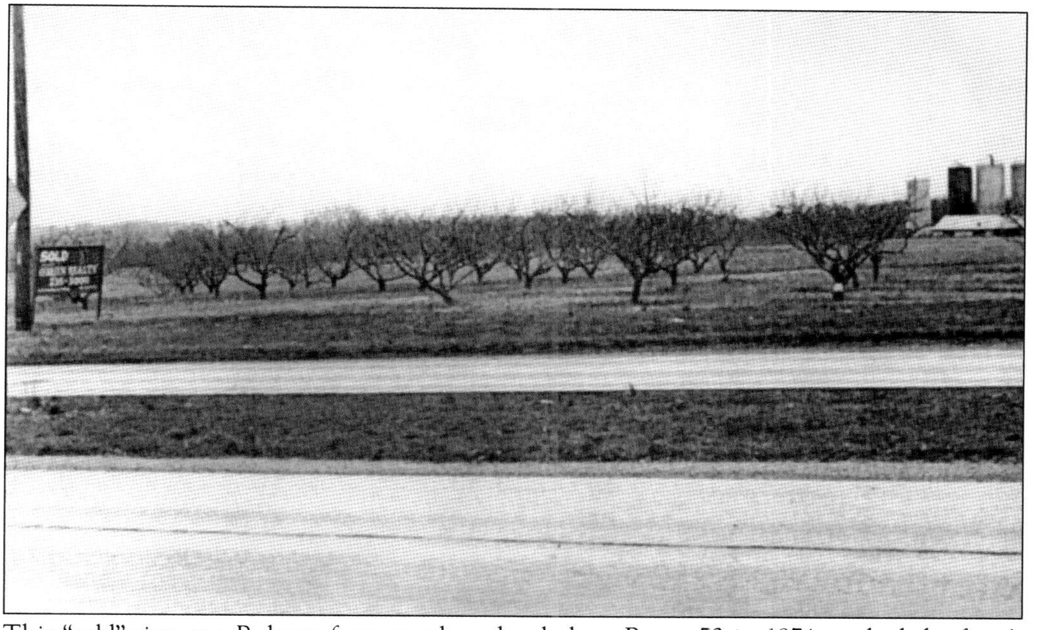

This "sold" sign at a Roberts farm peach orchard along Route 73 in 1974 marked the farm's sale to Lincoln Property, which developed the land into the Greentree Village planned-unit development. Construction began in 1977 and was completed in 1986. Between 1974 and 1977, the farm remained in operation under a leasing agreement between the developer and Moorestown farmer Tak Moriuchi.

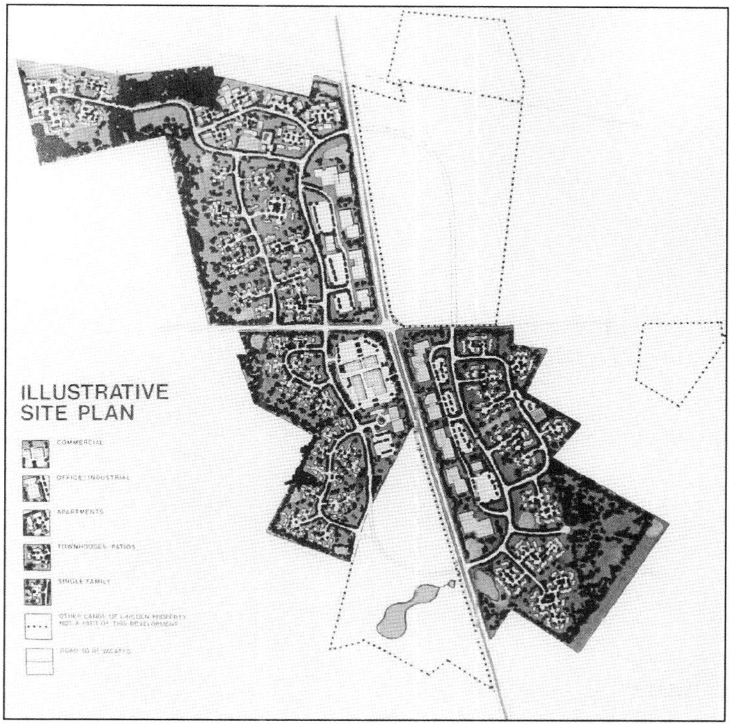

Pictured is the original plan for Greentree Village. When completed in 1986, the development did not differ much from this plan. There was local opposition to such a large-scale development, especially from residents of neighboring Woodstream and Evesboro West. Evesham had planned to purchase this tract using Green Acres funding, which it was unable to obtain.

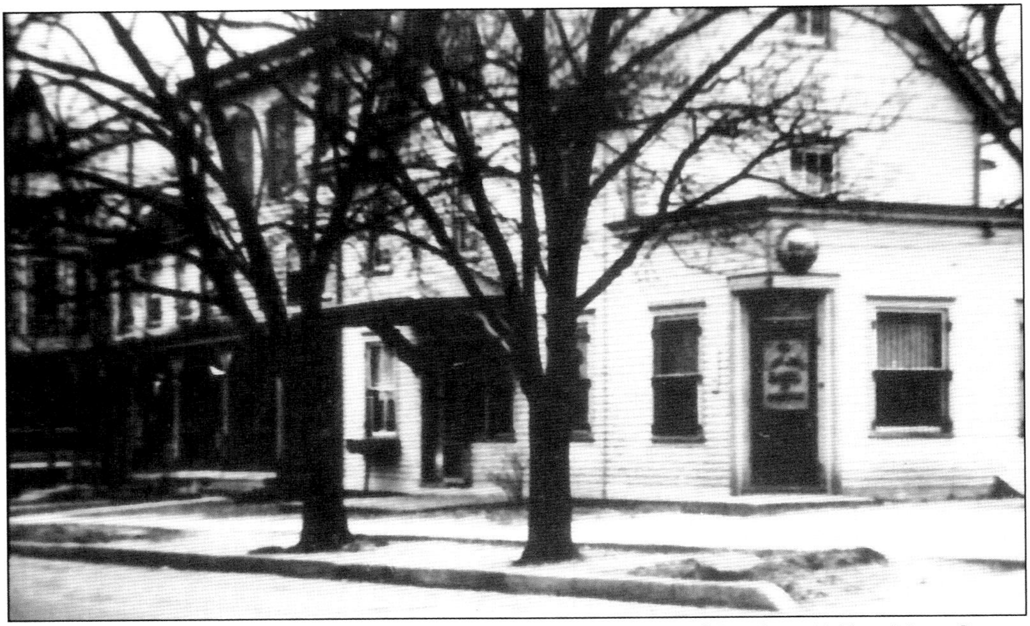

This photograph shows the original location of Marlton National Bank at 11 East Main Street. The bank opened here in 1927 and later moved to a larger building at 42 East Main Street. (Courtesy Edna Wirth.)

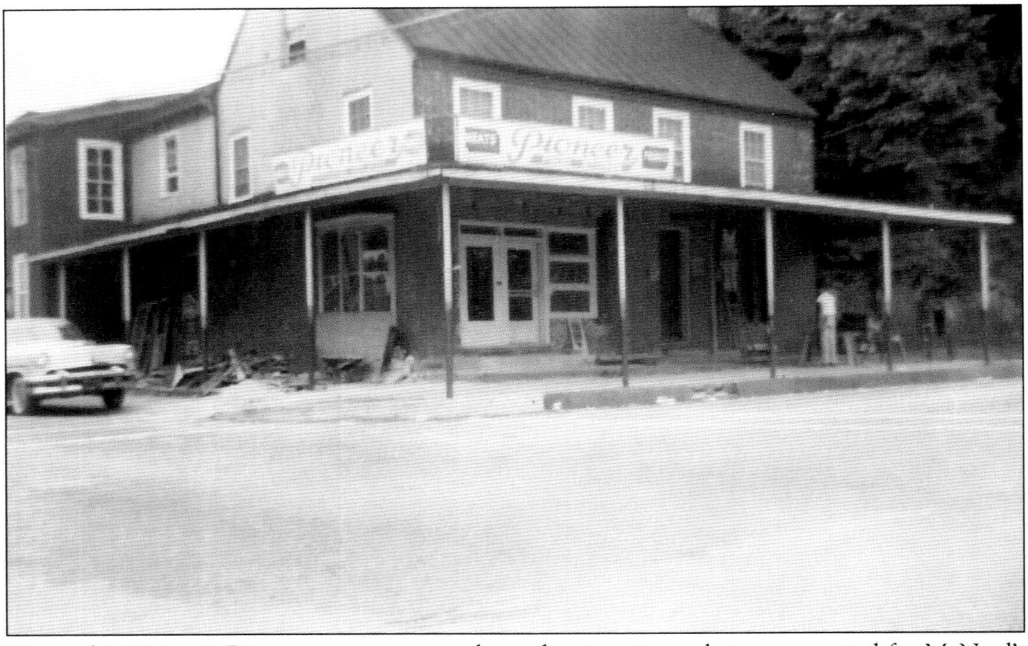

Pictured is Haines's Pioneer grocery store about the time it was being renovated for McNaul's Market in 1949. McNaul was the last grocer in this building, operating into the 1970s. (Courtesy Evesham Historical Society.)

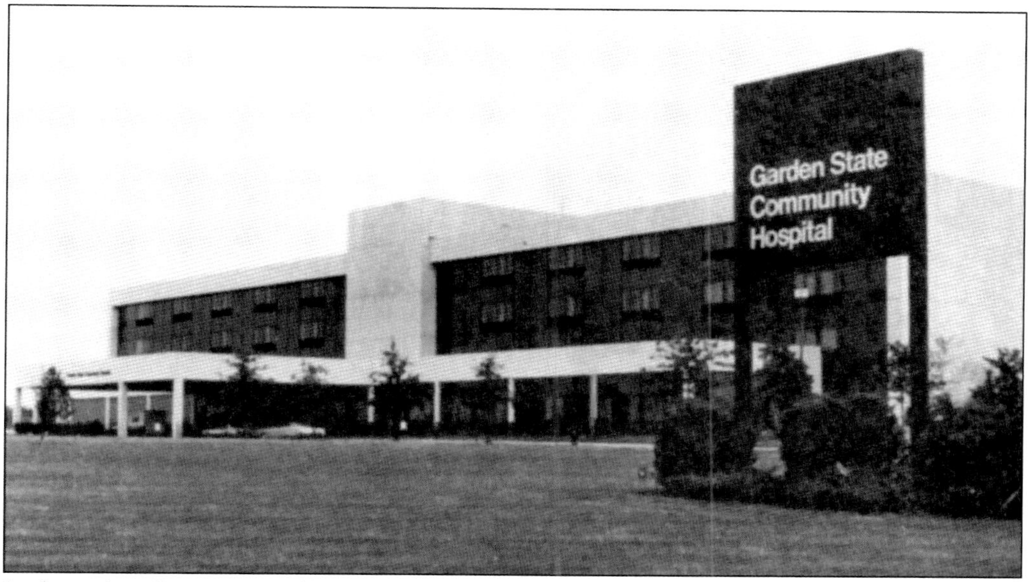

In the early 1970s, a group of local doctors recognized a need for a hospital in Evesham Township. They contacted American Medicorp, then one of the nation's largest hospital management and development firms, who after two years of planning and construction opened Garden State Community Hospital on June 4, 1973. Located at Brick Road off Route 73, the 200-bed hospital was purchased by West Jersey Health System in 1982 and in 1998 became Virtua Marlton with the merger of West Jersey and Memorial Health.

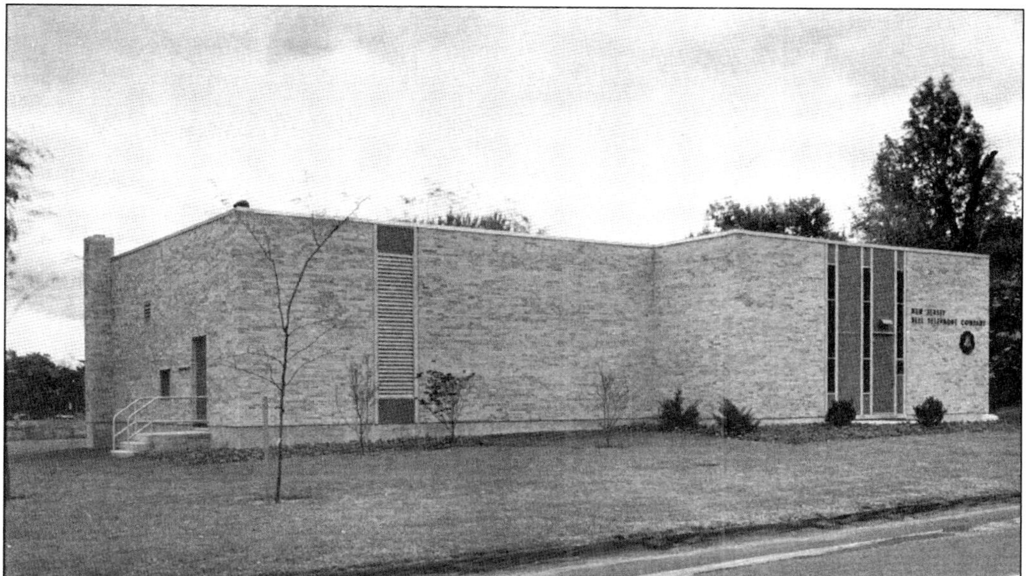

New Jersey Bell constructed this central office building on North Maple Avenue in 1961 to initiate all-number calling service here. It was placed in service in May 1962 and served customers in both Marlton and sections of Medford. The original "EAstgate1" and "YUkon3" exchanges for Marlton and the Medford "OLive4" exchange became simply 983. This building has been expanded through the years to accommodate growth.

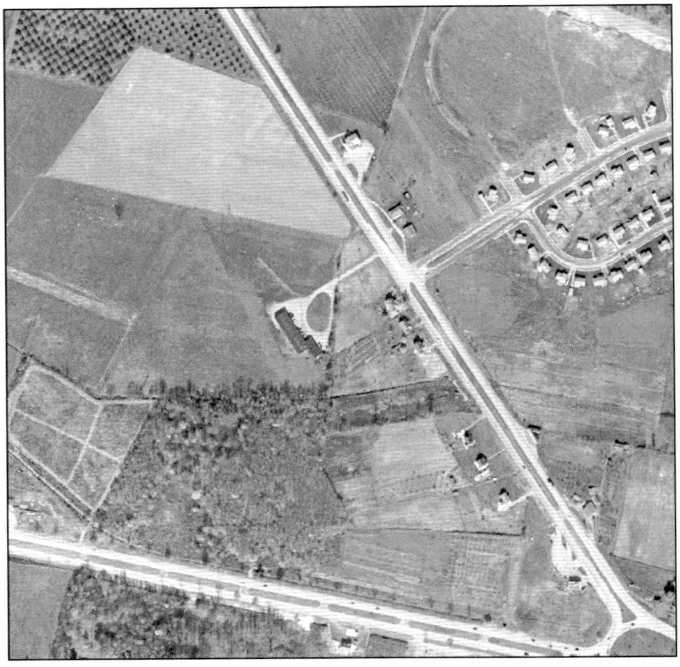

Shown in the center of this aerial view is the Hedges Diesel plant on Route 73 across from Baker Boulevard. Harry O. Hedges founded Hedges Motor Company on the West Coast and began designing and building engines. By 1949, the company had relocated to Philadelphia, and by the late 1950s it purchased 13 acres in Marlton and relocated here.

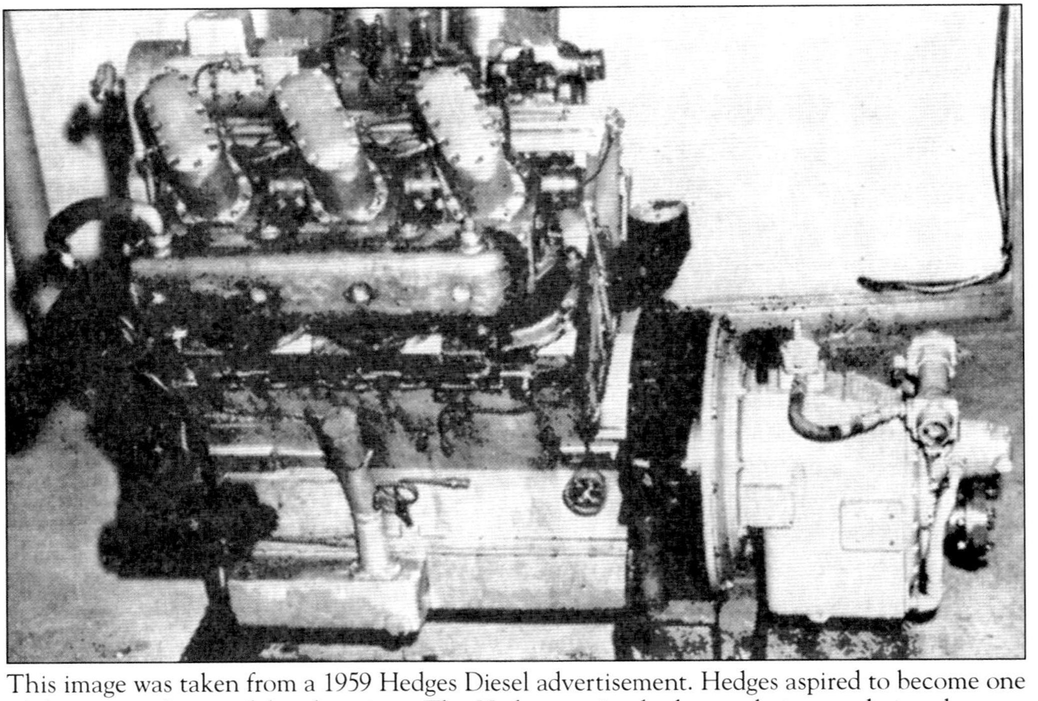

This image was taken from a 1959 Hedges Diesel advertisement. Hedges aspired to become one of the top producers of diesel engines. The Hedges engine had a revolutionary design that was claimed to make it one of the most efficient in the world. Unable to secure any major contracts or assistance from the Small Business Administration, Hedges Diesel lost its charter in 1963 for nonpayment of taxes. The property remained vacant for many years until becoming the site of Burns Honda.

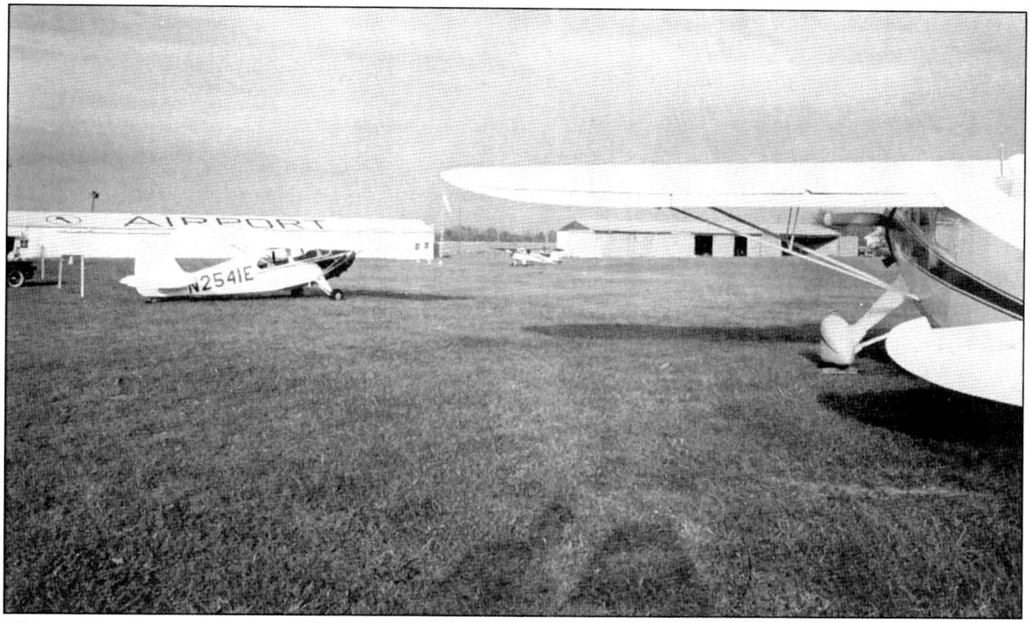

This is the former Marlton-Medford Airport, which was located on the south side of Evesboro-Medford Road at present-day Greenbrook Drive. The airport opened during the mid-1940s and was in existence until the mid-1960s. It had two runways and three buildings and offered fuel, hangars, and tie-downs.

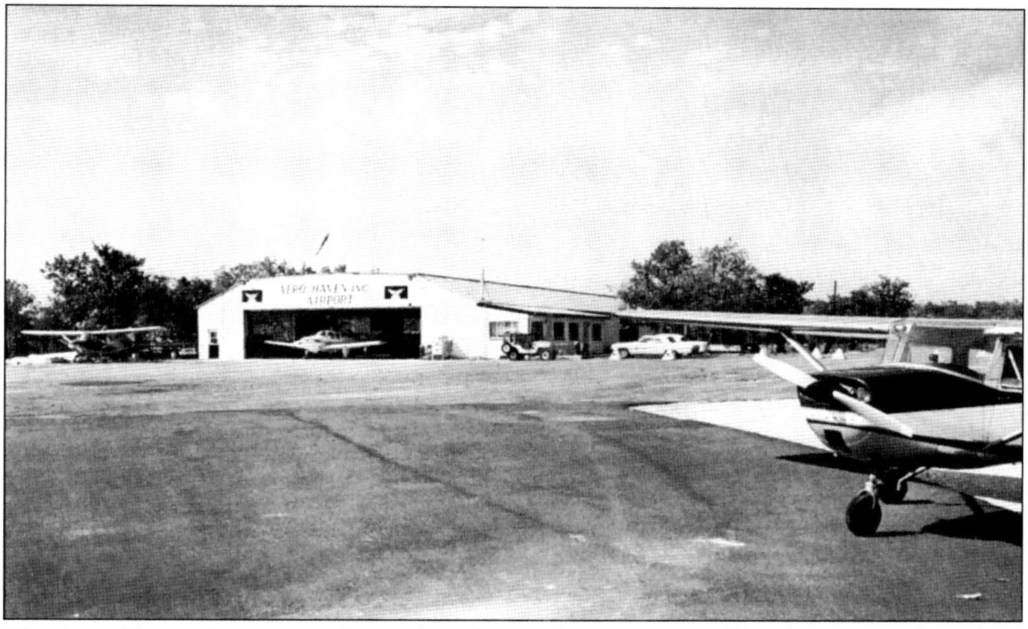

The Aero Haven Airport was located in the southern portion of Evesham Township along Kettle Run Road. It was built in the 1950s as a clearing in the woods with one runway. By 1962, a hangar and other improvements were added, such as taxiways, along with the runway being paved. It was later renamed Camden-Burlington County Airport and continued operation until the early 1980s.

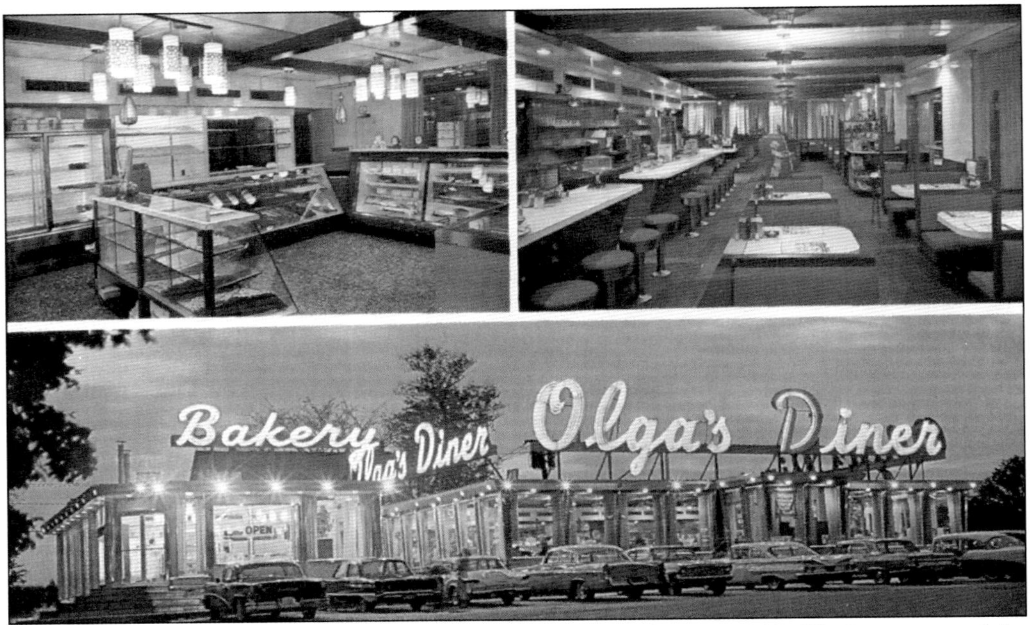

Pictured is the original Olga's Diner, which opened in Marlton in 1960. Olga's was named for Olga Stavros, who started a luncheonette in Camden in 1946 with her husband. The business moved in 1951 to a nearby location and became Olga's Diner. Olga took over the business after her husband died. The Camden location closed in the 1980s.

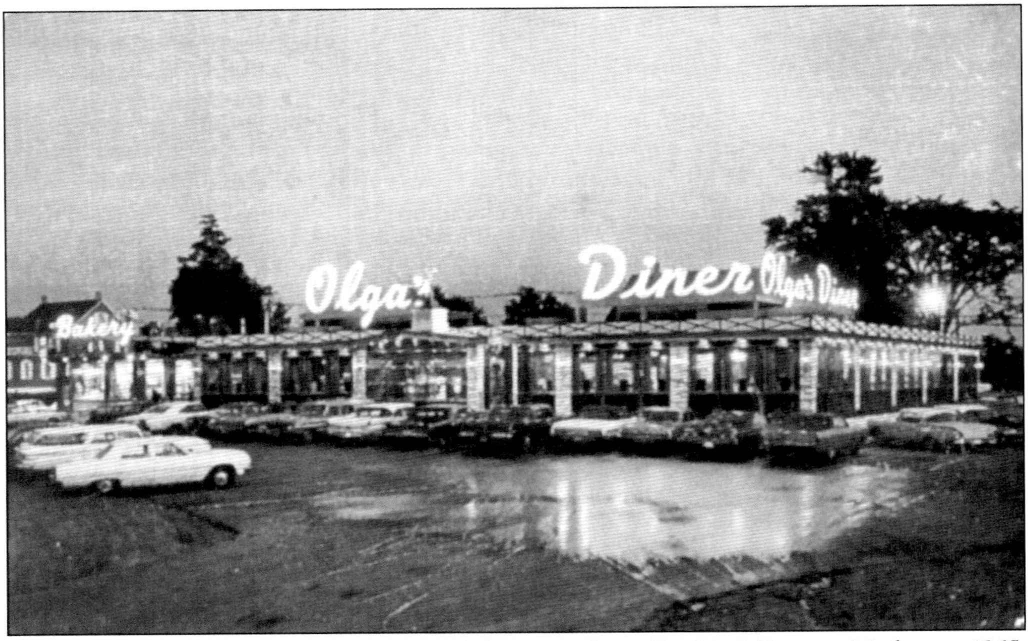

This 400-seat diner built by Fodero replaced the original, smaller Olga's Diner at Marlton in 1965. The bright neon sign could be seen for miles. Olga died in 1990, and the diner was then owned by her son John. The diner closed in October 2008.

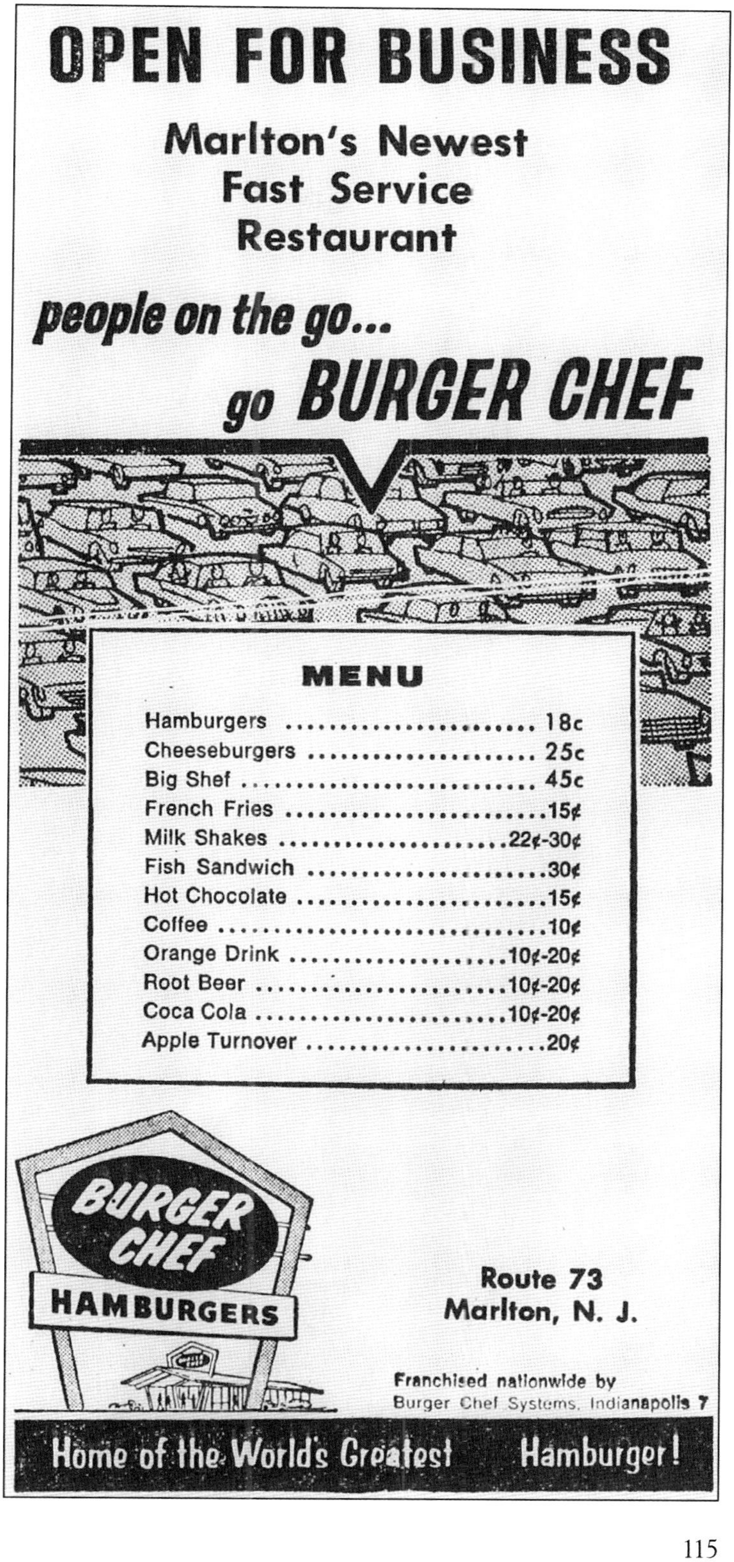

Fast food came to Evesham in 1967 with the opening of Burger Chef on Route 73 north of Route 70 behind present-day Kohl's. Burger Chef is remembered for its open kite–design building and for its open flame–broiled burgers with high meat content and homemade french fries. This ad from Burger Chef's opening shows typical fast-food prices at that time. The restaurant closed in the early 1970s.

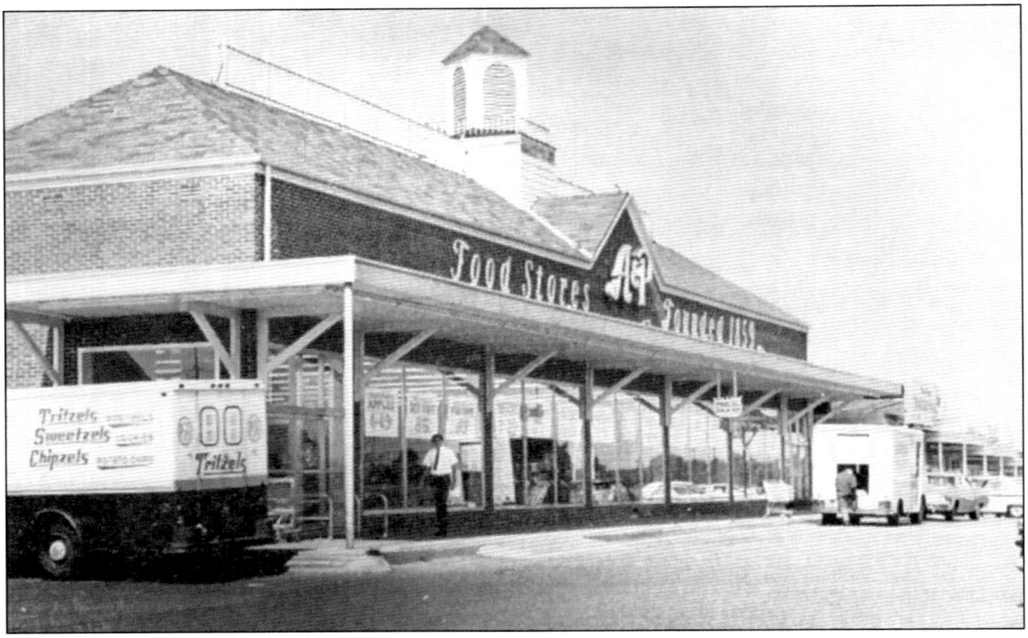

The first modern shopping center in Evesham was built in 1965 at Route 70 and North Cropwell Road. Known as Marlton Square, it contained 11 stores. Until 1975, the center was anchored by an A&P, the first supermarket to open in the township. In 1976, Grossman's Lumber became the anchor store, replaced by Staples in 1989. The center was later renamed Staples Plaza. The Marlton Square name was then used by a group of specialty shops on Route 73.

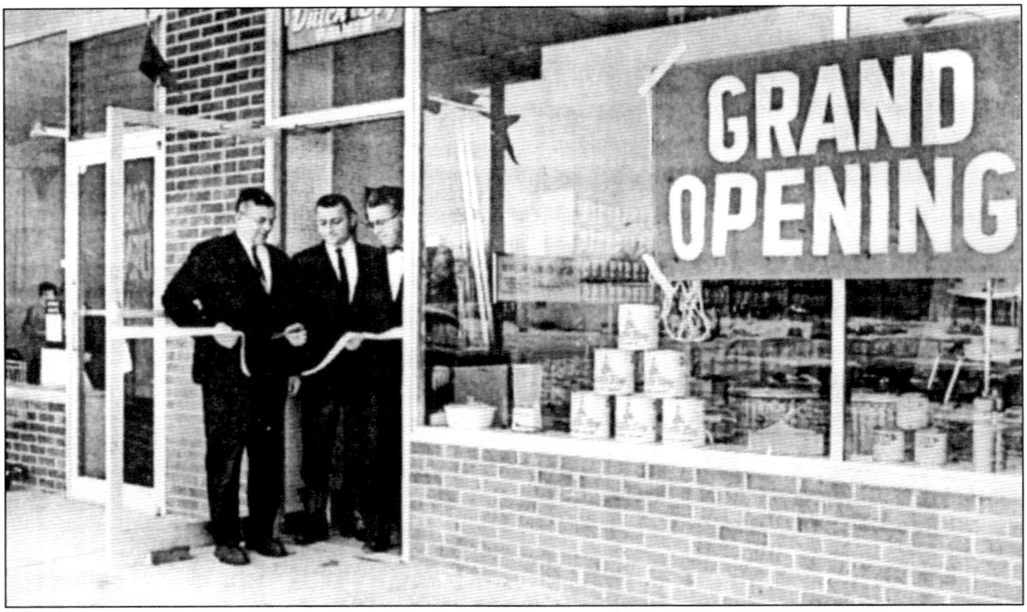

Mohan's Village Paint and Hardware opened in the Marlton Square shopping center on March 3, 1966. Shown at the store's opening from left to right are Cherry Hill mayor John Gilmour, Evesham mayor George DeChurch, and Samuel Lippincott, who was president of First National Bank of Marlton. Mohan Hardware remained here until the mid-1990s.

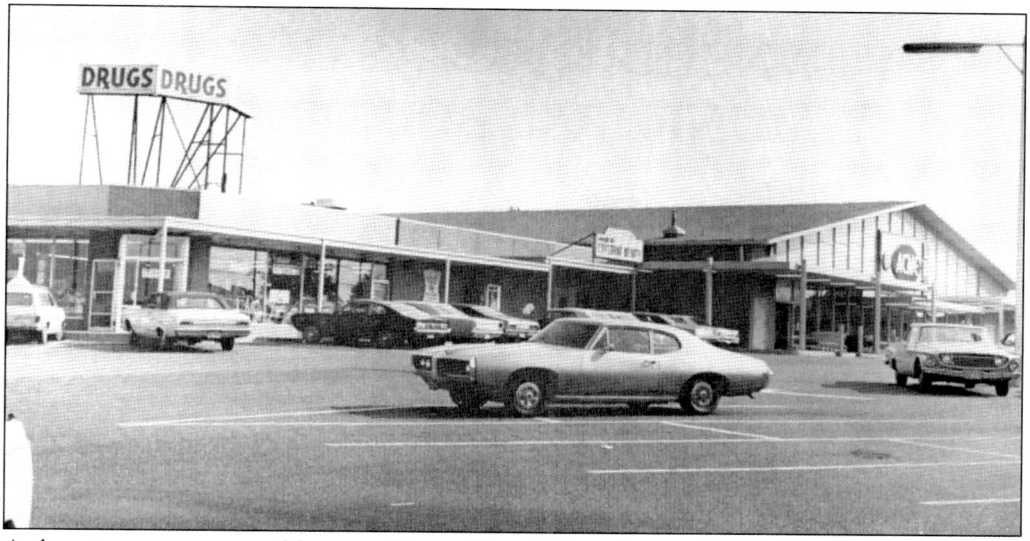

A shopping center opened between Route 70 and Main Street at Marlton Circle in 1966. The anchor store in this center was an Acme Market. Other stores included a Sears catalog store, a beauty salon, drugstore, and dry cleaners. The Mister Living Room furniture store occupied the former Acme space in 1976. The center was destroyed by a fire in 1977 and replaced with Marlton Greene Center in the 1980s.

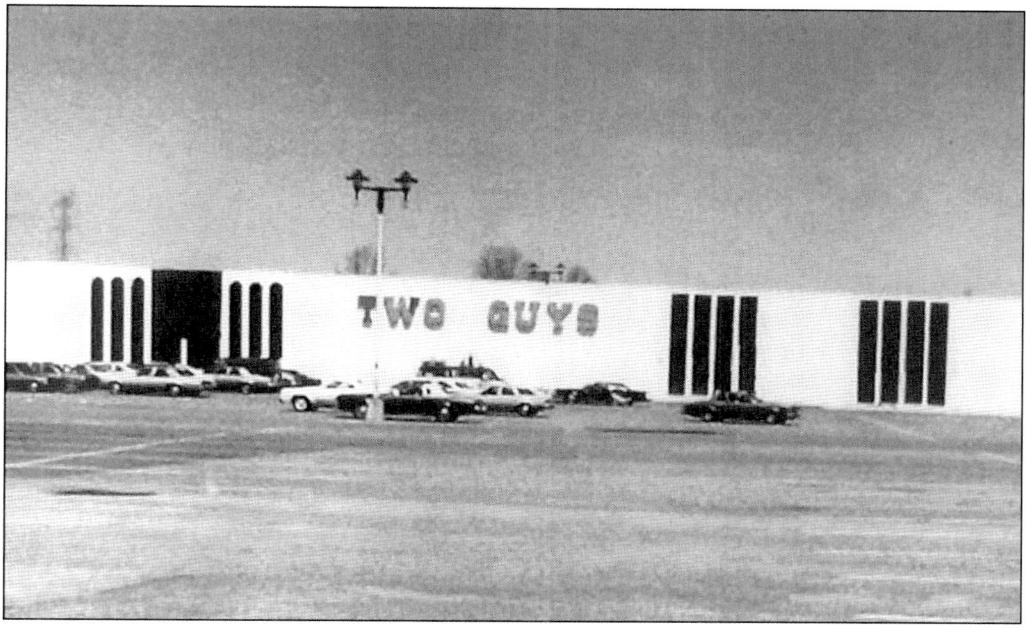

Two Guys was the first discount department store in Evesham, opening in July 1973 at Marlton Circle. This large store also contained a supermarket, which became Shop Rite in 1979. Two Guys closed in 1980, when the chain was liquidated. Later, the space was occupied by Jefferson Ward, Bradlees, and Kohl's. (Photograph by the author.)

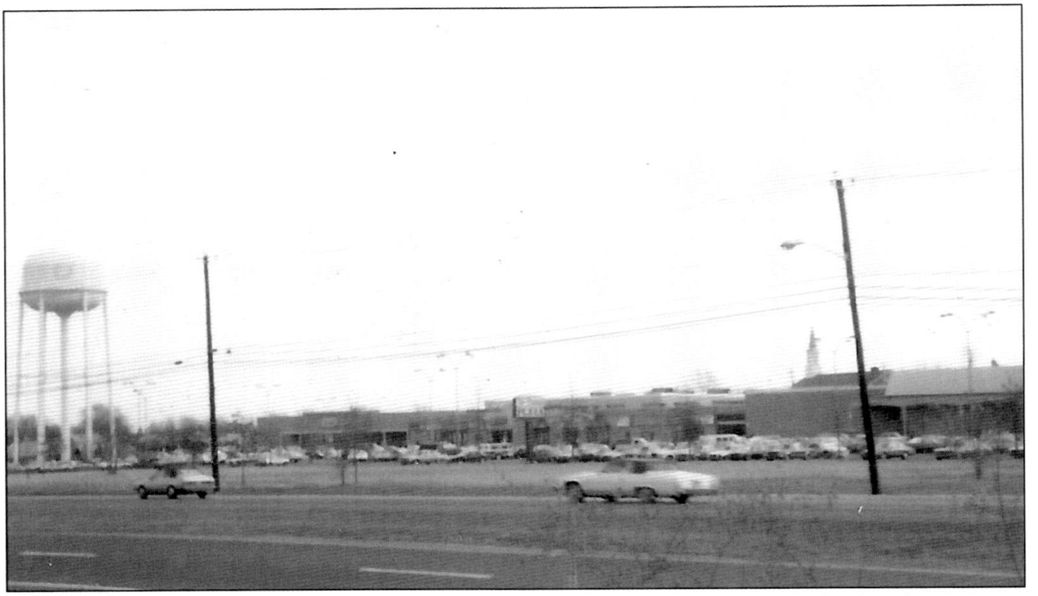

Tri-Towne Plaza was built in 1975 at Route 70 and Plymouth Drive despite neighborhood opposition and a rezoning battle. This shopping center originally opened with a Kmart and an A&P as anchors and contained an enclosed mall with several smaller stores. (Photograph by the author.)

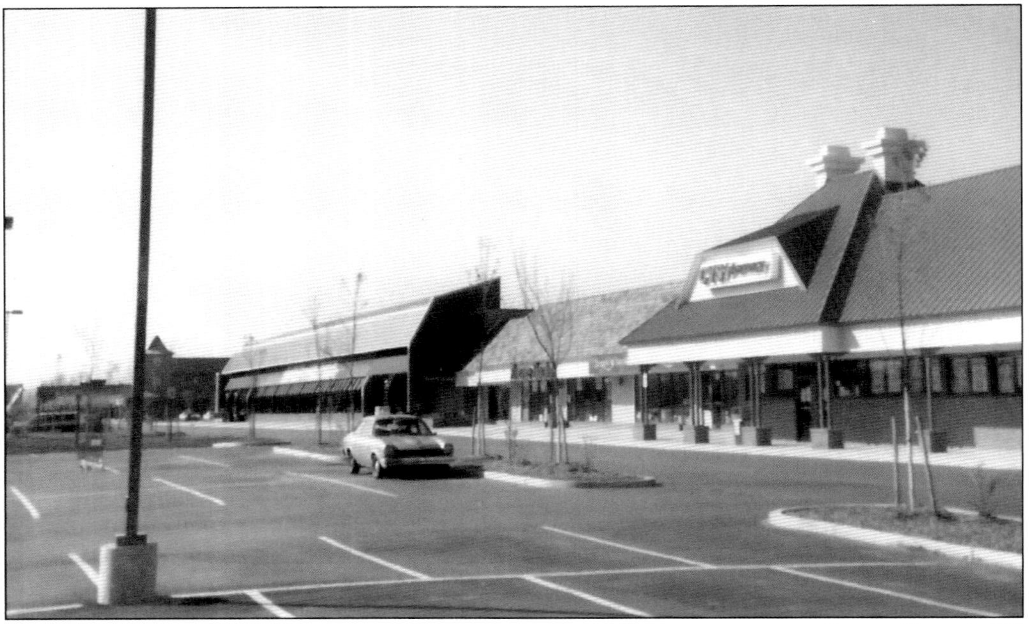

This photograph shows a portion of Marlton Crossing shopping center at Route 73 and Old Marlton Pike soon after it opened in 1987. Originally planned for this site in the early 1970s was an enclosed shopping mall that was to be called Marlton Center Mall. This mall was to be the centerpiece of Marlton Center, a planned-unit development. Only Marlton Village and part of Marlton Meeting were completed when the project folded in 1974. The remaining land was developed by different contractors in the 1980s. (Photograph by the author.)

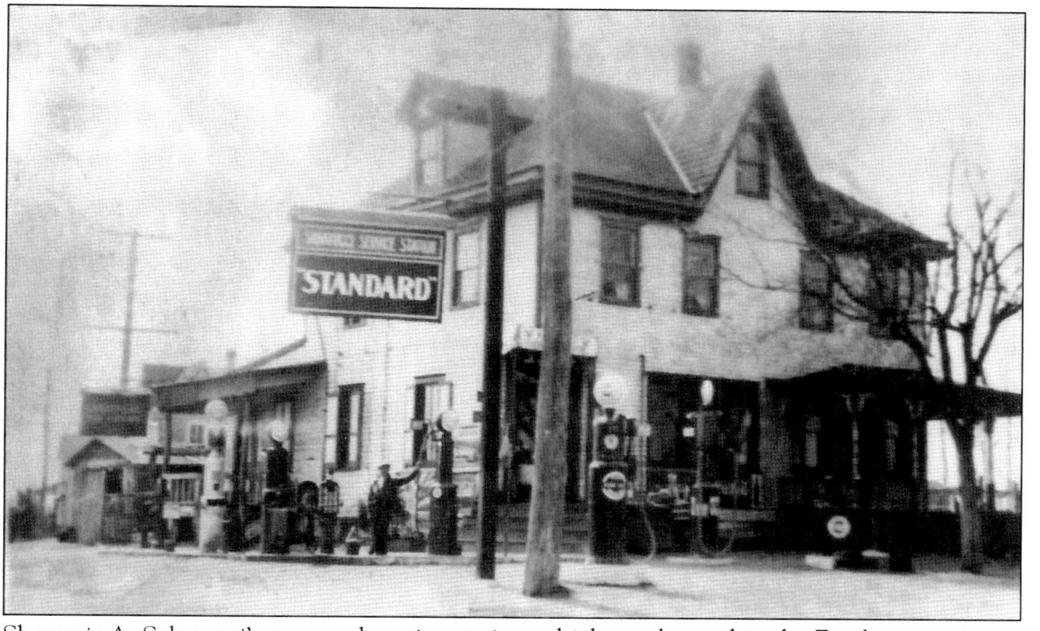

Shown is A. Sabatucci's store and service station, which was located in the Evesboro section at Greentree Road and Maple Avenue. (Courtesy Edna Wirth.)

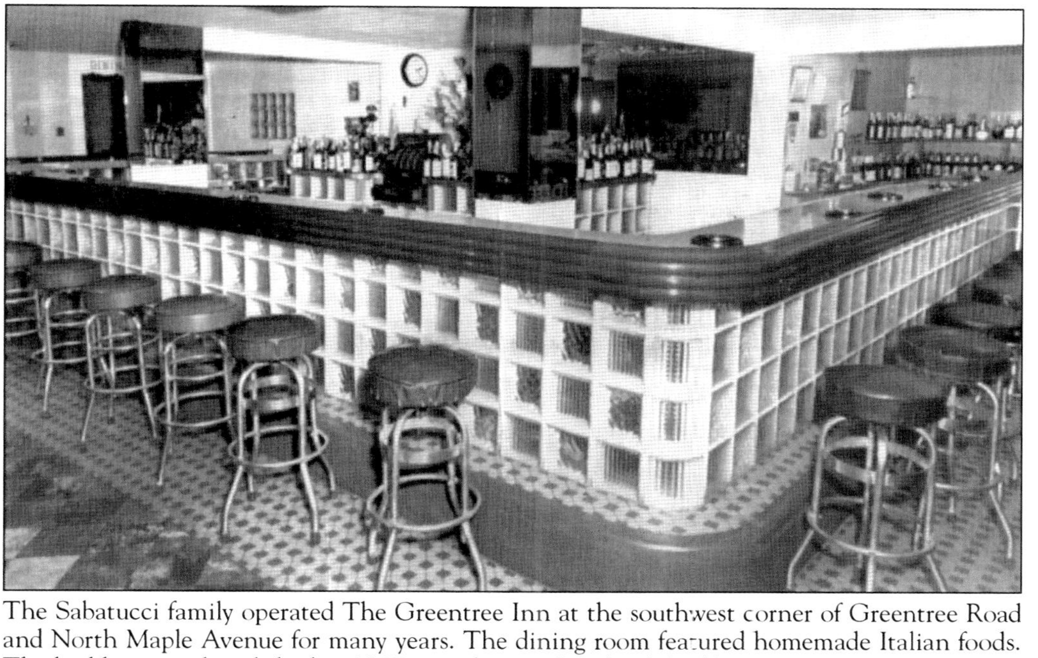

The Sabatucci family operated The Greentree Inn at the southwest corner of Greentree Road and North Maple Avenue for many years. The dining room featured homemade Italian foods. The building was demolished in 2007 to make way for a bank building.

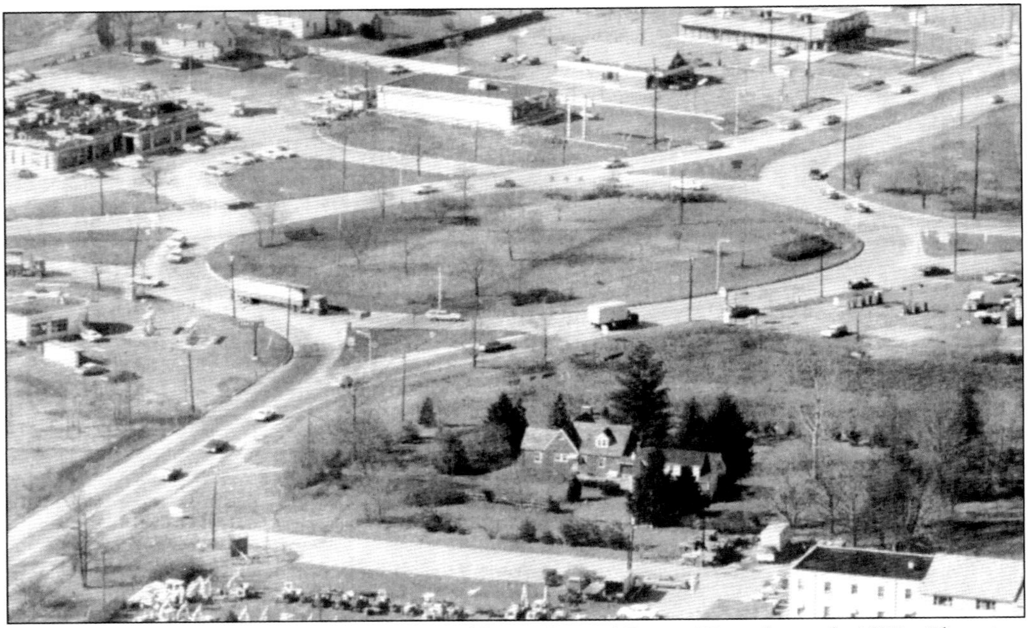

Shown is the Marlton Circle intersection of Route 70 and Route 73 in the early 1970s. Planning for these highways began in 1927. Both were built through Evesham during the 1930s. Route 73 was widened to four lanes in the early 1940s. Route 70 was built as four lanes from the west to Marlton Circle and two lanes eastward. Route 70 was numbered Route 40, and Route 73 was Route S41 until 1953. Route 70 was also named John D. Rockefeller Memorial Highway, but that name never became popular.

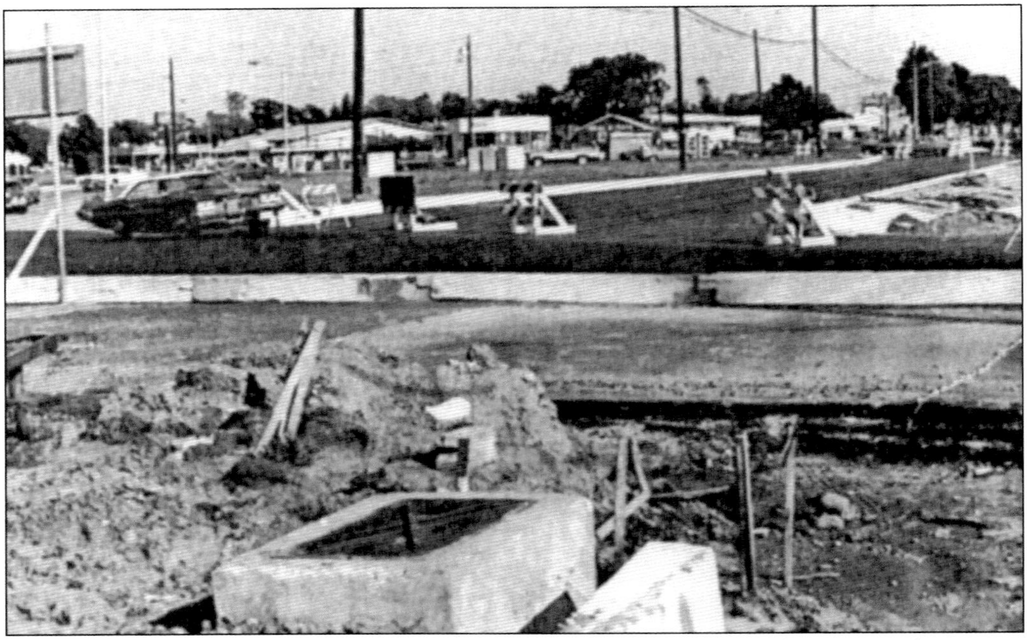

The four lanes of Route 73 were built through the center of Marlton Circle in 1974. This project helped relieve the traffic congestion that occurred at the intersection.

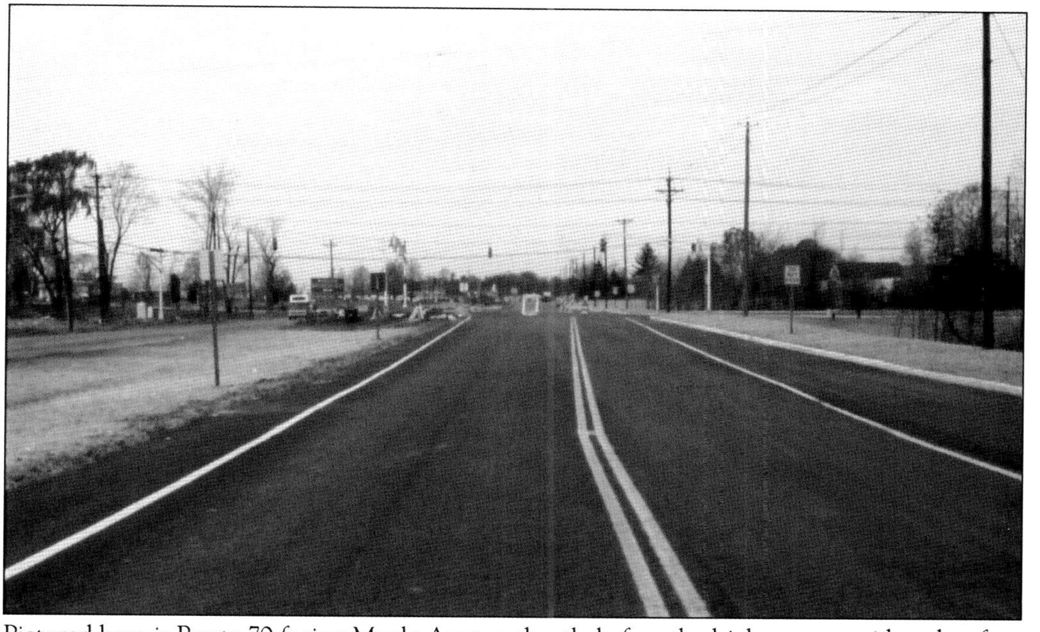

Pictured here is Route 70 facing Maple Avenue shortly before the highway was widened to four lanes in 1980. Route 70 was widened from Marlton Circle to a quarter mile before Greenbrook Drive. (Photograph by Guy Thompson.)

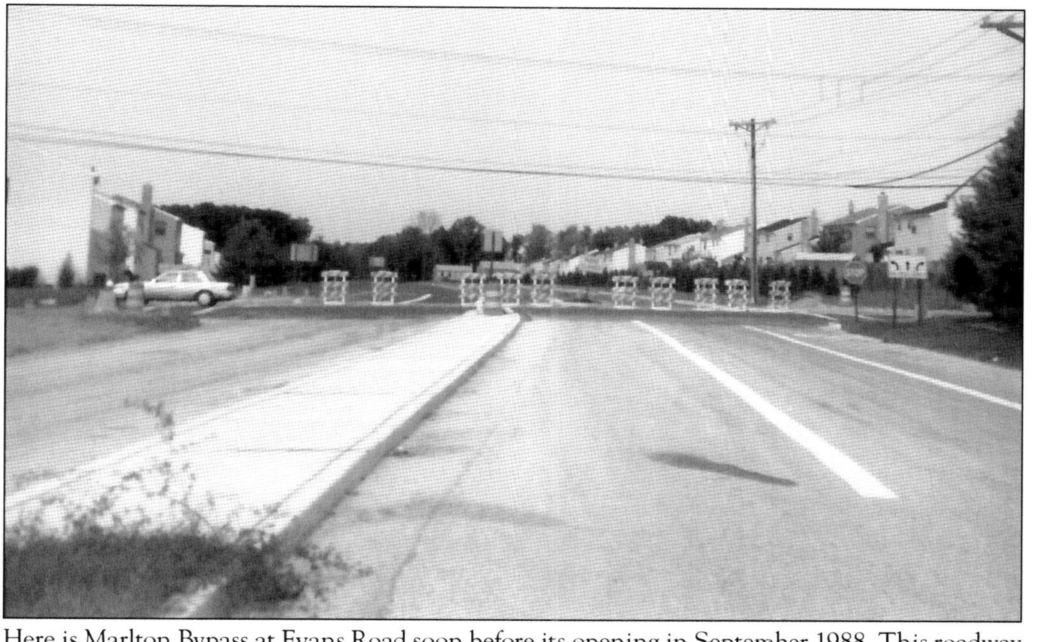

Here is Marlton Bypass at Evans Road soon before its opening in September 1988. This roadway was originally planned in 1959 to relieve traffic on Main Street. It was approved in 1968 but was shelved in the 1970s. A one-third mile portion was built with the New World development in the mid-1970s. The two portions that connected the original section to Route 73 and Taunton Lake Road were completed in 1988. The highway was later renamed Marlton Parkway. (Photograph by the author.)

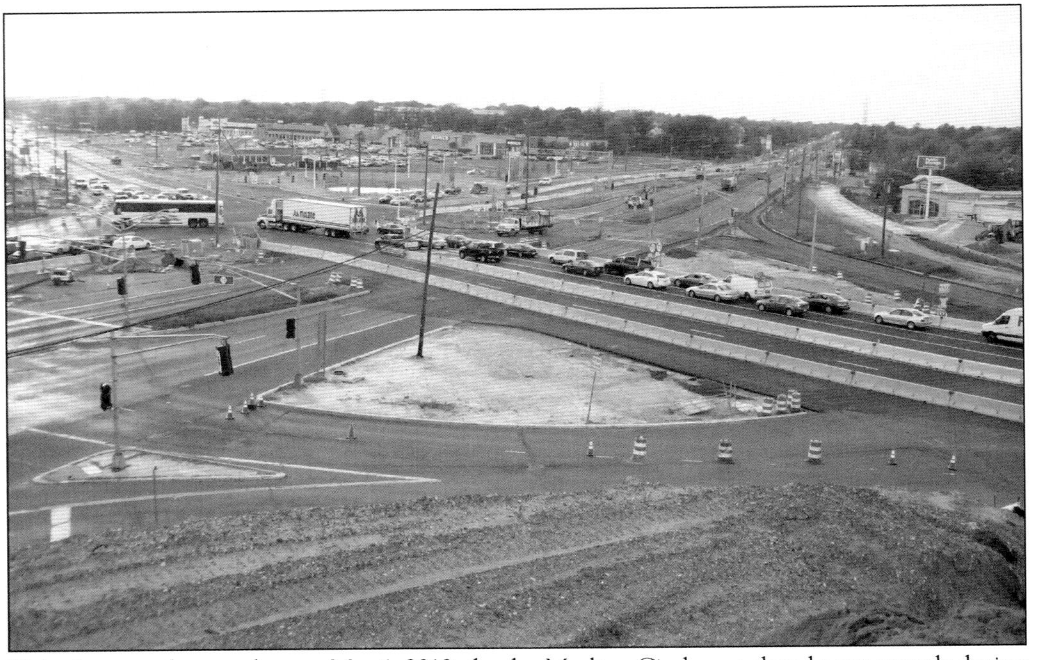

This photograph was taken on May 1, 2010, the day Marlton Circle was closed permanently during the construction project that replaced the circle intersection with an overpass. The project began in April 2009 and was completed in late 2011. (Photograph by the author.)

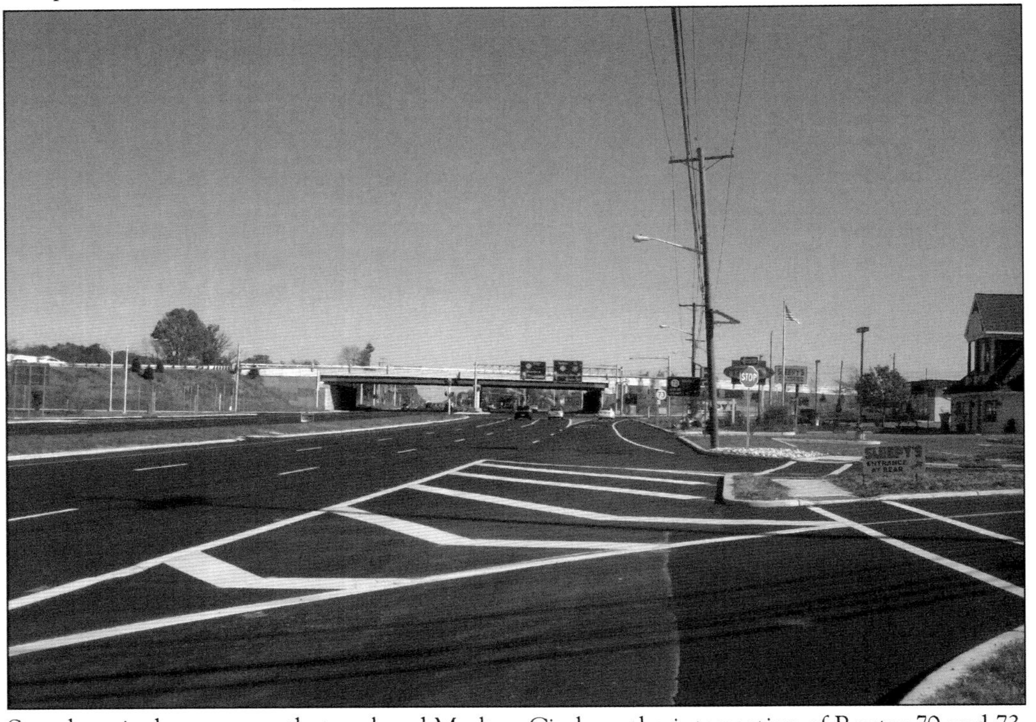

Seen here is the overpass that replaced Marlton Circle as the intersection of Routes 70 and 73. (Photograph by the author.)

George DeChurches was actively involved with Evesham's growth during the 1960s. He served as mayor, councilman, and director of public safety and was on the zoning and planning boards. DeChurches retired from the township in 1993 as director of public works. He died in 2011 at the age of 85.

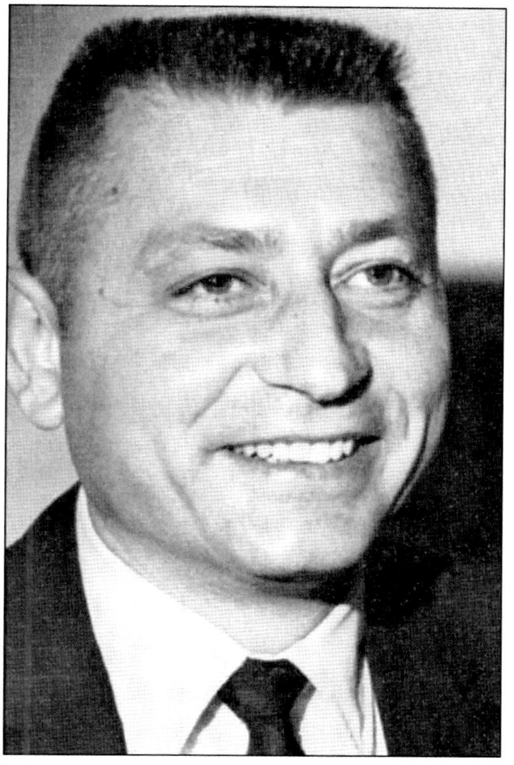

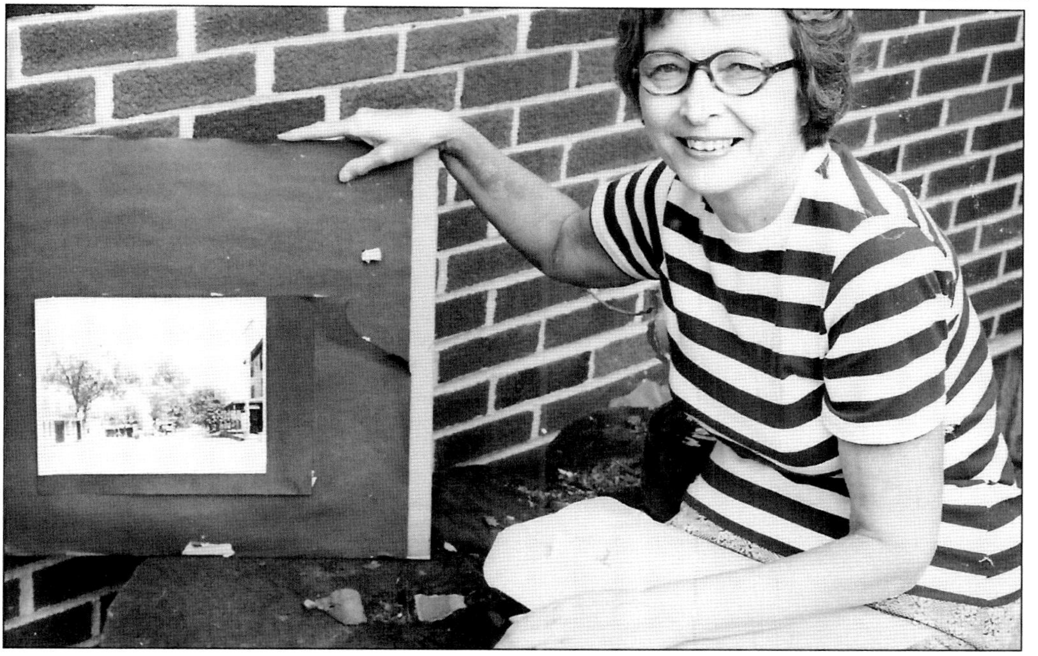

Shown is the late Edna Wirth working on a historical project in the 1970s. Wirth was an avid historian of Evesham. She spent countless hours documenting the township's past. Much of her work was used in the making of this book. (Courtesy Dolores Wirth.)

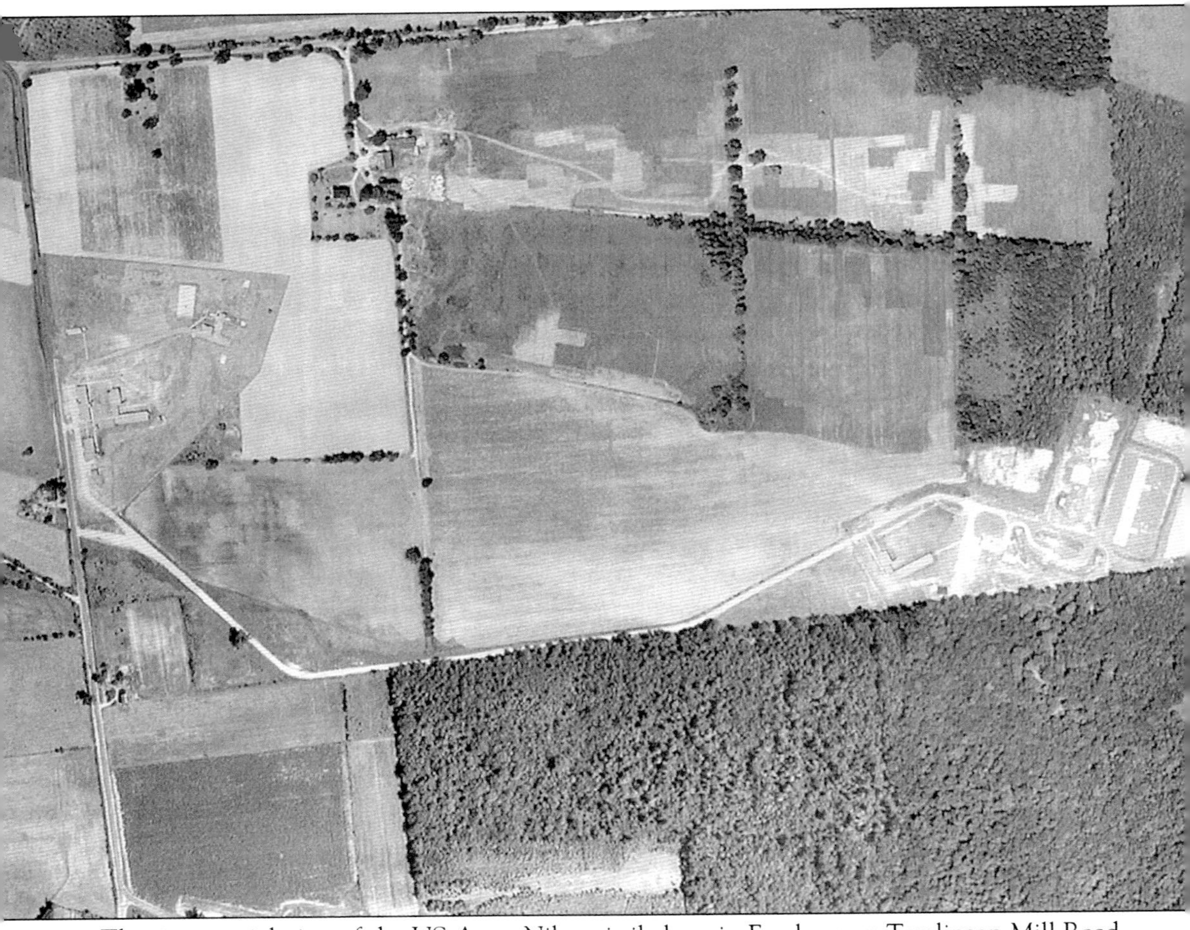

This is an aerial view of the US Army Nike missile base in Evesham on Tomlinson Mill Road between Elmwood and Taunton Lake Roads. The base was one of 12 that surrounded Philadelphia to protect the city from an air attack. It was numbered PH-32, the "PH" for Philadelphia Defense Area and "32" since the site was 32 degrees southeast of Philadelphia City Hall. The base in Evesham went into operation in 1955 and was transferred to the New Jersey Army National Guard in 1960, which operated the site until it was deactivated in 1963. During the early 1960s, some Nike bases were converted to house the updated and more powerful Nike Hercules missiles. The Marlton base was not upgraded, leading to its closing.

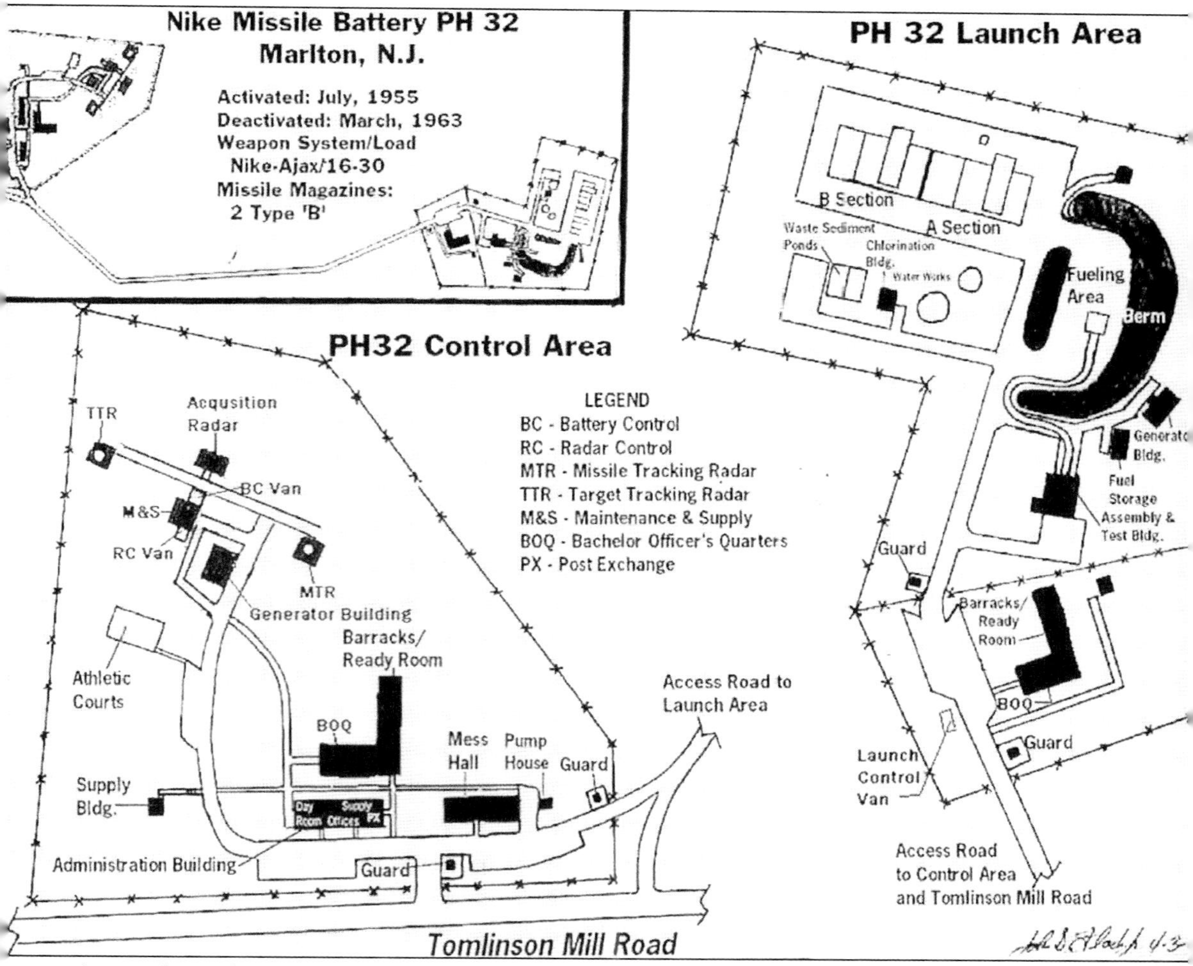

A map shows the two sections of the former Marlton Nike base. The control section contained the radars and computer equipment that searched for enemy aircraft and controlled the missiles in the event of an attack. This section also contained an administration building, barracks, athletic courts, and mess hall. The launch section contained two underground missile magazines that housed up to 30 Nike Ajax missiles, along with facilities for assembling, testing, and fueling the missiles.

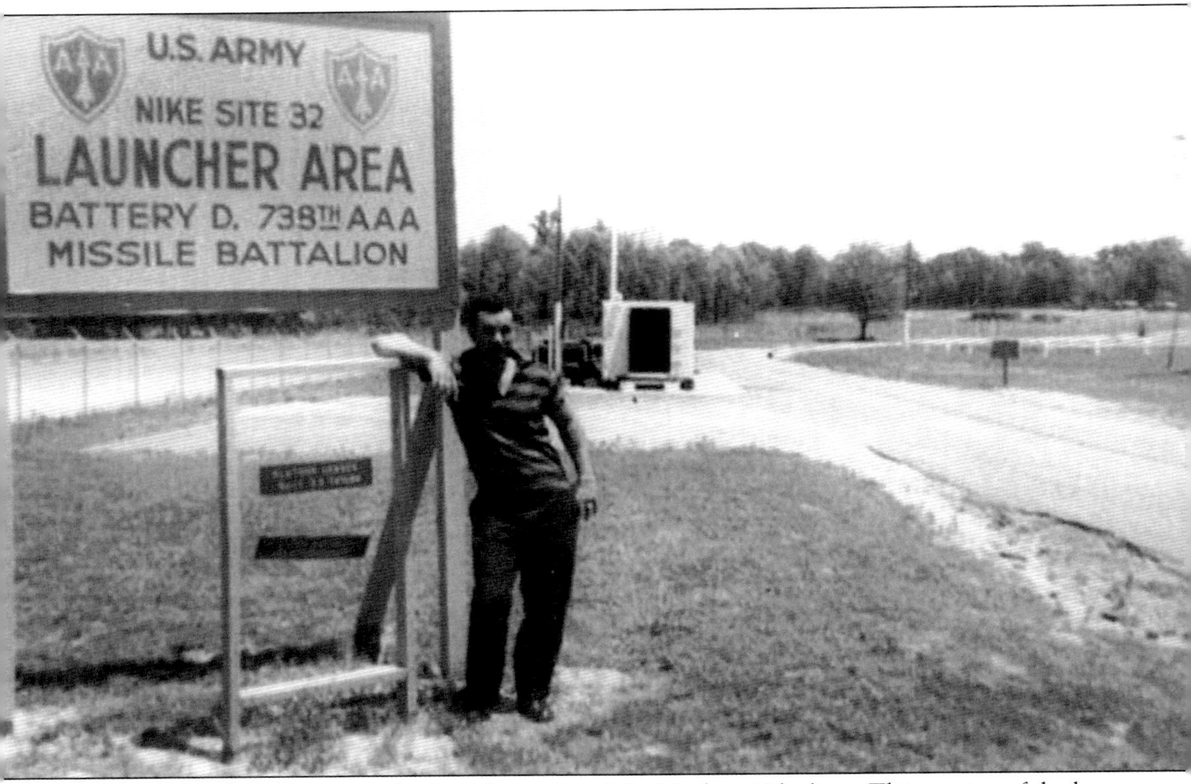

Pictured is the entrance to the launch section of the Marlton Nike base. This section of the base was located a half mile back from Tomlinson Road. (Courtesy Gene Ehrich.)

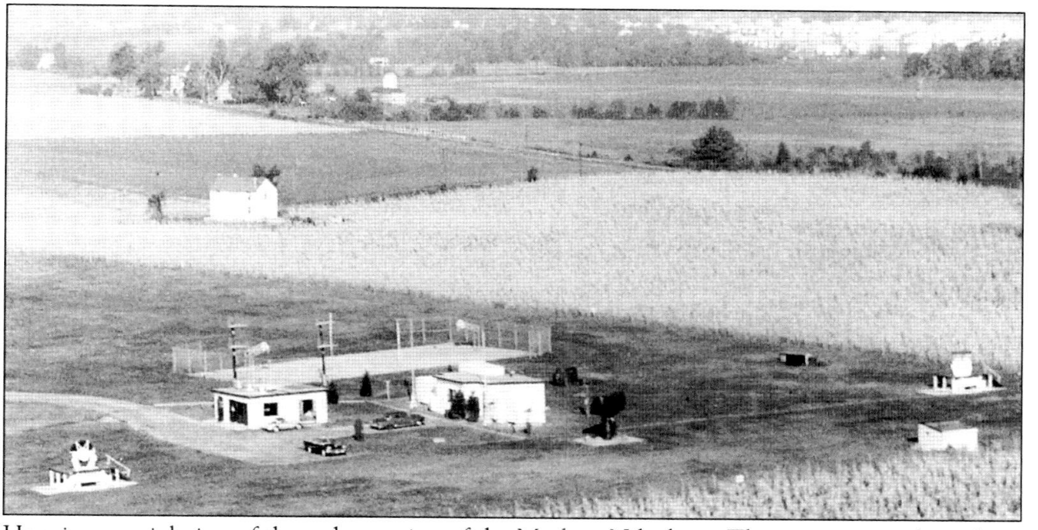

Here is an aerial view of the radar section of the Marlton Nike base. The antenna on the right is the target-tracking radar, the antenna on the left is the missile-tracking radar, and the antenna in the center is the acquisition radar. Close to this is the maintenance building with two trailers attached, housing the radar equipment. To the left of that is the generator building. Also seen are the base's athletic courts. (Courtesy Bernie Lorenz.)

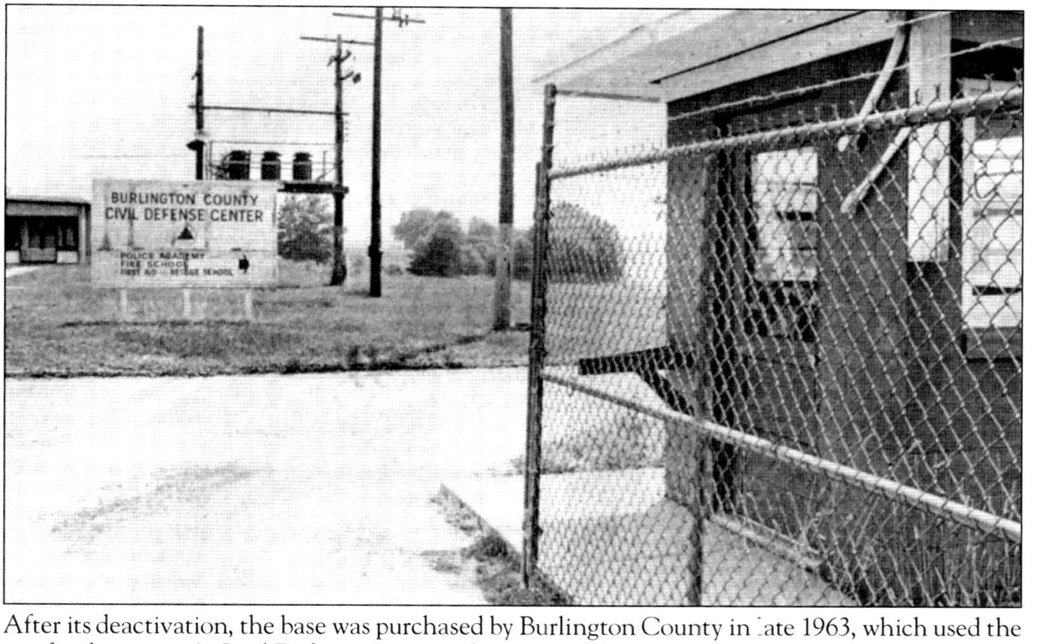

After its deactivation, the base was purchased by Burlington County in late 1963, which used the site for the county's Civil Defense Center. The county's fire and police academy was also housed here. The former base was also used by the Evesham Recreation Council, Civil Air Patrol, and South Jersey Radio Relay League and was the temporary headquarters for the Evesham Police Department when the force was started in 1966. The county closed the center in 1972 and auctioned the property in 1973 to a developer. The buildings at the site were demolished in 1977 after a planned residential development was approved. This project did not come to fruition, and the site was sold in the early 1990s and became the Briarwood development.